The Unvarnished Truth

The Unvarnished Truth

Personal Narratives
in Nineteenth-Century America

Ann Fabian

UNIVERSITY OF CALIFORNIA PRESS

Berkeley   Los Angeles   London

University of California Press
Berkeley and Los Angeles, California

University of California Press, Ltd.
London, England

© 2000 by the Regents of the University of California

Library of Congress Cataloging-in-Publication Data

Fabian, Ann.
  The unvarnished truth: personal narratives in nineteenth-century America / Ann Fabian.
    p.   cm.
  Includes bibliographical references and index.
  ISBN 0-520-21862-0 (alk. paper).
    1. United States—History—19th century—Biography. 2. Autobiography. 3. Poor—United
    States—Biography. I. Title.
  E337.5.F33 2000
  920.073—dc21   99-12652
                                                                              CIP

Manufactured in the United States of America
08 07 06 05 04 03 02 01 00 99   10 9 8 7 6 5 4 3 2 1

The paper used in this publication meets the minimum requirements of
ANSI/NISO Z39.48-1992 (R 1997) (*Permanence of Paper*).

For my mother,
Virginia Fabian

In democracies it is by no means the case that all the men who cultivate literature have received a literary education; and most of those who have some tinge of *belles-lettres* are either engaged in politics, or in a profession which allows them to taste occasionally and by stealth the pleasures of the mind. . . . They prefer books which may be easily procured, quickly read, and which require no learned researches to be understood.

Alexis de Tocqueville, "Literary Characteristics
of Democratic Ages," *Democracy in America* (1840)

In democratic communities each citizen is habitually engaged in the contemplation of a very puny object, namely himself. If he ever raises his looks higher, he then perceives nothing but the immense form of society at large, or the still more imposing aspect of mankind. His ideas are all either extremely minute and clear, or extremely vague: what lies between is an open void.

Alexis de Tocqueville, "Of the Inflated Style of American
Writers and Orators," *Democracy in America* (1840)

CONTENTS

ILLUSTRATIONS

PREFACE

Although most of the stories I investigate here were written in the nineteenth century, it was one of the more tawdry episodes of the late twentieth century that led me, I confess, to the idea for this book. That story begins with a Long Island garage man named Joey Buttafuoco, who took up
with one of his customers, a teenager named Amy Fisher. Some months
into their affair, Fisher went to Buttafuoco's house and shot an unsuspecting Mrs. Buttafuoco in the head. The three of them—Buttafuoco, the
wounded wife, and the teenage lover—paraded through the tabloid press
during the spring of 1992. Tabloid fame was enough to make them celebri-
ties, and celebrity status was enough to make each of their stories worth
money. When Amy Fisher's lawyer surveyed the crowd of reporters and
agents gathered around his client, he realized that her version of the story
could be sold at a premium, and he proposed peddling it to raise cash for
her bail and his fees. "After all," he told a reporter for the *New York Times*,
"she's just a teenager. Her story is her only asset."[1]

Or the only asset she could easily hawk from a jail cell. The lawyer's comment struck me as peculiar when I first read it, but of course, Fisher was not the first storyteller of modest literary talent to seek profit by offering the curious public a "true" eyewitness account, and, as we have learned in the wake of presidential impeachment, she will not be the last.[2]

Fisher and Buttafuoco may reveal the tacky side of personal stories sold for profit, but at times in the past such stories have had a more serious intent. The very possibility of telling tales based on experience has been a refuge for the weak and ruined, a means for those deprived of power, authority, and education to come before the great public. I wondered why people went public with tales of suffering and misadventure, and I turned to the stories told and sold by beggars, convicts, slaves, and soldiers to try to discover how poor people went about getting their stories into print. What did it mean to base a tale on experience? What rules governed the representation of experience? What happened when a storyteller was caught inventing the details of experiences described as "true"?

The writers whose stories appear in this book frequently announced on the page that they appeared in print only at the "urgent solicitation of friends." Perhaps they intended the phrase to assure readers that someone, at least, thought they had a good story to tell. Or maybe friends were just plain tired of hearing the same stories over and over again and figured that getting them into print would get bothersome talkers on to something else. Although I have had no urgent solicitations from my friends, I know I have tried their patience. I also know that without their solicitude I would never have finished this book. For their many kindnesses, I am deeply grateful.

For suggestions and criticisms, I thank Jean-Christophe Agnew, Joyce Appleby, Matt Backes, Dan Belgrad, Betsy Blackmar, David Blight, Kathryn Burns, Richard Bushman, Christopher Capozzola, Scott Casper, Kathy Compagnon, Cathy Corman, Michael Denning, François Furstenberg, Jackie Goldsby, Bob Gross, Lisbeth Haas, Karen Halttunen, Tom Head, David Jaffee, Regina Kunzel, Jill Lepore, Rich Lowry, Louis Masur, Tim McCarthy, Margaret McFadden, Meredith McGill, Susan McKinnon, Jeremy Mumford, Teresa Murphy, J. C. Mutchler, Franny Nudelman, Grey Osterud, Maureen Pearce, Jeffrey Pines, William Reese, Steve Rice, Joan Shelley Rubin, Laura Saltz, Scott Sandage, Marni Sandweiss, Fran Schwartz, Carol Sheriff, Catherine Stock, David Stowe, Alan Trachtenberg, Glenn Wallach, Lynn Wardley, Shane White, Christopher P. Wilson, and especially Jeanie Attie, who read the whole manuscript for me, and Elizabeth Kaspar-Aldrich, whose ideas appear on nearly every page. I am grateful as well for contributions from students in my seminars at Yale, Columbia, and the American Antiquarian Society and for comments from audiences at the Center for Literary and Cultural Studies at Harvard, the College of William and Mary, the Graduate Center of the City University of New York, the University of California at Santa Cruz, the Bowery Seminar, the Columbia University Seminar on Early American History, the Program in the History of the Book in American Culture at the American Antiquarian Society, and Doshisha University in Kyoto, Japan. Early in my research I had the good fortune to receive support from two institutions whose reputations for generosity to scholars are well deserved: the Shelby Cullom Davis Center for the Study of History at Princeton University, and the American Antiquarian Society in Worcester, Massachusetts. I am happy to think of this book as one of many made of materials found in Worcester, and I am pleased at last to be able to thank Joanne Chaison, John Hench, Caroline Sloat, and everyone at the American Antiquarian Society who had a hand in it. At the University of California Press, Monica McCormick took an interest in this project when it must have seemed pretty peculiar. I am glad that she did. I am grateful as well to Carolyn Hill, whose masterful copyediting improved the manuscript, and to Mary Severance and Marilyn Schwartz who shepherded it through production.

Thanks, too, to my family. Andrew read drafts of the first paragraph of each chapter, warning me about those that contained more than one muddled idea. Isabelle did absolutely nothing, she says, but she grew faster than this book, and that was good enough for me. Chris saw to it that we had music and food. And often that too was enough.

Introduction

Near the end of his novel *Israel Potter: His Fifty Years of Exile* (1854), Herman Melville inserted a meditation on the risks of making a pauper the center of a story: "The gloomiest and truthfulest dramatist," he wrote, "seldom chooses for his theme the calamities, however extraordinary, of inferior and private persons; least of all, the pauper's; admonished by the fact, that to the craped palace of the king lying in state, thousands of starers shall throng, but few feel enticed to the shanty, where like a pealed knuckle-bone, grins the unupholstered corpse of the beggar."[1]

In 1824 the actual Israel Potter, an aged veteran of the American Revolution, had produced a narrative of his sufferings, which he peddled for twenty-eight cents a book in an effort to ease the pains of old age and the burden of being denied a pension by the government.[2] Potter must have appealed to Melville as a figure who, in the face of hopeless odds, tried to escape poverty through authorship. But Potter's tale fared little better in Melville's hands than it had in his own: the professional author's reworking of the pauper's tale never found much of a market. Yet despite their

1

evidently limited commercial appeal, paupers' tales, in one form or another, pepper our cultural past. In the right circumstances and with the right collaborators, some became books, and some of those books sold well enough to have left traces.

In the middle of the eighteenth century, converts, captives, soldiers, sailors, beggars, murderers, slaves, sinners, and even wounded workers began to take advantage of opportunities to represent themselves in print, and the archive of these variously motivated personal narratives grew to vast proportions. By the early years of the nineteenth century, Americans were coming to see that the lives of both the noble and the ignoble not only had literary merit but also, as lived experience, had the shape of stories. An Enlightenment faith in the rational capacities of all human beings and a Romantic interest in individual lives lay behind the impulse to discern and articulate an order in the apparent chaos of a life. In the early years of the nineteenth century, sweeping intellectual, economic, and political changes moved the individual to the center of American culture. The growth of evangelical religion, the development of democratic politics, the rise of nationalism, the spread of print culture, and the expansion of the commercial relations of a capitalist society all fostered individual impulses toward personal narrative in printed form.[3]

Historians have documented the expansion of print culture in the early years of the nineteenth century and examined the high literacy rates that enabled men and women to become consumers of printed words. They have studied both the technological transformations that reduced the cost of printed matter and the developments in transportation and innovations in distribution that put books within easy reach of readers.[4] They have examined the ways a market for books shaped the profession of letters and investigated the ways common readings in newspapers and pamphlets characterized political life for citizens of the new nation. As the anthropologist Benedict Anderson points out, in the wake of the American Revolution, common readings in newspapers and pamphlets helped people scattered around the country to imagine themselves citizens of a single nation. Indeed, many experienced political life only as a series of printed exchanges. Literary scholar Michael Warner argues that disembodied forms of print offered citizens (in particular the white men who read and voted) opportunities to engage in the disinterested dialogue and debate that ensured the republic's health.[5]

There were, however, texts that circulated beneath or below impersonal and disembodied political debate. The poor men and women who set down their experiences in print produced texts that differed in important ways from those penned by more respectable authors. In the first place, their stories were insistently personal, both in their content and in the ways they were marketed. Many of these poor authors appeared in person before would-be readers, inviting questions about their stories. Some displayed for audiences their scarred or mutilated bodies, living proof, if you will, of the truth of the story being sold. Such personal sales methods carried over into texts that were distributed by less direct means. Authors described in print previous encounters with approving audiences and incorporated into books illustrations of their marred bodies. Perhaps such references represent a transition in the history of the printed text itself, from the primitive broadside or pamphlet hawked door-to-door or sold at fairs and executions to the book produced for wider distribution through intermediaries. In any case, these incorporated references to physical encounters remind us how close print sometimes was to speech.

We often think of reading, writing, and the world of books as aspects of the spread of refinement through the life of the expanding young Republic. Paupers' books, however, call forth a different history and a tradition far from genteel. The poor beggar with a story to tell carries into the commercial markets of nineteenth-century America the experiences and forms of marketplaces more nearly medieval. In modern print the impoverished narrator does not so much reject (or retard) the politeness, reserve, and polish so crucial to the culture of refinement, as predate it. Perhaps that is why these narratives can seem today, in contrast to some of the refined ("Victorian") popular writings of the time, paradoxically so modern:

they keep alive traditions that we are constantly reviving. They seem to regress to a preliterate, precivilized state while simultaneously staking out the territories of what is to come.[6]

Unschooled writers of the nineteenth century manipulated the particular forms of media available to them and made allies of those who provided access to print. They worked with small-town printers, politically minded editors, media-savvy ministers, and culturally adept abolitionists, the figures best able to help them turn misfortunes into assets, experiences into published books. The narratives that succeed—that are accepted as true by readers, book buyers, directors of charitable institutions, and makers of social policy—manage to balance contradictory demands of the self-effacement that is humility and the self-assertion that is publication. By studying these narratives in relation to the immediate contexts in which they were produced and to the more ancient traditions by which they were informed, I have set out to write what might be called the social history of a cultural form.

Most of the beggars, convicts, slaves, and soldiers who wrote and published chronicles of their experiences were men. Indeed, for some, publishing a story was a means to achieve and to assert a masculine identity, in that the expected profits were to free the poor writer from a financial dependency perceived as feminine. With the exception of captivity and conversion narratives, where a certain dependent passivity could be presumed, the narrative forms adopted by poor writers who traded on their stories were those traditionally associated with men: they wrote picaresque adventures and tales of travel, trade, and war. Occasionally, female cross-dressers appear, whose disguise leads them into "masculine" experiences. But their narratives cross-dress as well, adhering to masculine conventions.[7]

It may seem odd to lump together storytellers who recount such a wide array of experiences: beggars impoverished by imperial misadventures and determined to earn money by peddling their stories; fugitives from slavery encouraged to contribute tales to the cause of abolition; prisoners convicted of crime and urged by ministers, jailers, and popular publishers to confess their crimes in print; and heroic soldiers captured by an enemy, made ill in confinement, and invited by the federal government to tell their stories. But these stories deal with questions of truth and authority in surprisingly similar ways. When read together as episodes in a history of truth and true-story telling, they illuminate a shadowy corner in the cultural world of the nineteenth century. What did it take to turn experience into a true story? Why were some poor people's stories of experience labeled "true," whereas others were discounted as frauds or fabrications?

Confession, conversion, and captivity provided templates for poor sufferers with stories to tell. And for historians, the vast body of personal narratives has provided evidence of our deepest cultural concerns. Although the initial intentions of most poor and unschooled writers are frequently local, their publications have a greater reach. Personal narratives offer a popular version of the American past—a key both to our myths about ourselves (stories for a culture fabricated from the lives of so many freestanding individuals) and to our national literature.

Captivity narratives, for example, have been hailed as the first instance of an original American literature. Mary Rowlandson told her story in 1682, but tales of white captives held by Indians would be told time and again over the next two centuries. With the help of allies (ministers, doctors, journalists, and printers), hundreds of returned captives turned tales into small books, which they traded for money. For some, telling a tale of captivity provided a means to demonstrate that life among the "aliens" had not altered them beyond recognition. Stories helped former captives rejoin the society of neighbors and friends. Others had more concrete goals in mind; they hoped to gain compensation for property lost or the means to ransom friends and family still held captive. Those who bought the narrative of Reverend James W. Parker in 1844 helped him effect "the release of his daughter and her child, and many others who were also prisoners among the Indians, and having a niece, yet in bondage, he hopes to be able to realize from the sale of this narrative, a sufficient sum to enable him to successfully prosecute his exertions to release her also." Those who purchased his book thus participated in his yet unfinished project.[8]

Set in type, stories like Parker's circulated far beyond the world of close associations and small projects. As cultural artifacts, captivity narratives laid out ways for white readers to imagine contacts between European settlers and native peoples. The tales of suffering white women perhaps reinforced rules of gender and race; stories of heroic captives perhaps taught white boys a way to tap into the regenerative powers of violence that would make them men; and captivity narratives perhaps helped to turn an aggressive war against Indians into a noble defense of white women.[9]

Historians have also found evidence of large cultural themes in the published confessions of convicted criminals. Like captivity narratives, many confessional stories began as local projects designed to make a little money, sometimes even for those confessing to ugly crimes. Scholars have used the hundreds of confessions produced over the course of the eighteenth century to chart the gradual decline of unquestioned belief in a religious explanation for all worldly events. Working on narratives produced in the early nineteenth century, scholars have found in them the seeds of the taste for sensationalism so prevalent in popular culture today. Others contend that lowly popular culture bore great fruit, arguing that writers of the American Renaissance, Poe and Melville in particular, found literary inspiration in narratives describing lives of sin and vice.[10]

No doubt the most important of these personal narratives are slave narratives. As problematic as poverty might have been for white men and women, fugitives from slavery who found themselves reduced to their stories faced additional difficulties. To live, many turned stories into assets, persuading skeptical, even hostile, white audiences that they were telling the truth. Fugitives and their abolitionist allies recognized that the stakes were great, both for storytellers themselves and for the country as a whole.[11]

Fugitive narrators surely borrowed language and metaphor from captivity and conversion narratives, turning materials familiar to audiences to less familiar ends of abolition. But to lend authority to their voices and to make their narratives appear "true," fugitives borrowed the devices that poor and illiterate writers often used to present experiences as true stories. Slave narratives may be about race, but they are also about exercises of power and judgment that go beyond race.[12]

Some literary theorists have suggested that the articulation experience is a means to assert an imaginative propriety over events by giving them narrative form. As Raymond Williams wrote, "It is, in the first instance, to everyman a matter of urgent personal importance to 'describe' his experience, because this is literally a remaking of himself, a creative change in his personal organization to include and control experience." Individual articulations of experience launch the "process of communication [that] is in fact the process of community."[13] Williams placed great faith in the promise of community, and perhaps he is right to see in stories of experience a means of building bonds among people, a means of making visible to themselves and to others the history of those whose voices counted little. For those without genius, education, or expertise, experience offers a kind of authority, for are we not all experts on our own lives?

Unfortunately, much as we might long to believe otherwise, the authority derived from experience and the bonds built on its articulation are not necessarily either liberating or long-lasting. The articulation of experience follows rules; it is "discursively produced," to use a phrase of the historian Joan Scott. Sometimes in paying particular attention to the discursive production of experience we can witness a play of social forces that grants truth and authority to certain descriptions of experience and not to others. Writers who assumed the pose of poor and humble narrators often learned (sometimes to their great distress) that to follow rules for the articulation of experience was to accept humility and therefore to defer to those who claimed a right to exercise social and cultural power over them. These narratives provide us with an opportunity to explore conflicts over truth and authority, art and honesty, assertion and deference. These contests, their narrative manifestations and their social consequences, are the subject of this book.[14]

CHAPTER ONE

Beggars

In 1817 he once more endured extremity; this second peace drift-
ing its discharged soldiers on London so that all kinds of labor
were overstocked. Beggars, too, lighted on the walks like locusts.
Timber-toed cripples stilted along, numerous as French peasants in *sabots*. And, as thirty years before, on all sides, the exile
heard the supplicatory cry, not addressed to him, "An honorable
scar, your honor, received at Bunker Hill, or Saratoga, or Trenton, fighting for his most gracious Majesty, King George!" so
now, in presence of still surviving Israel, our Wandering Jew, the
amended cry was anew taken up, by a succeeding generation of
unfortunates, "An honorable scar, your honor, received at
Corunna, or at Waterloo, or at Trafalgar!" Yet not a few of these
petitioners had never been outside of the London smoke; a sort
of crafty aristocracy in their way, who, without having endured
their own persons much if anything, reaped no insignificant
share both of the glory and profit of the bloody battles they
claimed; while some of the genuine heroes, too brave to beg, too
cut up to work, and too poor to live, laid down quietly in corners
and died. And here it may be noted, as a fact nationally characteristic, that however desperately reduced at times, even to the
sewers, Israel, the American, never sunk below the mud, to actual
beggary.

Herman Melville,
Israel Potter: His Fifty Years of Exile (1855)

But let the reader consider that I am neither historian nor politi-
cian, and that I am barely able to relate, and that in an humble and
unskilled manner, my own unfortunate story.

Moses Smith,
*History of the Adventures and
Sufferings of Moses Smith* (1812)

BEGGARS AND BOOKS

During the cold winter months of 1807–1808, Moses Smith, a poor
cooper from Long Island, made his way overland from Maryland to
Brooklyn. He had escaped from a prison in Carthagena, a Spanish-ruled
city state in present-day Colombia, and returned to the United States
with nothing but a good story to get him home. Telling his story, he
begged passage, food, and shelter from those he met along the way. His
trip was difficult, and once back in New York, he turned to political allies
and produced a book in which he recounted his adventures and detailed
his sufferings.[1]

In 1812, after America declared war on Britain, Michael Smith, a
shabby Baptist preacher, gave up his property in Upper Canada, packed
his family in a wagon, and made his way south from Ontario to Virginia.
To earn money to feed them all, he preached, cut wood, begged, and
sometimes sold books in which he described the Canadian countryside,
the war in the northeast, and his personal sufferings.[2]

In October 1815, a merchant with designs on trade with Africa said that
he had plucked Robert Adams, a mixed-race and illiterate American
sailor, from among the "distressed seamen" and discharged soldiers who,
in the wake of Waterloo, crowded the London streets. Adams had attracted notice among the street beggars by including descriptions of the
"far-fabled" city of Timbuktu in his story of shipwreck on the western
coast of Africa and captivity among the Moors. The merchant, S. Cock,
lured Adams into his office with an offer of food and clothes ("of which he

stood particularly in need"), gathered a group of "gentlemen" to interrogate him, and transcribed for publication the tale that had made the ragged sailor a man of "consequence" on the street. The merchant promised that a portion of the profits from the book's sale would be reserved for Mr. Adams.[3]

To some of those they met, men like Smith, Smith, and Adams must have seemed annoying beggars, but they were also storytellers who rehearsed their woes aloud and then turned tales into printed books. It is clear that they wrote from the margins of the economy, but they also extracted from their experiences of economic marginality a kind of provisional cultural authority.[4] Much as reading and writing may have hastened the spread of gentility through American life, beggars' narratives remind us that stories set down in books did not necessarily foster high thoughts and fine manners. Storytelling beggars, carrying the books and briefs that detailed their woes, wandered from the courts of the old world into the marketplace of early nineteenth-century America. With help from political allies, wealthy patrons, sympathetic co-religionists, commercial scribblers, and friendly printers, people who had been reduced to begging got stories made up as books, using print to achieve their own ends and turning narratives of misadventure into commodities that could be transferred and sold.[5] These authors pocketed a little authority and a little cash. But exchanges between writing beggars and patronizing readers were complicated. Some prosperous readers who purchased beggars' tales discovered that good stories could mask shoddy motives and that clever dissemblers could pass as deserving sufferers.[6]

Peculiar witnesses beggars may have been, but beggars with stories had good tales to tell. They bore witness, of course, to their own suffering and to their own merit. They also witnessed the effects of an expanding maritime economy that tied men and women of the east coast into an Atlantic world where some prospered but others were sent wandering in search of money or work.[7] Some writing beggars described the stable folk who had grown suspicious of wanderers who asked for relief. Some participated in their country's first imperial adventures and described the beginnings of a world where claims of national identity could give order to a bewildering flux of experience. To be an American, they found, could be beneficial; it could also be risky. Although they described themselves telling tales aloud, they also witnessed a society becoming habituated to finding books in the hands of ordinary people.[8] In their books they described a world dominated by spoken exchange, but they put their descriptions into a form designed not to be spoken but to be read. They boasted no great skills as readers or as writers, yet they became the authors of books. What can we learn of the workings of culture in nineteenth-century America by exploring connections between behavior so socially marginal as begging and behavior so culturally central as writing?

THE ADVENTURES OF MOSES SMITH

Moses Smith, a Brooklyn cooper, was among those who participated (unwittingly, he maintained) in Francisco de Miranda's ill-starred initial attempt to lead Spain's South American colonies to independence. When local peasants failed to rally round Miranda, he abandoned the expedition. His underlings, Smith among them, fell into Spanish hands and were convicted of piracy by a colonial court. Ten of the convicts were hanged, and Smith and several others were sentenced to ten years of hard labor.[9] After an eighteen-month confinement, Smith tunneled out of a "foul and unwholesome" dungeon. A kind American captain took him as far as Maryland. Even though Smith had completed the longest leg of his voyage home, he still had to get to Brooklyn. He had only ten shillings, hardly enough to pay his way to New York, so he decided to tell his tale, in the hope that those who heard it would finance his travels through the wintry countryside. Once home, he sued the Federalist plotters who he insisted had tricked him into enlisting with Miranda. A judge found little ground for his accusations of fraud and dismissed his case. Determined to get the last word, Smith turned to political allies who helped him get his story printed as a book.[10]

Smith thought he had a good story to tell. It began simply enough: innocent and patriotic, he enlisted in a band of men recruited supposedly to

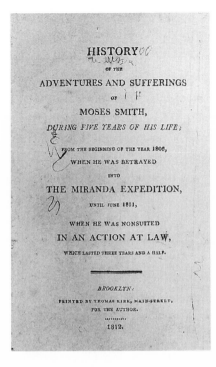

HISTORY*OO*

OF THE

ADVENTURES AND SUFFERINGS

OF

MOSES SMITH,

DURING FIVE YEARS OF HIS LIFE;

FROM THE BEGINNING OF THE YEAR 1806,

WHEN HE WAS BETRAYED

INTO

THE MIRANDA EXPEDITION,

UNTIL JUNE 1811,

WHEN HE WAS NONSUITED

IN AN ACTION AT LAW,

WHICH LASTED THREE YEARS AND A HALF.

BROOKLYN:

PRINTED BY THOMAS KIRK, MAIN-STREET,

FOR THE AUTHOR.

1812.

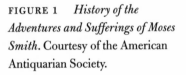

FIGURE 1   *History of the Adventures and Sufferings of Moses Smith.* Courtesy of the American Antiquarian Society.

ride guard beside U.S. mail stages on the road between Washington and New Orleans. He was promised, he said, a uniform, a monthly salary of twenty-five dollars, and, if he stayed on for three years, a bonus of fifty dollars and "one hundred acres of the lands of the United States." A good offer, he thought, for a young man "reduced in circumstances—and out of employ." To his surprise, the ship he boarded did not head south to Washington but set out on the high seas for Santo Domingo. When Miranda presented himself on deck, Smith said he realized for the first time that he was part of an adventure neither of his choosing nor to his liking.[11]

Miranda went on to plot revolution in London, eventually joining Simon Bolivar and returning to Venezuela in 1811 as dictator of an independent country. He fared less well in the succeeding years. When Miranda signed an armistice with Spain in 1812, Bolivar accused him of betraying the revolution and gave him over to Spanish authorities. He was transported in chains to Cadiz, where he died, still in prison, in 1816.[12]

In the meantime, Smith concerned himself with his story. Unfortunately, in the late fall of 1807 Smith found that Americans had lost interest in Miranda and his revolutionary schemes. Those determined to promote the settlement of the Mississippi Valley had supported the man because his plans for South American independence promised markets for American produce. But support was short-lived, and Smith complained that people he met that winter were more interested in Aaron Burr's newly exposed plots than they were in Miranda and in the injustices suffered by a poor cooper who had been seduced into Miranda's service. Burr's trial, Smith wrote in exasperation, had so "fatigued the public mind" that few now had patience for his story.[13]

Smith said that he had expected to endure icy nights and irregular meals but was surprised at the cold reception given his tale.

> Instead of that sympathy which the injured and oppressed in general meet with in this great community, I experienced more of aversion or contempt. As I proceeded on my weary journey, I related my story to such as were disposed to hear it. Besides that it was the story nearest to my heart and nearest to my tongue, it was also necessary to account for my condition and appearance, which was too like that of a convict escaped from legal coercion. It was mortifying, humiliating, and afflicting to find with what indifference, distrust and contempt it was sometimes received by my fellow citizens.

At one tavern, a sarcastic landlord dismissed Smith, telling him that "*such stories were good to tell some people.*" But certainly not his paying customers.[14] "Thus did I pass along," Smith whined, "trailing my wearied steps thru melted snow and ice, shivering and sinking with fatigue; unpitied and never regarded but with eyes of distrust or scorn, nor answered but with the tone of neglect and disgust."[15]

Smith was not the only poor vagrant of his generation trying to finance a journey with a tale of woe; others, however, were more successful. Henry

Bird, redeemed from captivity among the Shawanese in the Ohio Valley in 1811, remembered that "his story almost always gained him food and lodging, and, with very few exceptions, he was seldom turned away from any man's door." "Misery and poverty so seldom knock at the doors of an American farmer," he continued, "that his heart is not yet steeled to apathy by becoming familiar with objects of distress." Living off the "benevolence of his countrymen," Bird traveled from Vermont to Washington, where he arranged an audience with President Madison and registered a plea for his friends and neighbors still held captive on the Ohio frontier.[16]

Or consider the case of the Pequot writer William Apess. In 1813, Apess and a companion made their way from New London to New York by spinning a tale of their supposed ordeal on a captured privateer. Apess's companion (a man he described as the better storyteller and the more abandoned liar) gave a "great account of our having been captured by the enemy, and so straight that [our listeners] believed the whole of it," at least until they tried to convince a group of sailors that their captors had forced them to eat bread laced with ground glass. Torture heightened drama, but drama too lurid pushed a story beyond the plausible. Drama, which might well serve the needs of traveling entertainers, could discredit those whose tales had to sound "true" in order to gain the audience's sympathy and assistance.[17]

Moses Smith certainly tried to create a good yarn. He incorporated political intrigue (wily Federalists using guileless young men like Smith to discredit Jefferson and Madison), biography (a "biographical sketch" of Miranda concluded the second edition of his book), travelogue (notes on the climate and landscape of Colombia), and Gothic adventure (escape from an airless, damp, and "dark cavity" behind the moss-covered walls of a castle).[18] He described prisoners held in "gloomy seclusion," fed a "loathsome diet," deprived of "light and air," and subject to "irons, insults, and other means of terror, to break down the courage of the victim and weary him of life." Smith also depicted the ingenuity of ordinary Americans. He and his comrades dug through walls of a "thickness twice the length of a man's stature," using only a shoemaker's hammer. They covered the noise of their digging by rattling their chains and making rough music on the flute, fiddle, and fife they had purchased with money advanced them by a visiting American captain.[19]

By rights such stories should have interested American audiences who followed the misadventures of virtuous protagonists like Smith in popular novels. To avoid condemnation by critics suspicious of fiction, novelists often insisted that their tales were based on true stories. Like these novelists, Smith offered readers something akin to an intimate experience, but his tale had to conform to a higher standard of apparent truth, insofar as he asked of his audience something more than the emotional response invited by novelists. Smith had no choice but to create a credible narrative, because incredulity (as Apess and his friend learned) would break his contract with the reader. Moreover, Smith needed responsive readers to complete his story. No fictional hand could right the wrongs he had suffered. That task was reserved for the readers who invested mind and money in Smith's tale. Resolution of Smith's plot waited for readers who would believe his version of events and relieve his suffering.[20]

Smith sought out those who would listen to his story. He "did not like to beg," he said, but when he met a brewer on the road, he admitted that he "had not the wherewithal to pay my lodging for the night." The brewer invited him home and helped him arrange to insert a paragraph about his South American adventures in a Baltimore paper.[21] When he later spotted men reading the paper in the stage office in Philadelphia, he hailed them, presenting himself as a celebrity of sorts. They accepted this apparent confirmation of his story and gave him money to continue to New York, where, after a tearful reunion with his father, he launched a lawsuit against those he contended had tricked him into enlisting on the ill-fated voyage.

Smith's luck in the courtroom was little better than it had been in the tavern, and after three and a half years of motions and delays, the judge dismissed Smith's suit.[22] In print, Moses Smith prevailed, pursuing a back channel, if you will, into the archives and making sure his version of the events was on record. He republished the charges that the New York court had dismissed and favorably compared the swift, if severe, justice he had received in a Spanish colony with the arcane practices of the United States. Spanish judges, he declared, believed him but found it hard to accept the fact that a country supposedly ruled by law could harbor seducers of innocent workers.[23] Finally, Smith appended his opinion of legal writing, criticizing the excesses of lawyers and praising the plain and unadorned prose that characterized narratives such as his. "I am sorry," he wrote,

> that it becomes necessary to my story, to lay before my reader a law paper: for I know that it is the dryest, dullest kind of reading, and that such things are generally so skillfully drawn up, as to be unintelligible to plain people. The lawyers, call it my declaration; some for shortness call it my *narr*. It is as intelligible, I believe, as a law matter can be. . . . I am sure, if my counsel had been at liberty to use their own good sense, and tell my story in their own way, instead of this distorted manner of legal narrative, it would have been much better.[24]

We know Smith's version of the story of his story only because he recruited enough subscribers in New York City and Albany to produce two editions of his book.[25] Smith incorporated his adventure into a partisan narrative, blaming the New York Federalists for his woes and turning his Republican confreres into subscribers to his book. In the person of Thomas Kirk, Smith enlisted the help of a Democratic-Republican printer. He also found nearly five hundred men and women in and around New York City to subscribe to his book. He found some four hundred more upstate (more than 10 percent of them women) and hired the commercial printers, Packard and Van Benthuysen, to produce a second edition. Smith attracted supporters from a wide range of occupations: merchants, shipmasters, grocers, hairdressers, sailmakers, coopers, masons, sailors, cartmen, and laborers.[26]

An author like Smith who published his own books could minimize the risks of an uncertain market by finding buyers before the book appeared. Those willing to advance him money underwrote the costs of paper, printing, and binding and probably helped defray the costs of distribution as well. Like many such authors, Smith recruited friends and friends of friends, but his political claims remind us that such social and intellectual networks were also supported by partisan allegiance. In his publication, he reprinted for readers the charges that the New York judge had dismissed, and he criticized the long and futile legal process. At a moment of deep despair, he asked himself, "What had I done to merit so much anguish. To be disowned and abandoned by my country, unprotected by its laws. My only crime was my simplicity, and the ignorant credulity with which I listened to the vile and interested deceiver, who has wantonly plunged me into this complicated misery." According to Smith, the Federalist cause was clearly the cause of Satan, and Smith's cause was the "cause of every free-born citizen. It was the cause of every virtuous heart. It was the cause of a great community, whose honour was involved in the eyes of other nations."[27]

Although we recognize in Smith's appeal the strains of a populist rhetoric, Smith was not as simple and ignorant as he would seem to have his readers believe. Smith may have been a man of scant material resources, but he was not without intellectual gifts or social connections. And though he was, for a time, a poor vagabond, he knew that even wandering paupers could claim privileges of citizenship. By describing himself as a poor and persecuted American citizen, Smith made his personal experiences into something more than an eccentric misadventure. His unvarnished truths, he insisted, had to be read in a political context, as an episode in the history of the young nation.[28]

The pain he suffered in a Spanish colonial dungeon and the injustice he suffered at the hands of New York courts lent significance to his tale, and in describing pain and injustice, he drew comparisons that showed readers he was a man of judgment. Perhaps because he pledged to tell an artless tale in plain unvarnished prose, Smith could not embellish his account with elegant analogies. But even without access to rhetorical flourish, he established authorial expertise by expressing several straightforward judgments. He ranked the relative severity of the pain, suffering, and injustice he witnessed, developing devices perfectly suited to authority based on experience rather than genius, education, social position, or art.

This pattern of judgment becomes particularly clear as Smith describes for readers the events of his life between his return from Colombia and the composition of his story. He tried various jobs and finally shipped as a common sailor to London. He invested in a schooner that wrecked on the Rockaway shoals, but he deemed this loss a calamity not worth recounting. "[M]isadventures of this nature do not wring the soul like justice denied, or the triumph of iniquity, and make but a small part, indeed of my calamities, and do not demand public attention as public wrongs do."[29]

When Smith recomposed his story in 1811 and offered it to readers who were slowly turning their attention to war, he found that his eloquence could not bridge the seven years that lay between the time of his calamities and their publication as a story. To his frustration, interest in his story had proved brief and fickle; the political landscape had changed significantly since his departure on the ill-fated expedition. With eloquent appeals to national feeling, he invoked shared patriotism to lend significance to events that no longer had much popular currency.[30]

Smith began with a story of adventure that he exchanged for food, shelter, and passage home. Once home, he turned the story of his experiences into a vehicle to recover his good name. To recover his good name, however, he needed readers and interlocutors to accept not only his description of things he had seen and heard—his experiences—but also his explanation of why he had joined Miranda, and his conspiratorial interpretation of what had happened to him. Smith had not shipped out in the hopes of personal profit; he was a man duped by evil plotters. The structure into which he placed his own calamities—powerful plotters versus innocent pawn—is a recognizably political one. With claims of innocence, he made believing his tale of experience into a multilayered partisan act: he recruited readers as advocates of his personal cause, as supporters of a political faction, and finally as partisans of a nation, which had become a player on a world stage.

THE SUFFERINGS OF MICHAEL SMITH

The preacher Michael Smith had better luck with his publications, but he too suffered for his national allegiance, and he too learned something of the fleeting market for stories based on specific personal experiences. A particular combination of experience, suffering, and acquaintances made Smith a writer: experience among the British in Canada gave him something to say; suffering gave him the moral authority to say it; and Baptist friends and sympathetic printers gave him the wherewithal to publish it. Michael Smith suffered from hunger, cold, poverty, and ill-health. For all Baptists, he suffered the rebuffs of arrogant Presbyterians; for all Americans, he suffered the tyrannies of British authorities and the insults of their Mohawk allies, one of whom approached Smith with "hasty steps and terrific looks," shouting, " 'Where is de d___m Yankee? Me now kill him— oh, me kill him—his blood now spill—de Yankee must die.' " In his books, Smith combined a geography of Canada with an account of the war, adding to the last editions of his book depictions of his personal travails and spiritual growth. At the start of his career as a writer, he produced travel literature, offering readers the benefit of his "experiential knowledge" of Canada. By the end of his brief public career (1813–1817), he had replaced secular information with a narrative of spiritual experience.[31]

Lured to Canada by promises of cheap land and no taxes, the Pennsylvania-born Smith settled with his wife and two small sons on the shores of Lake Ontario in 1808. He tried various ways to earn money— teaching school, publishing a newspaper, and preaching—but he was never very successful. Even though ill-health and impending war dogged his ventures, he insisted in print that he found Upper Canada an excellent country for poor men. To encourage others to come north, he began a process of observation and notation necessary to produce a geographical and political account of British North America.

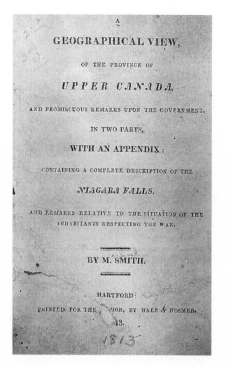

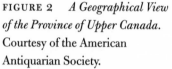

FIGURE 2   *A Geographical View of the Province of Upper Canada.* Courtesy of the American Antiquarian Society.

Judging from Smith's writing, he went to Canada in order to better his fortunes and not to spread the American version of republicanism. Nevertheless, as war approached, it became increasingly difficult to remain above politics, and British authorities, suspecting that Smith, like most of the American settlers who had come recently to Upper Canada, had little love for Britain, asked him to swear loyalty to the king. When Smith refused, they kicked him out of Canada and turned him and his family over to the American army. Smith seemed a suspect character to British authorities, who recognized that his geographical account could serve an invading army as easily as it could would-be settlers.[32]

To add to Smith's troubles, some of the people he met in the United States apparently read his praise for Canada as a sign of disloyalty to his native country. During the Revolution, American Loyalists fled to Canada in large numbers, and perhaps some of those in the United States who questioned Smith's patriotism recalled this earlier emigration.[33] To allay suspicion, Smith displayed his poverty like a badge of honor, insisting that readers see in it proof of patriotism. "Some may imagine, because I write thus, that I have a partiality for the English—but this I solemnly deny; I only describe things in their true characters, with the impartiality of an historian. I began this before the war; I undertook it with an earnest desire to benefit some, I care not who; if any are benefitted I should be gratified; in short, I write this *Pro Bono Publico.*"[34] Smith admitted later that he also wrote for "the benefit of myself, for I am needy enough, having lost all the property I had (chiefly land) in Upper Canada, rather than remain there and be obliged to fight against my own country."[35]

But even patriotic poverty was sometimes a hard sell. One man turned away the "*poor, cold* and *hungry*" family, insisting, "I do not lodge such mean looking people as you are, nor will I let you stay." Even the plea that he had forfeited all property in Canada rather than "bear arms against my *beloved countrymen*" found no sympathy. "You ought to have staid and helped the British to kill every one of the invaders," replied the householder. "Our government had no right to trouble that country! You see what your beloved countrymen have brought you to—then, if you love them so well, go and let them provide for you and your poor perishing wife and children."[36]

Smith may have lost what little property he had in Canada, but he recovered the portions of his manuscript on Canada that he had sent to an American printer. Unfortunately, he had no money to have it printed, so he joined the wandering poor, supporting himself and his family, including his little son Milton Paradise (who got sick but never did get lost), as a day laborer and preacher. When he could find no work, he begged. As he moved through a country where most people were poor, Smith saw no shame in his poverty. In fact, misfortune sometimes contained the seeds of small prosperity, and the poor preacher acknowledged a sort of good luck in following an outbreak of typhus through upstate New York. In the winter of 1812–1813, he survived by preaching funeral sermons to grieving Presbyterians ("the higher class of people in those parts"), who to their apparent consternation had no one to turn to but a man of "Indian appearance," an unprepossessing Baptist preacher in a shabby coat of "bearskin cloth, of drab colour, and quite ragged and patched and belted also around the middle with a strap of leather."[37]

Moses Smith had found sympathetic, believing readers among political partisans; Michael Smith found his among his co-religionists. In Bennington, Vermont, Smith met a fellow Baptist willing to invest in his "experiential knowledge" and to underwrite the publication of his manuscript. In exchange for several hundred copies of the book, the Bennington minister would pay to produce the book. "As I had no money," Smith remembered, "I thought this an advantageous offer, and of course accepted the same." As in many transactions engineered by rural printers and booksellers, no cash changed hands in Smith's initial venture.[38]

Smith went to Hartford, where he arranged to have the first edition of *A Geographical View, of the Province of Upper Canada, and Promiscuous Remarks upon the Government* set in type. It is likely that the Vermont minister's confidence in a market for Smith's manuscript was enhanced by Smith's willingness to append an account of the war to his already completed geography.[39] This was the first of several publishing transactions that financed the Smith family's trip back to Pennsylvania and then on to Virginia. Several times, Smith exchanged the right to print his manuscript and to sell copies of his book in a particular region for a portion of a print run. He worked out arrangements with printers in New York, Philadelphia, and Trenton. Each of these printer-publishers assumed control over a discrete local market, supplying Smith with updated reprints of his book, which he agreed to sell elsewhere. These publishing agreements pushed him south. "After my printing was done," he explained as he started for Virginia, after spending a few months in parts of Pennsylvania and Maryland, "as I had obligated myself not to sell any of my books in the above two states, and as I did not see any prospect of living here, and wishing to go to the south where I married, I concluded to start on that way."[40]

By the time he left New England, Smith estimated that he had left behind almost thirty thousand copies of his book. While he headed south with his little stock in his wagon, copies of his work probably moved out across the countryside in the packs of the itinerant peddlers who supplied New Englanders with reading material.[41] Smith's book was well-suited to readers attuned to what the historian David Jaffee has called the "village enlightenment," because he used piety and patriotism to offer readers a wealth of secular information about Canadian geography and American military tactics. Into these more public stories, he inserted his own opinions on everything from the proper compensation for itinerant clergymen to the best means of converting American Indians to Christianity. As Jaffee suggests, Smith's book, along with many others produced in the early years of the century, helped turn reading from a devotional practice into a means of acquiring secular knowledge. Smith took advantage of this market for knowledge, speculating on his experience just as he had speculated on Canadian lands.[42]

Smith distributed his books as he moved his family through the mid-Atlantic region, where support for the war was strong. Wartime mobilization brought prosperity to the farmers and manufacturers of Pennsylvania and New York who had contracts to supply the army.[43] As the war progressed, the price of Smith's book (like the price of produce) rose. For the first edition, he charged fifty cents. At the war's end, he was asking a dollar, a high price given that a skilled laborer (or an itinerant preacher like Smith) earned about one dollar for a day's work.[44]

When the war ended, he continued to seek out printers and Baptists willing to help him. He asked the Baptists to subscribe to his publications, and he asked the printers to lend him money. Like other itinerant peddlers (such as Washington's biographer Parson Weems), he sold his books where he could find crowds of potential buyers. He approached those willing to extend charity to him and his family and those curious to know more about Canada and the war. Smith went to Baptist meetings and militia encampments, selling books among those who did not know him personally but, by a kind of institutional affinity, were predisposed to accept him as a reliable witness of the events he recounted.[45] He often sold books to people who had heard him preach, who had seen his poverty with their own eyes and assessed his sincerity for themselves. With their help, his books moved from a society of close connections into a world of disparate readers. Late in his career, although he was still a poor man who depended on printers' advances to produce his books, he calculated that there were "about 50,000 volumes in circulation bearing my name."[46]

But profits were slow in coming to Smith. He remembered selling most of his Lexington edition "at a reduced price to the *pedlars;* of course, [I] did not gain much by the publication." He also learned that a wartime book market could be hazardous. He lost would-be customers when a militia company was mobilized; he lost several copies of his books in "transportation"; and, when the British set fire to Washington, most of the Baltimore edition he had stored in the Treasury Building went up in smoke. Without his stock of books to sell, he fell ever deeper into debt and found himself "unable to get money fast enough to pay what I had borrowed in due time," including sizable debts of twelve hundred dollars each that he owed a printer and a bookbinder in Lexington, Kentucky.[47]

As the war drew to a close, Smith added to his book a personal narrative entitled *A Narrative of the Sufferings in Upper Canada, with his family in the Late War and Journey to Virginia and Kentucky, of M. Smith.* When the war ended, he sold his personal narrative as a separate book by subscription, working again among Baptists and soldiers. He accepted the fact that he hardly appeared the most prepossessing of authors and admitted that many subscribed to his book "more from a wish to benefit me than from a desire to obtain such a book"—more, in other words, out of sympathy for the man and his family than out of curiosity about what he had written. Smith boasted about his knowledge of Canada and the war, but by eliciting sympathy from would-be purchasers, he seemed to invite those who bought his book to condescend to a needy man and his family.[48]

A litany of his sufferings, a list that echoed both the sufferings of Job and tragedy of Lear, appears near the conclusion of his narrative.

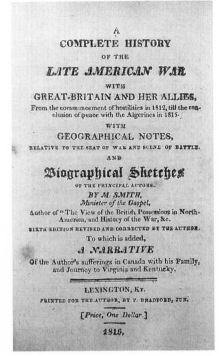

A

COMPLETE HISTORY

OF THE

LATE AMERICAN WAR

WITH

GREAT-BRITAIN AND HER ALLIES,

From the commencement of hostilities in 1812, till the conclusion of peace with the Algerines in 1815.

WITH

GEOGRAPHICAL NOTES,

RELATIVE TO THE SEAT OF WAR AND SCENE OF BATTLE.

AND

𝔅iographical 𝔖ketches

OF THE PRINCIPAL ACTORS.

BY M. SMITH,

Minister of the Gospel,

Author of "The View of the British Possessions in North-
America, and History of the War, &c.

SIXTH EDITION REVISED AND CORRECTED BY THE AUTHOR.

To which is added,

A NARRATIVE

Of the Author's sufferings in Canada with his Family,
and Journey to Virginia and Kentucky,

LEXINGTON, KY.

PRINTED FOR THE AUTHOR, BY F. BRADFORD, JUN.

[Price, One Dollar.]

1815.

FIGURE 3   *A Complete History of the Late American War.* Courtesy of the American Antiquarian Society.

In the first place, I have been brought to the gate of the grave, and seen that vain was the help of man. I have been brought to bow at the feet of the ignorant and wicked savage of the woods; to beg my life at the hand of children. I have been stripped of all I had in this world, and with it my prospect of early joys.—I have been obliged to bear the ridicule of the polished and the laugh of fools.—I have begged bread for myself and family to eat and have been denied the boon.—I have laid on the floor like a dog, and have been refused that privilege; and at other times I have been drove from the ashes to the piercing wind.

Retreating from a description of lonely suffering, Smith concludes his complaint by reminding readers that he is a family man: "In all these sufferings my little babes and affectionate wife have participated, though unused to such things. *My soul hath them still in remembrance, and is humbled in me.*—Jer."[49]

Smith's account of his suffering was clearly intended to move his readers to pity, yet at the lowest moment of beggarly debasement, he played his author card. He was, he reminds us, a writer, a man of experience, with information to sell, or, if he preferred, to give away. He was grateful to those who had helped him, but in his turn he too could be generous. He distributed "gratuitously" some eighteen hundred copies of his narrative to soldiers encamped in Virginia. He said that "the reading thereof did some good by inducing the soldiers to trust in God." However indirectly, reading also encouraged them to support literary projects like Smith's. Some of limited means who chose to buy Smith's books surely did so at the expense of purchasing books by more celebrated authors. Smith wisely prepared for the end of the war by setting aside his narrative of current events and cultivating an evangelical market that valued discussions of a person's relations to the eternal. Although he announced his intention to publish a journal of his life and history of evangelical revivals in the west, his last book was *The Beauties of Divine Poetry, or, Appropriate Hymns and Spiritual Songs*, a project he thought "likely to be the most profitable book I ever published."[50]

Smith had as little talent for accumulation of wealth as he had aspiration for refinement, and it is probably his candor about his economic position that makes him such an appealing character. Even debt, Smith reckoned, could be a sign of his good character, because who would lend money to a bad man? According to Smith, Mr. F. Bradford of Lexington "agreed to print the work, which would amount to nearly $200, without requiring an obligation from me. I mention this to show the reader in what estimation I was held, though nearly a stranger."[51]

Down and out when he finally reached Richmond ("an expensive place"), he refused an offer of charitable funds to maintain him and his family through the winter: "I declined receiving one cent in that way, especially as I had some money. I thought it would be time enough to beg, when I should have nothing to live upon."[52] Writing, Smith sensed, was an honorable substitute for begging—readers could buy his books to benefit him, if they wished, but he offered them something in return. He never forgot that he was as likely to need charity as were many of the poor to whom he preached.

As a wandering man, Smith would have had a hard time obtaining relief from municipal authorities in the towns he passed through. In the first few decades of the nineteenth century, even poor residents who stayed put had to meet increasingly stringent criteria in order to obtain relief. During the years in which Smith traveled the northeast, communities abandoned an easy tolerance for the poor. At the start of the century, those reduced to dire poverty by death or accident could still turn for relief to a patchwork of public and private organizations. As the number of poor people increased during the Embargo Crisis of 1809, during the War of 1812, and following the Panic of 1819, towns adopted measures to restrict begging on the streets. During the 1810s and 1820s, municipalities discouraged public begging; they sent on their way non-residents like Smith and his family, and they passed measures designed to limit outdoor relief and confine the permanent poor to almshouses and workhouses.[53] Unlike reform-minded municipal authorities, Smith was willing both to give to the poor and to listen to their stories. Although he had used his experience in Canada and the war to produce a series of books that turned him into something of an expert, he acknowledged that his social position was little changed. He sustained sympathy for the lot of the beggar, hesitating to draw distinctions between the worthy and the undeserving poor. "For my part, I am so well convinced that nothing is lost, but much gained, by the exercise of a liberal disposition, that I am determined to be so to the extent of my power, and do encourage it in my children (and others); for which purpose I have often put money into their hands, and then led them to the *beggars' shed* in the large cities, to listen to their *tale* of woe."[54] It is hardly surprising that a minister like Smith, who believed that the rich should help the poor, would urge readers to perform acts of charity. What is surprising is that he did so by encouraging them to go to the places where beggars congregated and to listen with hearts and purses open to the tales that beggars had to tell. As we shall see, beggars with stories could muddy the waters of charity.

THE TRAVELS OF ROBERT ADAMS

Robert Adams and his sponsors brought to press just such a narrative from the "beggars' shed." Although Moses Smith and Michael Smith both launched their publications from the margins of society, they were confident that writing would lead to profit, and they retained control over the production and marketing of their books. In their printed works, they argued that their experiences mattered, especially to an American public concerned about world events. They presented themselves as witnesses and offered their words as the testimony of just the sort of free white men whose experiences were coming to define the nation. They insisted, moreover, that poverty was a passing thing, the result of misfortune and not of moral failing. Robert Adams's book differs in several respects, notably in the likelihood that the whole story may have been an elaborate hoax, although it is not clear whether Adams duped London gentlemen or whether a London gentleman tricked the book-buying public. Adams's account of his adventure takes up a mere fifty pages of a two-hundred-page book; the rest of the publication consists of devices of authentication: preface, introduction, footnotes, commentary, an elaborate map, and two appendices containing speculations on African geography. Extensive appendices were common in African travel narratives, particularly when explorers claimed credit for significant discoveries, but the appendices in Adams's book were designed as much to prove the man a plausible narrator as to document his discoveries.[55]

Adams's story was distinctive in other respects as well. It appeared by grace of a peculiar literary patronage; after extracting the story from an illiterate, mixed-race, American sailor, Mr. S. Cock offered it "to the Committee of the company of merchants trading to Africa." "Gentlemen," he wrote,

I beg leave to present to you the NARRATIVE of the Sailor ROBERT ADAMS, in the form which I conceive will be most interesting to you and to the pub-lick, and most useful to the poor man himself, for whose benefit it has been committed to the press.

I have the honour to be,
>   Gentlemen
>>   Your faithful and obedient Servant,

S. Cock[56]

Perhaps Cock's salutation was designed to alert readers to a ruse, suggest-ing that, like the long story that concludes Laurence Sterne's *Tristam Shandy* (1759–1767), Adams's tale was a "cock and bull" story. It is also possible that Cock's "African Committee" was a deliberate play on the African Association, the group of aristocrats and businessmen underwrit-ing the European exploration of Africa. As fabrication, *The Narrative of Robert Adams* can perhaps tell us more about how devices of authentica-tion worked in an early-nineteenth-century beggar's tale than about a trip to the African interior.[57]

Cock acknowledged that the recent departure of Major John Peddie's expedition from London bound for Timbuktu had heightened interest in the sailor's account of a similar voyage. In addition, he and his friends were surely aware of the rapid sale of Mungo Park's recently published African travels.[58] But Adams was neither a Scottish adventurer like Park, nor a British officer; he was an innocent, ignorant, and illiterate American who had managed, through no particular virtue or effort, to reach the mys-terious city that had lured a number of European explorers to their deaths.[59]

To demonstrate for readers the value of the story they now held, Mr. Cock said that the sailor's African tale had made him a "man of conse-quence" on the streets of Cadiz. Adams's account of a shipwreck, a Bar-bary captivity, and a voyage to Timbuktu was so good that he had used it to work his way from North Africa to Portugal, from Portugal to Wales,

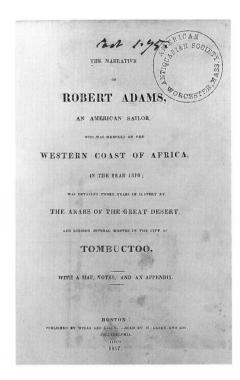

THE NARRATIVE

OF

ROBERT ADAMS,

AN AMERICAN SAILOR,

WHO WAS WRECKED ON THE

WESTERN COAST OF AFRICA,

IN THE YEAR 1810;

WAS DETAINED THREE YEARS IN SLAVERY BY

THE ARABS OF THE GREAT DESERT,

AND RESIDED SEVERAL MONTHS IN THE CITY OF

TOMBUCTOO.

WITH A MAP, NOTES, AND AN APPENDIX.

BOSTON :

PUBLISHED BY WELLS AND LILLY....SOLD BY M. CAREY AND SON,

PHILADELPHIA.

......

1817.

FIGURE 4   *The Narrative of
Robert Adams.* Courtesy of the
American Antiquarian Society.

and finally to London, where, according to Cock, he hoped to trade on his tale one more time and persuade the American consul to pay his passage home.[60] Cock said that he and a group of "gentlemen merchants" who had heard tell of a sailor with a tale intercepted Adams on his way to the American consulate.

Adams explained that he had been forced to leave the United States because of an "amour, which he was unwilling to make good by marriage." Like Moses Smith and Michael Smith, he set high value on his national identity. A British consul in Cadiz was touched when Adams let out "an involuntary exultation at the sight of the American flag, which seemed quite convincing."[61] Although Adams's American identity may have been a marketing ploy designed to give audiences in the United States a tie to his experiences, American identity also gave Cock an excuse to ship an unreliable narrator off to New York, far from English readers who might have questioned his story. A few years later an American reporter found no trace of Adams or his family.[62]

In fact, the begging sailor had no firm identity—national, racial, or personal. The introduction, which at first glance seems to tell readers enough about Adams to make them believe the man and his story, ends with a note from the British consul at Cadiz that clouds rather than clarifies Adams's identity. In the note, the consul admits that the name Robert Adams was unfamiliar to him but suggests that the man calling himself Robert Adams was a sailor he had ransomed who was then known as Benjamin Rose.[63]

According to Cock, Adams was the son of a sailmaker from Hudson, New York. On June 17, 1810, he sailed from New York in the ship *Charles* bound for Gibraltar with a cargo of rice, flour, and salted provisions. In Gibraltar, the *Charles* took on wine, "blue nankeens[,] and old iron" and headed for the Isle of May. The ship ran aground some "400 miles northward of Senegal," and Adams and his shipmates were taken prisoner by the Moors. He was put to work tending goats and sheep. In these respects, his story resembled that of many Barbary captives. But either Adams or Cock soon found a way to make it more interesting.[64]

Adams insisted that he had accompanied the Moors on a slaving expedition through the Sahara. Captured by "a large party of Negroes," the slavers were taken to Timbuktu. While the Moors sweltered in a prison, Adams and a Portuguese boy were free to roam the city. For six months, Adams observed the commerce and customs of the residents of Timbuktu. Cock induced Adams to answer questions that had vexed and troubled a generation of Europeans. Was there an opulent city on the southern edge of the Sahara? Who ruled Timbuktu? Did the natives traffic in gold? How far south did the empire of the Moors extend? How far was Timbuktu from the Niger River, and did the Niger flow toward the east or toward the west? And finally what was "*the extended and baneful range of that great original feature of African society—Slavery?*" The last was no innocent question, and a generation later, African American abolitionists would object to its underlying assumption that slaves were somehow responsible for slavery.[65]

Adams, or the character of Adams invented for the purpose of publishing a little book about Timbuktu, had an answer to every question, and the editor had an explanation for his every answer. As for gold: "He never saw the Negroes find any gold, but he understood that it was procured out of the mountains, and on the banks of the rivers, to the southward of Tombuctoo." As to the site of Timbuktu: the city was situated on a level plain, "on the south-east side" of a river he called the "*La Mar Zarah.*" The houses were "square, built of sticks, clay, and grass, with flat roofs of the same materials," and the king was not a Moor, but a Negro, probably affiliated with the King of Bambarra. The editor pointed out that contradictory accounts about who ruled the city should little surprise Europeans, who had recently witnessed so many changes in sovereignty on their own continent. "[A]n African traveller (if so improbable a personage may be imagined) who should have visited Europe in these conjunctures, might very naturally have reported to his countrymen at home, that Russia, Germany, and Spain were but provinces of France; and that the common sovereign of all these countries resided sometimes in the *Escuriat* and sometimes in the *Kremlin!*"[66]

According to Cock, Adams's interlocutors found his adventures and sufferings so extraordinary that they suspected that his account of residence at Timbuktu was "invention." They asked him to repeat it. Over a period of several weeks, they asked him questions, and they looked for discrepancies in his answers. Internal consistency reassured them, but it was not enough. They felt better when they found in Adams the "artlessness" they considered necessary for impoverished storytellers.

> In Adams we find an individual relating travels and adventures, which are indeed extraordinary, but are told with utmost simplicity and bear strong internal marks of truth. Placed in a wide and untravelled region, where a mere narrator of fables might easily persuade himself that no one would trace or detect him, we find Adams resisting temptation (no slight one for an ignorant sailor) of exciting the wonder of the credulous, or the sympathy of the compassionate, by filling his story with miraculous adventures, or overcharged pictures of suffering. In speaking of himself, he assumes no

undue degree of importance. He is rather subordinate to the circumstances of his story, than himself the prominent feature of it; and almost every part of his Narrative is strictly in nature, and unpretending.[67]

In other words, Adams was the very model of a deferential beggar with a great story; he bowed to the "facts" of his experience, like every "modest witness" to empirical truth, but in doing so, he also bowed to the interpretive powers of wealthy gentlemen.

In the preface, the editor informed readers exactly how Adams came to know the things he now recounted. Late in the story he reminded them that Adams was an illiterate man, an "unscientifick [sic] individual," who had learned nothing from books. His uncorrupted knowledge came, instead, from physical observation. Adams knew the "exact number of *days* occupied in his long journeys" because he had been "obliged to travel almost naked under a burning sun . . . and always inquired, before setting out on a journey, how long it was expected to last." He knew "the precise number of *miles* which he travelled each day" because "he could easily recollect whether camels on any particular journey, travelled well or ill." Heavily burdened camels, he knew, would not travel more than ten to fifteen miles a day; fresh and lightly laden camels would travel from eighteen to twenty-five miles a day. He knew the *"directions"* in which he traveled because, constantly plotting his escape, he "always noticed in a morning whether the sun rose in his face, or not." But what he could not know was what his tale meant.[68]

As a raconteur, Adams grew so deferential that he declined an invitation by the editor to elaborate on a story about witchcraft. "Is it unreasonable to suppose," the editor asked, "that having found his miraculous stories . . . discredited and laughed at, both at Mogadore and Cadiz, Adams should at length have grown ashamed at repeating them, or even outlived his superstitious credulity? This solitary instance of suppression (the particular stories suppressed being of so absurd a nature) may be rather considered as proof of his good sense, than as evidence of an artfulness, of which not a trace has been detected in any other part of his conduct."[69]

In effect, the editorial frames stripped from Adams, the storyteller, all opportunity for self-assertion and made of him a man who deferred to social and intellectual betters. There were instances, of course, when his account appeared preposterous (he described, for example, an enormous elephant with four tusks), but his editor excused these exaggerations as what one would expect from "an uncultivated individual like Adams." All the apologies and explanations for Adams's inconsistencies might be read as simple literary conceit, but, as the editor noted, in 1815 the streets of London were crowded with men like him. The editor may well have been aware that if the sailors milling about the streets began to see themselves as men of "consequence" (as Adams, remember, was wont to do), their discontent could turn to revolutionary violence. In the structures of "truth" that the editor so carefully built into Adams's story, we see a means of taking knowledge (even accidental, experiential knowledge) and its promise of power from a poor man.[70]

Upwards of "fifty gentlemen" (men who carried by grace of title and social position a capacity to pass on the truth of stories told by men like Adams) had seen Adams and "interrogated him at different times; among whom there was not one who was not struck by the artlessness and good sense of Adams's replies, or who did not feel persuaded that he was relating simply the facts which he had seen, to the best of his recollection and belief."[71] The documents surrounding Adams's tale contained several phrases designed to mark its "truth"—the social standing of the gentlemen interrogators, the artlessness of the modest witness, and the consistency of repeated reports—but none was quite enough to prevent questions about the sailor's peculiar tale.

Although Adams's book is often listed among the tales of white men enslaved in Africa, his racial identity, like his tale, was more complicated.[72] To his British friends, Adams was a mixed-race American: "His mother was a Mulatto, which circumstance his features and complexion seemed to confirm," and his "pronunciation of Arabick resembled that of a Negro." But to his black hosts at Timbuktu, he was a white man. His editor noted that Adams called himself the first white man to visit the city of Timbuktu, because the value of the tale rested in part on such a claim. But

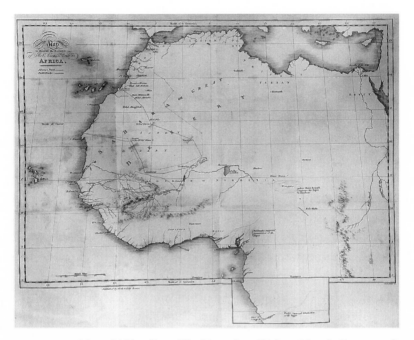

FIGURE 5   Map of Africa (from *The Narrative of Robert Adams*). Courtesy of
the American Antiquarian Society.

a parenthetical aside qualifies the contention: "He believes, as well from
what he was told by the Moors, as from the uncommon curiosity which he
excited (though himself a very dark man, with short curly black hair,) that
they never had seen [a white man] before." The British consul suggested
that it was Adams's religion rather than his race that excited the natives of
Timbuktu. Among the Africans he may have passed as a Christian, but he
described himself as a Christian "who never prayed."[73]

Nor was Adams always the "stupid, unthinking, simple being" his
sponsors suggested him to be. One reviewer, convinced that London merchants were trying to dupe the gullible public with the tale of a guileless
sailor, quoted a "gentleman" who had seen Adams on the streets of Cadiz
and insisted that "he was shrewd, intelligent, and proud, and valued himself highly on the reputation of having been at Timbuktu. He saw it gave

him consequence, and was disposed to take advantage of it." If Adams were "craft[y] and observing," precisely the virtues that might have made him better able to describe the peoples and landscapes of Africa, he was, paradoxically, not to be trusted. The better his intellect, the more likely he was either to take advantage of kindly gentlemen or to inspire his peers to dissent. It is this paradox that makes his book more than just a good Barbary captivity, more than just a good yarn about Timbuktu; it is also a tale about how a story from the beggars' shed served the purposes of gentlemen.[74]

The supporting documents, the appendices, the map, and the commentary by the British consul who had ransomed him failed finally to establish either Adams's identity or the facts of his tale. Contemporary reviewers in the United States were skeptical about both the man and his book, although their concerns differed from those of the British gentlemen, who perhaps used the story to belittle a street person suddenly grown into a man of consequence. American reviewers were less concerned about the revolutionary potential of a propertyless, wandering proletariat than about the history and future of slavery. Editors of the *North American Review* were sure that Adams's publishers had launched the narrative—"a tissue of lies" made credible by the sanctions of "distinguished men"—to take advantage of a reading public made vulnerable by their curiosity about "the city of Timbuctoo, about which so much has been said and conjectured, and so little is known" and by their sympathy for the "accumulated ills of Africa. . . . The natural disadvantages and privations to which it is subjected, had already awakened the sympathy of the friends of humanity. It became now the subject of general attention and interest." Africa, according to the reviewer, had excited two of the most powerful principles of the human mind—"sympathy and curiosity."[75]

Cock positioned Adams's narrative at a precise point where the interests of traders in African markets coincided with recently awakened sympathy for enslaved Africans. Adams's narrative appeared in its American edition in 1817, less than a year after the founding of the American Colonization Society, an organization dedicated to resettling free black men and women in undeveloped regions in Africa. According to *The North American Review*, the good hearts of American readers had made them the easy victims of a scheming beggar and his clever British patrons. A reviewer pointed out the "improbabilities, inconsistencies and contradictions" in Adams's story and asserted that he had searched in vain for an Adams family in Hudson, New York. He also described a letter from the collector of the port of New York, who said that no vessel matching Adams's description of his ship *The Charles* had sailed on June 17.

The reviewer finally dismissed the book as a "gross attempt to impose on the credulity of the publick. To us, indeed, this appeared so obvious, that we should not think it worthy of any serious examination, had it not excited so much interest, and gained universal belief in England." And he concluded, "We leave our readers to draw such inferences from these facts, as they think proper. To us they appear conclusive, and connected with the fabulous character of the narrative, they impress a conviction of deception and bold imposition, on the part of Adams, which we think no one, who examines the subject with much interest or candour can resist."[76] Some fifteen years later, *The North American Review* again dismissed Adams's story as a "motley concoction,"[77] suggesting this time that the begging sailor and not S. Cock and his friends had engineered the fraud.

What are we to make of Adams's African tale? On the one hand, if we assume that there was an historical Robert Adams, a poor and illiterate sailor who begged his way from North Africa to England, then we can read his story as an episode in the social history of a particular kind of experiential knowledge. He told his yarn to his sailor friends, and, apparently, they liked it. To circulate his experience into the world of print, he had to make allies of gentlemen who possessed the authority to label it true, authentic, and, therefore, valuable. On the other hand, if we assume that the story was a hoax, we have an implicit acknowledgment on the part of both hoaxers and those who tried to expose the hoax of the appeals to sympathy and curiosity that made it so hard for readers to know how to respond to a poor man with an extraordinary tale to tell.

THE NARRATIVE OF ISRAEL POTTER

Not long after Robert Adams supposedly headed home from London, another displaced American, "clad in tattered garments," presented a request for passage to the American consul. By 1822, the aging Revolutionary veteran Israel Potter was at the end of his rope. His wife had died; his health was failing; he had exhausted his reserve of rags, nails, paper, and broken glass scavenged from the refuse of the streets; and his young son Thomas ("a child of my old age") was trying desperately to support the two of them by mending chairs, sweeping the cause-ways in front of "gentlemen," and making and selling matches. In the years after Waterloo, competition at the bottom of the economy was stiff, and Potter suffered from the added disadvantage of being known in London as an American. (According to the overseer of the poor who turned him away from the almshouse, he was nothing but a "d—d yankee vagabond.") Despite his hardships, Potter consoled himself that his sufferings were real and that he had never resorted to the fraud so common among the fraternity of the street.[78]

> Among the latter class, there are many; however, who so far from being the real objects of charity that they represent themselves to be, actually possess more wealth than those who sometimes benevolently bestow it.—These vile imposters, by every species of deception that was ever devised or practiced by man aim to excite the pity and compassion, and to exact charity from those unacquainted with their easy circumstances—they possess the faculty of assuming any character that may best suit their purposes—sometimes hobbling with a crutch and exhibiting a wooden leg—at other times "an honourable scar of a wound, received in Egypt, at Waterloo or at Trafalger, fighting for their most gracious sovereign and master King George!"[79]

With effort, Potter persuaded the consul that he was indeed an American, and the consul arranged to send both Potter and his son back to the States. Young Thomas sailed immediately for Boston, but Potter had to

FIGURE 6   "'Old Chairs to
Mend'" (from *Life and
Remarkable Adventures of Israel
R. Potter*). Courtesy of the
American Antiquarian Society.

wait a few months before a berth could be found for him. The consul provided the old man with the wherewithal to sustain himself. Lodged at a
public inn, Potter rediscovered "civility" among the American seamen,
who, like him, "were boarded there at the Consul's expence [sic], until
passages could be obtained for them to America." The displaced sailors
formed a fellowship of storytellers. "[B]y hearing them daily recount their
various and remarkable adventures, as well as by relating my own, I passed
my time more agreeably than what I probably should have done in any
other society."[80] As had Moses Smith, Michael Smith, and Robert Adams,
Potter told his story aloud before a "live" audience, who approved of it.

Potter had long dreamed of returning to his native soil, but his welcome
home was less warm than he had anticipated. Family members he had
hoped to find in Rhode Island "had many years since removed to a distant

part of the country." And his brothers, before departing, had divided their father's estate among themselves. Disappointed in his inheritance, Potter turned to the government, petitioning Congress (as had many of his surviving comrades) "to be included in that number of the few surviving soldiers of the Revolution, for whose services they had been pleased to grant pensions." Congress refused his petition, even though he had submitted his request "accompanied by the deposition of a respectable gentleman (which deposition I have thought proper to annex to my narrative) satisfactorily confirming every fact as therein stated—yet on no other principle, than that *I was absent from the country when the pension law passed*—my Petition was REJECTED!!!"[81]

Other disappointed veterans protested in the streets, but Potter took to the page. Once more, a story of begging resulted in a book, and once more, a writer who was an object of charity became the subject of a story. His twenty-eight-cent book would have to provide his pension, and it was as carefully constructed as a formal petition to the government.[82] Like Moses Smith, whose story was similarly discounted by an official audience in a court of law, Potter composed his book as a motion for a rehearing. Like the books of other poor men turned writers, Potter's story established his patriotism, describing his services in the Revolution and the abuse he subsequently suffered when he refused to renounce his country. He established his need for relief by detailing his poverty and sufferings, his honesty by exposing the lies of other beggars, and his skills as a storyteller by describing himself at home among the raconteurs at a public inn. His story was all that he had to persuade those he met that he was a "hero" and not a fraud. He said in his book that the American consul believed him and so did a "respectable gentleman" whose affidavit he attached to the story.

Of course, Israel Potter is remembered today because Melville rewrote his story (never mind the obscurity of Melville's novel). In Melville's retelling of his tale, Potter found symbolic justification, but symbolic elevation was not initially what the old beggar intended.[83] Like the two

Smiths and the sailor Adams, Potter tried to win an audience by inserting his tale of personal suffering into a larger story. Moses Smith had wanted readers to see him as a victim of the political and diplomatic intrigues of powerful men heedless of those whom they abused. Michael Smith had two great stories at his disposal—a history of war and a history of spiritual striving—and he used them both to lure readers to a tale of woe. Robert Adams embellished a sailor's yarn with information designed to appeal to explorers and merchants who had their eyes on Africa. Or, if you prefer, S. Cock embellished a beggar's tale with information designed to appeal to readers curious about Africa and sympathetic to her sufferings.

All these stories turn on dramas of identity. Who were these men? Were they beggars or entrepreneurs? Were they long-suffering heroes, or practiced liars; innocent victims, or escaped convicts; patriots, or traitors? Each asserted national identity in order to avoid questions about their ambiguous personal identity. Whatever they were, they were Americans, "d___m Yankees," if you will. But American identity was a category as unstable as all the others—not something fixed and permanent, but something claimed and demonstrated. These early-nineteenth-century stories offered readers lessons in how to claim the rights and privileges of citizenship. What would a country do for ordinary citizens caught up in international adventures? Would a government ransom filibusterers from foreign jails, rescue settlers from enemy nations, provide pensions for old soldiers, or pay passage home for the elderly, impoverished, or infirm? If the filibusterers, settlers, soldiers, and others spun a good story, maybe. But official aid was never enough. Begging writers needed a second audience, a democratic readership who would right the wrongs they had suffered by buying and believing their stories.

ENTREPRENEURS OF EXPERIENCE

Most of those uprooted by the political and economic events of the early nineteenth century had modest aspirations for their stories of disaster.

Poor men and women with tales of loss and suffering first turned to family, friends, neighbors, and the agents of organized relief. When these failed them, they resorted to print, exchanging their tales of woe for charity. As municipal agencies came to see poverty as the fault of the poor, they demanded explanations from those who sought help. Explanations involved stories. And good stories got results. For example, several victims of shipwrecks and fires took stories of misadventure to the New York City Clerk's Committee on Markets, which could waive the fee for a license to sell the cheapest of goods—such as coffee and vegetables—in established markets. Stories thus became means to edge into the legitimate commercial economy.[84]

For some, they were a means to edge into the literary economy. In the 1840s, the poet John Greenleaf Whittier took a nostalgic look at the wandering beggars whose tales, recitations, and songs had sometimes broken the monotony of his rural youth. His story "The Yankee Gypsies" opens with the arrival of a beggar carrying a written account of the shipwreck in which he lost his worldly goods. The narrator weighs the beggar and his tale, listening first to the promptings of an angel of benevolence, who urges him to give generously to the man, and next to an angel of prudence, who warns him to be wary of fraud. And indeed the beggar is a fraud. The narrator recognizes him as a man he has seen begging many times before, in the guise of a poor Penobscot Indian, as a widowed father, and as a fever-afflicted immigrant. The narrator discovers that the beggar has purchased the written description to support his latest disguise "from one of those ready-writers in New York who manufacture beggar-credentials at the low price of one dollar per copy, with earthquakes, fires, or shipwrecks, to suit customers."[85]

Whittier recognized that social relations in an increasingly complex economy tried the feelings of sympathy that he liked to think once governed relations between the poor and their more prosperous neighbors. He longed for a world of fixed and stable communities, where few disputed the obligations of the propertied to care for the indigent. The nature of obligation was more difficult to define in a commercial society that depended more and more on transactions between people who did not know each other. Poor men and women, often well-deserving of aid, were forced to move from place to place in search of work. How, Whittier asked, was one to separate these deserving poor from "vile impostors"? And how was one to tell the storytelling impostors from professional poets and writers like Whittier, who made a living arranging words?[86]

Was an author a beggar, a philanthropist, or a businessman who gave good value to discriminating purchasers? Surely some who contemplated the question recalled the opening lines of *The History of Tom Jones, a Foundling* (1749): "An author ought to consider himself, not as a gentleman who gives a private or eleemosynary treat, but as one who keeps a public ordinary, at which all persons are welcome for their money." Henry Fielding's advice to engage the market no doubt suited many writers, but as we have seen, there were "authors" who presented themselves not as peddlers of goods or dispensers of charity but as receivers of alms.

These "authors" proved particularly troublesome to the mid-nineteenth-century reformers who were anxious to systematize the distribution of alms. By providing a foil for professional authors (like Whittier), begging writers played a small part in the commercialization of literature. But they also played a part in the transformation of philanthropy into a profession whose principal activity was distributing money (rather than kindness and love).

Social reformers and philanthropists assumed the task of vetting beggars' stories. The best-known example of this literary side of social reform can be found near the end of English reformer Henry Mayhew's *London Labour and the London Poor* (1851), where Mayhew and his colleague Andrew Halliday denounce the "systematic impostures" of the current generation of beggars. Mayhew and Halliday recognized that dissembling beggars had been around for at least two hundred years, but only recently had the dissemblers made fraud into an organized system. Like Israel Potter, Mayhew and his associates found on the streets of London a motley fraternity of burnt-out tradesmen, blown-up miners, old soldiers, shipwrecked mariners, and fugitive slaves, some of whom had suffered the misfortunes they complained about; many of whom had not.

Fraudulent beggars enraged Mayhew and Halliday, especially those who carried printed accounts of suffering, which were often carefully produced and accompanied by affidavits signed by "honest" men. One of the tasks of Mayhew's Mendacity Society was to protect a credulous public from imaginative schemes hatched by the clever poor. In exposing such schemes, the society also guarded against the misappropriation of the devices of verification so necessary to a commercial world dependent on honest communication in printed documents. To help those who would protect themselves, the Mendacity Society published a list of the poses most common among the dissembling fraternity. The list included men and women (like Whittier's friend) who carried printed accounts of the deaths, disasters, shipwrecks, earthquakes, storms, and fires that had reduced them to poverty. Among the writing beggars, they also found "decayed literary gentlemen" who carried greasy copies of their "works," tales designed sometimes to document suffering and sometimes to serve as evidence of writerly talent worth supporting.[87]

The beggars whom Mayhew questioned knew that some stories were more effective than others. For example, a man who had lost an arm working in a brickyard dressed up as a sailor when he discovered that it was easier to make money posing as a one who had been maimed at sea than to explain his accident in the workplace. Dressed as a sailor, but saying nothing, he could conjure in the minds of would-be philanthropists a long history of nautical adventure. Brickmakers (a job that, as the unfortunate Israel Potter learned, was reserved for the desperately poor) had no such adventure stories.

To their consternation, agents for the Mendacity Society discovered that other beggars were using tales of a more recent vintage. They found men making a living on the London streets by pretending to have escaped from slavery in the United States. Some of the supposed runaways were actually white men "fortunate enough to possess a flattish or turned-up nose" who had "*dyed themselves black*." All the fugitives, black and white, were telling stories of suffering and escape that Mayhew and his colleagues assumed they had learned from reading *Uncle Tom's Cabin*. Americans and American stories had washed up on English shores.[88]

That antislavery sentiment could be inspiration for fraud would not have surprised the genial defender of slavery, George Fitzhugh. Fitzhugh incorporated a long section on storytelling beggars into his defense of slavery, *Cannibals All! or, Slaves without Masters* (1856). He reprinted a catalogue of "*Lurkers*"—poor people armed with stories and preying on the prosperous—that had first appeared in *The Edinburgh Review*.[89] Fitzhugh's catalogue of beggars resembled the compilation of the Mendacity Society, but Fitzhugh used it to defend slavery, not to warn against the wiles of the poor. Beggars were a blot on the free labor economy, a reminder that capitalism had unsettled everything. If wealthy philanthropists were gulled into supporting lying beggars, they had no one but themselves to blame. Fitzhugh knew it would make the prosperous uncomfortable to be reminded that they might be victimized by the clever poor, and he used his knowledge to turn an indictment of heartless capitalism into a warning against abolitionist methods.

Fitzhugh evoked lying beggars to warn those who listened to tales of former slaves: sympathizing with poor storytellers made listeners vulnerable to fraud and trickery. Fitzhugh admitted that he had scrutinized abolitionist strategy and tactics and confessed that he had borrowed for his own projects an art of using poetry and song he learned from " 'our Masters in the art of war' [abolitionists] when we carried their camp and their whole park of artillery (which we are now using with such murderous effect against their own ranks). We also captured their camp equipage, books of military strategy, &c."[90] It was apparent to Fitzhugh, as it was to Mayhew, that storytelling fugitives could be the near relatives of storytelling beggars. By hinting that fugitive slaves adopted the tactics of scheming beggars, Fitzhugh evoked for readers troublesome figures who reminded middle-class abolitionists that their purses, as well as their hearts, were vulnerable.

With Fitzhugh's passage on beggars and stories, we have come full circle. We began with beggars who cast themselves as the victims of circumstances they could not control; we end with middle-class philanthropists who worry that they have become the victims of beggars. Stories of suffering (and the ways stories were told, ratified, and sold) played critical roles for victimized beggars and for victimized philanthropists. It is possible that Moses Smith, Michael Smith, Robert Adams, and Israel Potter found some satisfaction in ordering their experiences into stories and in getting stories made into printed books they could exchange for cash. But they learned that interest in their stories could be ephemeral and that their stories' value depended on their being taken as true. Sometimes they vouched for the truth of their stories by standing up for them, by presenting themselves in person to answer questions. On the printed page, such vouchers lost force.

For poor men, printed truths were tricky things. To ensure the truth of their tales (and therefore their tales' value), they relied on processes of verification exercised by individuals and organizations with acknowledged social weight. In many transactions, such printed verification was the only available guarantee of truth—and yet, as readers and writers knew well, ratification was easy to fake, and certificates designed to assert a tale's truthfulness were as often made to serve the interests of fiction as those of fact. All in all, it was hard to have full confidence in the power of written assurances. They served to acknowledge the power of "gentlemen" to designate "truth," but who was to protect readers from beggars who invented gentlemen to back their lies? A necessary faith in printed forms came back to haunt middle-class philanthropists who opened themselves to the tales they read. Mayhew and Fitzhugh recognized that storytelling beggars exposed faults in a system meant to separate those who spoke and wrote the truth with authority from those who borrowed the trappings of legitimacy and retailed experiences from the margins. As we shall see, the lives and confessions of condemned criminals, long staples of popular print culture, helped readers learn to accept truths asserted on the printed page.

CHAPTER TWO

Convicts

Without a knowledge of the lives of the vile and abandoned, we should be wholly incompetent to set an appropriate value upon the charms, the excellence and the worth of those principles which have produced the finest traits in the characters of the most virtuous.

James E. Seaver,
A Narrative of the Life of Mrs. Mary Jemison (1824)

As a dying man, I certify that what the Rev. Mr. Ogilvie has read to me, is the truth and history of my life.

John Johnson,
Trial and Sentence of John Johnson, for the Murder of James Murray (1824)

WRITING OF CRIME

"It is common among authors, to beg an introduction to their works to the public, by making an humble apology for the crime of writing." Or so said our wandering preacher Michael Smith in a preface to the first edition of his geography. Smith's formulaic apology was surely ironic, but with it he acknowledged that writing was a questionable activity, an imposition on the public, for a man like himself.[1] In contrast, neither the early-nineteenth-century convicts who wrote confessionally of their lives and crimes, nor those who published their accounts, saw a need to apologize for printing such material. This is hardly surprising, especially if we assume that printed confessions serve as tacit acknowledgments that the courts do right to convict and punish. As admissions of guilt, published confessions have considerable social value. Unlike beggars who sought to benefit from their writing, convicts (particularly those headed for the gallows) had little to gain. By offering stories to the public, they committed no further crimes; in fact, they began to atone for previous crimes.

Beggars took liberties in telling their stories, whereas convicts condemned to death were urged by jailers, reporters, printers, and confessors to deliver a version of a life story that could be circulated to the public. As published documents, the lives and confessions of the condemned had epistemological value for people learning to place trust in printed words. Wandering beggars sometimes told strange and outlandish tales that were amusing but hard to believe. To take such tales as true, to believe the affidavits and testimonials they sometimes carried, was to risk being made the victim of a scam (as Henry Mayhew and George Fitzhugh reminded readers). In contrast, the convicts who appeared in print had been *convicted*: their crimes had been proved at trial. With jury verdicts registered, facts in criminal cases were rarely in dispute, and readers could turn to accounts of crime with confidence that, at least on some level, what they read was true. Confidence was further bolstered by the popular belief that those on the verge of death spoke nothing but the truth.

Convicts who produced their tales in the 1820s took advantage of a significant shift in attitudes toward the testimony of convicted felons. Common law had long operated on the assumption that one guilty of a felony was not to be trusted in any respect, and certainly not in testimony. But it was absurd, Jeremy Bentham argued in 1827, to shut the door of the witness box against the testimony of any "such men as happen to have been in the way to see, or to say they have been in the way to see, what, had it depended upon the actors, would have been seen by nobody."[2]

Producing and publicizing the truth about crime, however, has never been a simple matter. "The last words of the criminal, and the ritual of execution," as the literary critic Lennard Davis puts it, "permit paradoxically the lawbreaker to become the law-affirmer, the liar to become the speaker of final truths, and the thief to become the giver of good advice." On occasion, criminals have used the gallows as a podium and challenged the authority of the state.[3]

In the early decades of the nineteenth century, conviction also offered printers, confessors, and sometimes criminals themselves a chance to profit from the sale of a story. The most valuable stories contained the "authentic" voices of confessing convicts. In a criminal population that contained a fair number of illiterates, writing a story in an authentic voice could be difficult. Some literate convicts wrote their own confessions; others, even though they admitted they could neither read nor write, attested (in print) to the validity and accuracy of confessions that had been written for them. In printed criminal confessions, stories declared "true" by juries made their way from the courtroom to the marketplace, where publishers peddled them to a growing population of working-class readers. Readers who paid attention to the testimonials and affidavits so common in criminal confessions perhaps learned to trust the truth of printed stories and by extension to accept the authority of printed documents.

But the market's interest in profit did not always correspond with the court's interest in truth, and sometimes convicts with good stories to tell chose not to cooperate with the authorities who wished to circulate their stories. We know from Michel Foucault that the role of the condemned was crucial to the spectacle of execution: from their own mouths, criminals produced "truths" about their crimes. The condemned—who, in effect, had surrendered their lives to authority—were granted in return permission to speak and to write. When the market for stories made speaking and writing into commodities, however, some of those condemned for misdeeds discovered they had a means to profit from their crimes.[4] In the first few decades of the nineteenth century, dozens of those condemned to die produced pamphlets on their lives and crimes, usually with the help of ministers, reporters, printers, and lawyers who launched them into the burgeoning markets of popular print culture. In published documents, many of the convicted confessed; some also protested, complained, and took advantage of notoriety to publish philosophical speculations and poetic musings.[5]

A BRIEF HISTORY OF PRINTED CONFESSION

Criminals and accounts of their crimes have been staples of popular print culture in America since the end of the seventeenth century. Several scholars have used rituals of execution, criminal confessions, and gallows sermons to better understand how seventeenth-century New Englanders thought about transgression, sin, and salvation. Ministers reminded those gathered at the gallows, and those who later read what had been said by and about the condemned, of the capacity for evil in every person. A community torn by murder was made whole by recognizing "the sinfulness that was shared by all," as historian Karen Halttunen puts it. Rituals of execution reminded witnesses that only God's sustaining grace separated them from those who stood before them convicted of wrong and condemned to die.[6]

This close collaboration of ministers, criminals, and audiences deteriorated over the course of the eighteenth century; confessions published after 1750 show signs of the declining Puritan consensus and ministerial authority.[7] Printers, lawyers, hack writers, sentimental poets, and murderers themselves began to interpret crime for a reading public, and in the increasingly secular world of the late eighteenth century, the law, and not theology alone, seemed the means to make most sense of crimes and criminals. Pamphlet publishers such as Christian Brown in New York profited from the public's taste for crime literature. They produced transcripts of trials, constructed murderers' autobiographies, and reprinted confessions, last words, and fragments of intimate correspondence. Enterprising printers reproduced the lessons of spiritual advisors, published the opinions of experts, and circulated verses inspired by crime and punishment. Struggling newspaper editors seized on local interest in sensational stories and produced hasty pamphlets dealing with trials and executions.[8]

Sensational stories described crimes in lurid detail, but they did not explain the source of human depravity behind the act of murder. By the end of the eighteenth century, murderers had become "moral aliens," monsters who stood outside human society. Stories of murder, which once presented a coherent understanding of the spiritual and social consequences of sin, had, according to Halttunen, become narratives of "noncomprehension, whose thrust was to try *and fail* to come to terms with crime within an Enlightenment liberal view of human nature."[9] Audiences who once had been enjoined to respond to murder with a shock of recognition were now encouraged to shudder at monstrosity that could never be explained. Incomprehensible monstrosity encouraged the curiosity that drove the market for murderers' stories.

Curiosity intensified as the convicted and condemned were moved to locations increasingly further from the public eye. By the early decades of the nineteenth century, convicted criminals were physically isolated from communities, incarcerated in large penitentiaries, where they disappeared from public view. The spectacle of public execution also began to disappear: in the 1820s, essayists argued that executions carried out behind prison walls better served public interest, and reformers denounced public hangings as "festivals of disorder that subverted morals, increased crime, excited sympathy with the criminal and wasted time." Middle-class moralists bent on promoting self-control and private discipline, and merchants and investors worried about riotous crowds, thought that private executions, duly covered in the press, were a better means to extract moral lessons from crime. Pennsylvania abolished public executions in 1834, and by 1845, all New England and Mid-Atlantic states had given up public hangings.[10]

The fact that print provided an alternative means to display crime, criminal, and contrition helped those who worked to abolish public execution. Whatever lessons were to be learned by people gathered at the gallows could be better taught on the page.[11] Printers, publishers, reporters, and ministers pursued those who had once gathered to watch hangings but were now dispersed; they approached them as so many isolated readers, who might, in print, absorb the lessons once taught through public display. Although one printer admitted that "a prejudice generally exists amongst the respectable individuals against works of similar description," the disreputable were market enough. Published confession was one of several means by which early-nineteenth-century Americans absorbed lessons and learned of events that their parents and grandparents might have absorbed and witnessed in person. By midcentury, pamphlets, once intended for local audiences, reached readers scattered across the country.[12]

Through most of the eighteenth century, publication on crime mirrored a spiritual consensus on the sorry state of fallen humanity. When spiritual explanations for human behavior lost their unquestioned force, publication on murder took a secular turn. By the middle of the nineteenth century, sensation, and not moral lesson, drove publication. In telling the story of the transformation of crime literature from spiritual document to sensational story, even in telling it very well, historians have often overlooked two other strains that run through this literature—a story of the cash value of criminal confession, and a set of lessons on how to produce an authentic document about an individual's inner life. Criminal confessions published in the 1820s and 1830s often revealed as much about market value as they did about evil, as much about the production of an "authentic document" as they did about the weight of sin and the horror of crime.

For centuries, ministers had encouraged the condemned to confess their sins before they died; in the 1820s, pamphlet publishers urged them to do so in print. The results were curious documents, designed sometimes to serve the interests of confessing criminals as well as the interests of the state and its agents, jailers, and executioners. By the 1830s, it was commonly accepted that a person sentenced to die should write such an account. "It is natural," wrote Charles Boyington, a journeyman printer convicted of murder in 1835, "that the public should anticipate some statement from me: yet it is not for the gratification of curiosity, however laudable, that I have been induced to commence this exposition, but a deep sense of duty to my distant relatives and friends and to my memory." He reiterated the "plea of innocence" that a jury had rejected, but he also apologized for his rough prose.

> Owing to the great inconvenience under which I have written, there will doubtless be many faults observable, in the language which I have used, but this is not an article, the composition of which will likely call forth criticism from the reader. It is the *matter* not the *manner* that will meet with success or failure, and if through haste or inadvertency I have written any sentence that admits constructions contrary to my intention, let the *words* be disregarded and the *meaning* defined.

Boyington asked that every word be read as evidence of his innocence—the *matter* foremost in his mind. With his pamphlet he tried to get the last word on the question of his guilt. The judgment against him was a local matter, its text confined to archives in a courthouse. His pamphlet, however, was available to a widely scattered readership.[13] His personal history countered the judgment against him; it asserted his innocence, and it reached readers who knew neither the circumstances of his crime, nor the evidence against him.

With a premium placed on their words, with their stories and confessions set in type, the condemned reached beyond village talk and courtroom argument and addressed themselves to audiences of interested strangers who purchased and read what they had written or had had written for them. Criminals who put out versions of their lives acknowledged the advantages offered by publication. A pamphlet, as one publisher put it, created "a memorial" more permanent than either the gossip of the street or the coverage of the press.[14] Memorials to malefactors, which once had helped unite the spiritual community of the fallen children of Adam in a shared sense of common sin, now served an imaginary community composed of the descendants of Gutenberg. Children of Gutenberg, as we shall see, were also consumers of print—children of Adam Smith, if you will—who were ready to spend a little of the nation's wealth on the words of malefactors.

The fact that they possessed in their stories small commodities with market value was not lost on condemned prisoners. Take the case of John Lechler, a miserable Pennsylvanian, who sometime in 1822 caught his wife Mary in bed with his friend and neighbor, Bernhart Haag. Haag tried to get away, but while he cowered bare-bottomed in the cellar, Lechler strangled his wife. Rid of Mary, he turned his attention to Haag. Haag ran home, but Lechler followed, gun in hand; when he fired at Haag through the door of his house, the enraged husband missed, killing Mrs. Haag instead. Before he was hanged for the double murder, Lechler arranged to publish his dying confession, hoping, he said, "to raise a small pittance for the assistance of those innocent orphans who are rendered destitute by the crime of their father and the justice of their country."

Lechler was not confident he had full control over his story, and he concluded his confession with words designed to discredit a pirated version his jailer threatened to print.

> My good old friend, Samuel Carpenter, agrees to receive my confession, and have it published to raise a little money, after paying the printers, to educate my poor children. And I declare with my dying breath that it contains the whole truth. The jailor has frequently, as I have told several people, told me that I must give him my confession, because he gave me such good victuals—and at last I was *compelled*, for I am his poor prisoner, in chains to write a *history* for him, which he intends to have published also.[15]

Few jailers were so bold in their efforts to extract value from a prisoner, but Lechler used his ill-treatment to remind readers that he was a victim not only of a predatory neighbor and a powerful state but of a cruel and greedy jailer who, like so many others, saw financial opportunity in a notorious prisoner. His story had multiple, sometimes competing, purposes.[16]

Other convicts made better allies of their jailers. In 1829, George Swearingen, a Virginian who murdered his wife, remembered men around him fighting to market his confession. "I would here observe, that a few five-penny-bit catchers endeavored to have the Sheriff prohibit my confessor from coming to the jail to write my life and confession, supposing that they might do this service for me, but the Sheriff had too much manliness and honor to pay any regard to them." In contrast, Amos Miner, an itinerant mill-worker who killed a "town-sergeant" in Rhode Island, honored a "five-penny-bit catcher" with his tale, exchanging his story for "all the little services" a reporter had rendered him in his daily visits to the jail.[17]

To represent such a contest in print was to tease readers with the idea that they now held a valuable prize. Printed descriptions of the crowds who came to witness executions served a similar function, offering readers a chance to join those who had made great effort to attend a hanging. Mobs at the gallows surely made clear to publishers the market for their goods, but to depict these crowds in pamphlets produced after the fact helped to persuade readers that they had missed a noteworthy event. The case of John Tuhi is instructive. The sheriff who arranged his execution took into account the "excessive desire to witness the scene" and had the gallows built on open ground. He described the crowd as follows:

> [A] large proportion of the multitude were females, many of whom were at the place of execution by eight or nine o'clock, remote from any building, without shelter or anything to defend them from excessive heat, and there remained scorching in the sun for six hours, rather than relinquish the design, or be deprived of the opportunity (shall we say pleasure and gratification) of seeing a wretched malefactor sent, with violence and ignominy, into eternity.[18]

The story of Rose Butler, a nineteen-year-old girl convicted in 1819 of trying to burn the house where she worked as a servant, also made readers vicarious witnesses at her death. She remembered that she, herself, had once set out to join a crowd on its way to watch a hanging. Distressed, she turned back before she got there. Before her own execution, she observed those who had turned out to see her die. The execution of a woman, a rare event, had attracted several thousand spectators. Butler was surprised that she had become so important. Ministers, sheriffs, marshals, constables, a visiting physician, a pious Quaker lady, the deputy keepers of the prison, a platoon of civil officers, and "a carriage filled with ministers and pious persons" joined her procession to the gallows. "My head feels wild," she told the physician. And then to a "Reverend Gentleman" standing nearby, she commented, "What a great number of people are going to see one person."[19]

Few criminals wrote because someone chained them up and forced them to do so, but many wrote and published to defend themselves against rumors circulating outside their cells and to discount pirated versions of their lives. Lechler behaved like the dying men described by Daniel Defoe in 1726—men who "have been so often injured by the false and imperfect accounts given from those that have pretended to write from their own mouths, that such people generally give (what they design to say) in writing to the Sheriff or Officer appointed to attend the execution, and desire it may be made public, leaving copies with some of their relations, in order to be sure that nothing should be added, or omitted, and so that no wrong be done them."[20]

Lechler also employed devices often used by insecure, one-time authors, criminal or not: he blamed his literary venture on others who urged him to appear in print, and he claimed a compelling need to counter those who misrepresented him and his life. Like many confessing criminals, he tried to use a written text to police speech outside his cell, to check the spread of malicious rumor and mean gossip, and to admit to some misdeeds but to deny others. Similarly, John Schild, who was executed in Pennsylvania in 1813, confessed in print to bestiality and incest but asserted that "he had stolen no cloth of one Hartman; neither had he given poison to Hartman, nor to one Hertz, nor killed the wife of Michael Gehret: but he must confess that he had committed some thefts."[21] Likewise, it was the circulation of "idle and cruel reports" that finally com-

pelled Michael Powers to write. A Catholic, Powers reserved his full confession for a priest, and had

> intended to die without making any observation on his fate, or giving any
> particulars of his life; but there were so many idle and cruel reports in cir-
> culation, and each one ornamented with so many horrors, all told with
> such assurance of the truth, that he was constrained, if not on his own ac-
> count, yet in consideration of his friends, for friends he has, and those dear
> to him, to give the public some sketch of his humble walk through life.[22]

In 1832, Amasa Walmsley published his confession not only to counter
"false reports" that he had killed for revenge, but also to stop a story "stat-
ing that he had sold his body to the surgeons for rum. The story is false in
all its parts. His body, the last curious legacy he can give to his friends, he
has submitted to the disposal of his brother Uriah and his friends." Although Walmsley did not specify the value of his legacy to Uriah, he did
try to control the fate of his body, using his one chance to appear in print
to announce that he did not want to be disinterred "for the promotion of
science."[23]

It is rare to find in tales of the condemned a bequest like Walmsley's: it
is far more common to find a story made over to heirs than it is to find a
corpse. Like Lechler, many recognized that a story, if properly handled,
could be an asset. Together, Lechler and a friendly collaborator wrote a
tale designed to make money. Lechler knew that his performance as a confessing criminal would be valuable to his heirs only if it were published.
Lechler made the purchase of his tale into a charitable act by inviting readers to sympathize with his poor orphans and, through his unfortunate
children, with him. He had killed their mother, but the state was about to
kill their father.[24] He managed to cast himself as a victim and to use a victim's privilege to designate the direction of profits from the sale of his narrative.

Thirteen years later, John W. Cowan, a man who murdered his wife and
children in Cincinnati, got the coroner's consent to use part of the proceeds from his story's sale for the "the pious task of raising a monument

over the grave in which repose the victims of his barbarity." The preface to his confession ends with an affidavit, which bestows all his property, including "right in a certain manuscript, written by myself, and containing my confession and narrative of my life," on the men who "arranged" his narrative for the press and published it. He asked that one hundred dollars be set aside for gravestones.[25] Cowan's friends probably did not grow rich on the hanged man's legacy, but editors and printers did not scoff at the modest profits they could squeeze from a notorious criminal's life.

ILLITERATE AUTHORS

The most successful ventures in publishing criminal lives depended on at least three factors: the nature of the crime (particularly violent, particularly strange), the notoriety of the criminal (surrounding publicity), and the ability of a publisher to produce an "authentic" account (access to the convicted). Publishers often asked readers to witness the negotiations that produced a published text about crime, and when they did so they often considered what it meant to publish as though they were written by themselves the words of those who could neither read nor write.[26] Those who produced printed confessions of illiterates faced two problems: how best to reproduce in writing the spoken confession of an illiterate and how best to persuade an audience of its authenticity.

In some cases, it was fairly easy to solve these problems: after the illiterate John Earls was convicted of poisoning his wife Catharine in 1836, he told his story to six ministers, who wrote it down and read it back to him for his approval. All six of them witnessed "his mark" at the end of his account. The ministers transcribed a conversation and, employing privileges of office, deemed their transcription true and accurate. Although it is surely possible that the ministers accurately transcribed murderer Earls's lies (for they attested only to the process of writing down his confession), their testimony seems designed to extend an aura of truth to the content of Earls's entire story. The published version of the murderer's confession worked because readers brought to it assumptions about the honesty of ministers and the true contrition of the condemned.

In other cases, the exchange of information was more complicated. For example, when the publisher Herman Mann went to extract a confession from Ebenezer Mason, who had clobbered his brother-in-law with a shovel, Mann undertook to construct a conversation that would attest to Mason's sanity. "As it has been a singular trait in his whole life, that he never voluntarily introduces any topic of conversation, it could not be expected that a methodical speech could be obtained without questioning him." The Mason who responded to Mann's questions and appeared in print was hardly methodical, but apparently his responses assured the Dedham residents that his fate was due to want of a "moral education, rather than a total imbecility of mind," and he was hanged on May 18, 1802.[27]

The task of representing Mason in print was unusually difficult. Most illiterate murderers acknowledged the skills of those they addressed in print and tried to explain why they had failed to learn to read and write. Some acknowledged that they missed the interpretive skills that came with literacy. "Being an illiterate man," the murderer Charles O'Donnel confessed in 1797, "I kept no journal; and consequently many acts of wickedness have escaped my memory." Now that he was appearing in print, his journal of wickedness would have been valuable indeed. John F. Van Patten, who watched a man taking speedy notes at his trial, thought a lesson in fast writing could prove useful for a man on the brink of death with a lot to say. He asked someone "to give him the rules by which he might learn to write so well."[28]

Adding to the difficulties of publishing such accounts was the at-times loose definition of *illiterate*. John Cowan, the Cincinnati man who hoped his story would pay for his victims' gravestones, produced a confession and life's account in which he acknowledged both the commercial value of murder pamphlets and the devices necessary to represent in print what were supposedly an illiterate man's own words. An editor introduced

Cowan as "what is commonly called an illiterate man," but apparently by the 1830s those labeled "illiterate" could possess considerable skill in reading and writing. Cowan's amanuensis allowed that the prisoner read the Bible, but that his only prior attempt at composition had been a "slight epistolary correspondence with his friends." The editor found Cowan's orthography "rather good," his syntax "better than expected," but his skills at punctuation entirely wanting. In his prefatory remarks, the editor told readers that Cowan wrote best about intemperance and about the necessity and vitality of religion. Although the editor attributed such rare passages of clear composition to divine inspiration, it is more likely that they reflect earthly borrowings or simple transcriptions from sermons and temperance lectures. Cowan, in fact, had learned to read and write, but he had failed to absorb the self-discipline thought to be part of the practice of literacy. For the murderer, reading and writing had not been steps in a gradual process of refinement. Better for the editor to label him an illiterate than to explain how a man whose principal reading had been the Bible had gone so wrong.

Cowan's carefully structured and clearly written pamphlet concludes with this sample of his own writing: "I want my name signed Amedeately under this—I have it in my power to Ru two familyes in this place and satisfy the world of its correctness. . . . I remain until death your most humble murderer."[29] Like many amateur writers, he signed his publication as he would a letter. His valediction, however, served many purposes: it was a confirmation of the contents of the pamphlet and an affirmation of his new identity as a humble, writing murderer. But it also contained a threat, a reminder that the murderer on the brink of death still had the power to ruin two families. Michael Smith had considered offering a "humble apology for the crime of writing"; Cowan instead cast himself as a "humble murderer" who had become, thanks to crime, a writer.[30] If we read the contents of the pamphlet retrospectively through the final paragraph, it is clear that when his editors set about to manufacture an asset designed to bring in sufficient cash to pay for his victims' tombstones, they did more than correct Cowan's grammar. They provided the logical conventions that made sense of the murderer's life and dressed the "illiterate" man in linguistic trappings to match the black suit they described Cowan wearing at his execution. They framed his story with the devices of authenticity designed to give it added value in the market for murderers' confessions.[31]

Two years later, in 1837, another malefactor met his fate in Cincinnati. The condemned, John Washburn, had covered a good deal of territory in his short and dramatic life of crime, and the publishers of his confession aimed for readers just as geographically diverse. His *Life and confession of John Washburn: (partner of Lovett, Jones, &c.,) the great robber and murderer* was sold wholesale at 38 Strawberry Street in Philadelphia, not in Cincinnati where the murderer lived, killed, or was executed. Dead at twenty-four, Washburn took credit for a prodigious thirty murders—an early serial killer, perhaps, but one entirely free of the sexual tension that fueled the crimes of his Victorian descendants. Washburn killed for money. In his autobiography, he said he was the son of a poor but honest shoemaker who saw to it that his son at least learned to read. Young John went to work for his brother in a brickyard in Memphis, but he fell in with a gang of murderous thieves who took the whole of the Mississippi Valley as their criminal domain. His tale "dictated by himself and written by a fellow prisoner," was a cold-blooded chronicle of his thirty murders: "This last murder was committed in the winter of 1828," Washburn reported. "This murder happened in March 1833. . . . This murder I committed in July 1833."[32]

Anticipating readers' doubts about the accuracy of his calendar of criminal mayhem, Washburn displayed a curious moral fastidiousness and swore on the "Holy Evangelists of Almighty God" that his story was true. Why should readers believe that a man who had forsworn so basic a moral convention as the value of human life could adopt a verbal convention of veracity? Despite his criminal past, he was ready to assent to the obligations, if not exactly of a God-fearing Christian, then certainly of a truth-telling writer.

Washburn concluded by thanking Thomas Walker, the fellow prisoner who had written up his "particulars," declaring himself "perfectly satisfied with the manner in which he has performed his service; but I have no way to recompense him for his services and kindness, except by sincerely desiring the welfare of himself and family, both in this world and the world to come, which thing I do."[33]

AUTHENTIC ARTIFACTS OF EVIL

The content of Washburn's chronology may have been unusual, but many confessing criminals who had only the most rudimentary literary skills also organized their lives as lists. Although one historian has dismissed the detailed recitations that appear so frequently in early-nineteenth-century criminal confessions as "dry, naively empirical itineraries of names, dates, locations, and crimes," such naive empiricism served the needs of those who made and marketed narratives of criminal lives.[34] Chronologies of crimes, lists of addresses, names of victims, employers, and cellmates, and details of the local landscape provided a rough organization for tales told by admitted illiterates. Some editors and publishers preserved local details, recycling them as external signs of the authenticity of the tales they sold. Even if the moral content of confession could not be verified, surrounding detail could, and lists of particulars lent an aura of verisimilitude to grisly tales. The technique was an old one, but it would prove most useful in the 1840s to narrators who escaped from slavery. Many fugitives who wished to add their voices to the abolitionist cause strengthened a moral attack by the accuracy of local detail. An account of particulars made it possible to move on to the general tale.

A good list also displayed the powers of memory of those who, like the murderer O'Donnel, "kept no journal." On the eve of his hanging in March 14, 1808, Peter Matthias recounted his life by listing his own addresses and the names and addresses of those who had employed him. Having bought himself from his Maryland master, he made his way to Philadelphia. He remembered staying three months on George Street, three months on Plumb Street, and three months in the house of Mr. Raybould. Or take the case of Miner Babcock, a Connecticut man who killed his stepfather—perhaps accidentally. Babcock told the story of his life as a history of employment, a litany of small jobs. He noted that he had earned six dollars a month farming, but left the land when offered seven dollars a month to work as a shipboard cook. At sea, he earned eight dollars and then nine dollars a month. He told readers that he worked as a day laborer through the winters and returned each spring either to cooking or farming, and he remembered just what he had earned in each situation. As a writer, Babcock depended on the list, and after he finished his account of his own life, he listed, under a heading "misery loves company," all those who had spent time with him in the Norwich jail.[35]

In 1834 a reporter published the confession of Amos Miner, a cantankerous mill hand who bartered the facts of his life for the "little services" rendered by a reporter to a man in jail. Miner remembered his life in detailed incident, but local detail was not what the reporter wanted. Miner had traveled through the New England countryside in a wagon with his wife and nine children, working in cotton factories. In the manuscript, which we are assured "has been derived from the mouth and pen of the condemned culprit," Miner listed his employers and recounted wrongs that he suffered at each of his many jobs. Or so the publisher tells readers inside square brackets that explain his deletions from Miner's version of his life: "As the detailed account he gives of the sufferings and wrongs he received at those institutions may be exaggerated, as we have reason to believe that some of the direct charges he prefers against the proprietors of the factories are not consistent with facts, we have deemed it unnecessary and improper to give his statements to the public."[36] Miner's publisher may well have been protecting himself from libel, but he was also conversant with the demands of the market, and he aligned Miner's story not with the history of local grievances, but with "biographies of the inmates of Newgate" and "sketches of the more noted villains of this country, from Blackbeard the famous down to the history of Wamsley [sic] the infamous and unlucky."[37]

The publisher's language is significant because it helped to move the story he published into the national market for criminal literature. Local knowledge helped those with little skill as readers and writers structure their memories for print and persuade local readers that, even if the stories were short on insight, they were long on accuracy. Such local detail probably meant little to readers scattered across the country; sensation (an emotional appeal to readers' sensibilities) better served a national market. The popularity of compilations that compared the accounts of several criminals suggest that by the late 1830s readers responded to crime through shared memories of the malefactors they had met on the pages of books and not through knowledge of the misdeeds of friends and neighbors.[38]

Yet even if a text circulated far from the crime scene, a true version of events, particularly one obtained with the cooperation of a confessing criminal, was still worth a premium. Truth was worth more than invention; a murderer's uninstructed voice was more valuable than a polished sermon. And publishers denigrated competing productions. One New Yorker touted the value of his own pamphlet by acknowledging that although it was customary, particularly in large cities, to "palm upon the community pretended narratives, in which little or no regard is paid to accuracy or truth," his own pamphlet was "a plain unvarnished tale—presented as such, not revised," and "worthy of perusal by the enlightened and intelligent portion of the community." He suggested that those whose "delight it is to '*sup full of horrors*'" should satisfy themselves with fiction.[39]

Published confessions also made use of the old assumption that only the most alien of individuals would leave the world having last uttered a falsehood. To remind readers that a confession had been extracted from a person on the brink of death was to offer a warrant for that confession's truth. "Strange as the adventures of my life may appear," Samuel Green, a robber and counterfeiter wrote in 1822, "there is not a word specified herein but what is strictly true, and as these are nearly the last words I shall ever write, I do not intend to go out of the world with a lie upon my tongue, for I have not got to receive the just punishment of my crimes by suffering death upon a Scaffold."[40]

Prisoners had to do more than acquiesce in their own punishment. They had to produce, and to produce from bodies facing death, the language that substantiated and thus made real the justice of the state. The body "lent its truth" first to the story now published, and second to the fictions beyond the story—fictions that sustained the state's ability to take the lives of those condemned by its courts.[41] To keep the body in the text, publishers took words "from the prisoner's own mouth" (or lips or tongue). They wrote, they said, words that "proved to have dropped from his own lips" or that had been "obtained in part from his own mouth and partly from the testimony of others."[42]

Frequently those who exercised "authority" over prisoners vouched in print for a confession's authenticity. In the absence of a body to bear witness to truth, a signature was the next best thing. "It has been generally believed," wrote the publishers of *The Confession of Winslow Curtis*, "that Curtis could not write; therefore a *Fac Simile* of his name, as signed by him at the close of his CONFESSION, has been taken, and will be found within, in its proper place. The original is in the possession of the publishers, and may be seen at No. 4 Exchange Street, by such persons as may desire to view it." We do not know if readers took advantage of the offer to view the murderer's signature.[43]

For others, a promise to vouch for authenticity was sufficient. In 1807, Samuel Hull, an assistant keeper in the New York jail, announced himself willing "(if required)" to testify to the truth of John Banks's confession, as taken and published by one Thomas Mills. Hull had stood by while Banks admitted to Mills that he had hit his drunken wife with a fire shovel. Hull apparently was "required" to come forward, because the confession concludes with Hull's signature. But the statement he signed was not about Banks's transgression; it was about the transaction between Banks and his confessor, and it was designed to enhance the market value, rather than the legal value, of the confession. "No other person has had access to the prisoner for the purpose of taking his confession; that the one alluded to was voluntarily given by Banks."[44]

Many confessions made a fetish of the document, calling on the public to witness the act of transfer. Even if the contents were pure fabrication, the document was authentic. For example, in a preface addressed "to the public," the editor of Abraham Johnstone's confession asserted that Johnstone had "handed" the document "out of the dungeon he was confined in on the morning of his execution." Jesse Strang, an adulterer who became famous for killing his lover's husband, mounted the gallows carrying the text of his confession. "Then, holding a pamphlet in his hand, he said, 'This contains a full confession of the great transaction for which I am about to die, and every word that it contains, to the best of my knowledge and belief, is true: if there is a single word in it that is not true, it has been inserted by mistake and not by design.' " He then handed the pamphlet to the Rev. Mr. Lacey, rector of St. Peter's Church in Albany, who arranged to have it published.[45] And in 1836, when Simeon Crockett handed his confession to the Rev. E. T. Taylor, his publisher, the Boston Society for the Promotion of Temperance deemed the act worthy of woodcut illustration, consecrating it as one of the four great moments of his brief life.[46]

Such explicit testimony of physical transfer was rare. More often, signatures of several men attested to the transfer, offering a provenance for the confession now available for purchase. Three men, "Frederick Wolfersberger, esq., Sheriff of the county, John Downey, esq. and John Wyeth, esq. printer," acknowledged the truth of the confession of James M'Gowan.[47] A minister, a sheriff, a clerk, a turnkey, and the murderer himself swore to the authenticity of George Swearingen's confession, and each attested to the veracity of the others. Swearingen swore the confession was his; the clerk swore Swearingen had signed it with his own hand; the sheriff swore he saw him deliver it thirty seconds before his execution and that he was not the type to "die with a lie in his mouth"; and the turnkey swore that he had sat with the Rev. N. B. Little, the man who held the copyright to the published document, while he was writing it and reading it back to Swearingen. And, the clerk added, "this is it."[48]

FIGURE 7   "Rev. E. T. Taylor Receiving Crockett's Confession" (from *A Voice from the Leverett Street Prison*). Courtesy of the American Antiquarian Society.

Antoine Le Blanc, a Frenchman convicted in 1833 of a murder spree in New Jersey, demanded an even more careful collective rendering of authenticity, but, as in Swearingen's case, the number of figures made authenticity seem more the product of conspiracy than a simple act of ratification. Five individuals, a dead family, and an unspecified group of "proper persons" graced the title page, which read "S. P. Hull's report of the Trial and Conviction of Antoine Le Blanc for the Murder of the Sayre Family at Morristown, New Jersey on the night of the eleventh of May, 1833. With his CONFESSION as given to Mr. A. Boisaubin, the interpreter. Lewis Nichols, Printer, Corner of Pearl and Beekman streets. New York." The following statement appeared in the center of the title page, on either side of a portrait in profile of a man identified as the murderer: "Every document certified as correct, by the proper persons. I certify the above to be a correct Likeness of Antoine Le Blanc. August 30th 1833. George H. Ludlow, Sheriff of the County of Morris."

The publisher knew Le Blanc's place in the genre, and he concluded the confession by recommending the stories of Gibbs the pirate, William Teller, Caesar Reynolds, and George Swearingen. His mention of other published confessions—probably an indirect form of genre advertising—suggests that he advised Le Blanc to address himself to a new kind of audience: an audience of scattered readers who enjoyed shuddering at any representation of evil, no matter how distant, rather than to a local community that gathered at the gallows to shudder at the person of the condemned, the embodiment of evil in their very midst.[49]

SILENCE

Protestant ministers also saw value in publishing the stories of criminals. For ministers and lawyers, criminal autobiographies offered a means to advertise their skills before the literate public.[50] In a world where expertise flowed increasingly from the command of information contained in printed material, ministers and lawyers who had once earned professional recognition for their oratorical skills used published confessions as one of many means to reassert their authority on the page. In many cases, those who read of murder would learn of the labor of ministers.[51]

Sinners and their confessors who refused to share accounts of crime with printers irritated those who catered to a public curious to read sensational stories. Some of those who were thus irritated used the silence of Catholic criminals to attack the efficacy of confession and to appeal to readers who were increasingly hostile to Catholic immigrants.[52] Joseph Sager, a man from Maine who murdered his wife, blamed his downfall on a serving girl, "an Irish Roman Catholic who believes they can have all their sins pardoned by the Priest at all times." Similarly derogatory, a "Protestant Divine" waxed poetic when he was refused admission to a condemned man's cell: "The Priest sat by / To shrive his soul from purgatory—vain hope! / That man in reason could commit a crime, / Repentance, caused through fear, would pardon. / The judgment seat of God, alone, unfolds this mystery."[53]

But the problem of confession was commercial as well as moral, because without a murderer's voice, it was difficult to fill a pamphlet with "authentic" material. "We understand," wrote the two men who published Thomas Barrett's confession in 1845, "that he has made a full confession to the priest, but of what nature no one can tell, as the Catholic confessional is held sacred. We have been at great pains, and have gathered all the particulars which can be obtained." The particulars included the contents of the stomach of Barrett's victim—a gruesome list of meat, potatoes, and berries—offered as a sort of substitute for the contents of the murderer's mind.[54]

A man like John Erpenstein proved more useful to Protestant ministers. Erpenstein, an immigrant from Prussia, murdered his wife when she arrived to join him in New Jersey in 1851. His published confession detailed his gradual progression toward Protestantism, and he structured his life story as one long attack on the Catholic Church, especially its drunken priests. Personal animosity augmented intellectual dissatisfaction, and he insisted that it was the absurd disproportion between the enormity of his sin and the paltry penance demanded by his confessor that started his conversion to Protestantism. A priest "heard me confess, and afterwards imposed on me 8 ave marias, to be repeated three times a day. The following week he came again and shrived me once more. I told him everything. One day I received holy bread." He was absolved, he wrote, "yet found no peace."[55]

Not all murderers moved so gracefully toward a published confession. The Baptist minister John Stanford encountered a recalcitrant man in New York in 1823, and the story of Stanford's dealings with John Johnson illuminates with particular clarity the cooperation necessary to bring a criminal confession to the marketplace. The story of Johnson's published confession also tells us something about the fate of those who refused (for whatever reason) to produce a story for an expectant public. For ministers and printers, Johnson's statement was apparently a valued prize, but the condemned man did not make it easy to obtain.

John Stanford, who helped produce several printed confessions, was born in England in 1754 and was ordained a Baptist minister before coming to the United States in 1785. He served as pastor of the Church of Christ in New York City from 1795 until 1801, when the church was destroyed by fire. Lacking a fixed congregation, he took under his "ministerial charge" those confined to the "various humane and criminal institutions" in New York. In 1812, Governor Dewitt Clinton appointed him chaplain of the state prison in New York City, giving Stanford unlimited access to inmates and their stories, and Stanford served his captive flock with dedication until his death in 1834. In the 1820s, he began to keep a log of the sermons he delivered to the city's institutionalized populations. Without careful record keeping and publication, little of his work among the incarcerated would have been visible to the public. In a personal diary, he also recorded his daily rounds of visits, charting his congregants' slow progress toward divine grace. He took "short notes" on all the prisoners whom he visited, and in the late 1820s he published a collection of his notes, "to show the benefit of the institution and to magnify the riches of a Saviour's mercy to the chief of Sinners!" Stanford hoped his book would guide other people who came to work in prisons. He advised ministers to maintain humility in the face of sin and cautioned against either complacency or curiosity.[56]

Instead of pride and curiosity, Stanford carried piety, humility, and prayer into the prison, and he carried stories out, arranging for the publication of several criminal biographies and confessions. He worked closely with a printer named Christian Brown, and together they produced several criminal confessions in the 1820s.[57] In most cases, Stanford appended his own notes to these publications, describing in detail the work it took to make a convict confess. Publishing his notes served many purposes for Stanford. For example, the portions of his diary that are reprinted throughout his *Last Dying Words and Confession of James Reynolds for the Murder of Captain Wm. West* documented his work as a minister without church. They gave him something to show for his labor, something to offer the prison keepers who allowed him privileged access to their charges. Through Stanford's notes, prison keepers extended the range of their surveillance from body to soul. "I shall now close these notes," he wrote after presenting Reynolds' "full disclosure." "As usual they are given to Messrs. Grant and See, of the City Prison, as their perquisite. It is requested that should their Printer obtain any other papers on the subject of James Reynolds, that they should be kept separate from these Notes, as the writer is not answerable for any other communications."[58]

Although Stanford traced his work among condemned convicts back to Puritan ministers who had acknowledged that only the grace of God separated the worthy from the unfortunates who stood on the gallows, his work was drawn into a competitive market that placed a monetary as well as a moral value on criminal narratives.

One of Stanford's prisoners who refused to confess publicly about the murder for which he was eventually hanged became the subject of popular conjecture and, as an object of speculation, the subject of several competing pamphlets. John Johnson kept a sailor's boardinghouse in lower Manhattan—perhaps not an occupation of great respectability, but one at which Johnson earned enough to purchase a small farm in upstate Orange County. Early on Sunday morning, November 23, 1823, the body of an unidentified man who had been hacked in the head with a hatchet was found in a downtown alley. The corpse proved to be one of Johnson's lodgers, a man named James Murray. When a bloody sheet was found in Johnson's cellar, he was arrested, tried, and convicted of the slaying.[59]

Shortly after his arrest, Johnson, worrying that his wife and daughter would be implicated in the killing, confessed orally to murder. A few days later, he retracted his confession and then steadily refused to sign for Stanford any written version of his remarks. He admitted that he had plotted with another man to rob and murder Murray, but insisted that he had not been the one to deliver the fatal blows. Apparently the crime that bothered Johnson most was his failure as a landlord to protect a lodger. He did not see himself as a man who had neglected his duty to God, but as a man who had failed in his obligation to protect a paying customer. Johnson's murder of Murray seemed to fit an image of the city teeming with villains ready

LIKENESS OF JOHN JOHNSON.

FIGURE 8 "Likeness of John Johnson" (from *A True Account of the Confessions and Contra Confessions of John Johnson*). Collection of the New-York Historical Society.

JOHN JOHNSON, born in Antrim, county of Antrim, Ireland, is now in his 47th year.—Married his wife in Antrim ; her name was Ellen McFalland ; Mary his first child, was born at Albany, and is now in the 17th year of her age.—He has five children, four boys and one girl.—His Farm at Newburgh, consists of 35 acres of land, valued at $25 per acre ; the frame house on the premises cost $525

to set upon innocent travelers. That Johnson's story conformed so easily to notions about urban villainy likely made it easy to tell. What would be the fate of a commercial metropolis if all stories entertained in the imagination were proved to be true in the courts? Johnson's repeated apologies, not for the murder of Murray but for neglecting his duty as a host, may have been designed to support his contention that he was a mere accessory to murder; they certainly served also to reassure commercial travelers that even a drunken and villainous lodging-house keeper recognized an obligation to protect his guests.[60]

Stanford began to visit Johnson in December 1823, and he continued to urge him to confess throughout the spring of 1824. His efforts intensified in March; he recorded ten visits to the prisoner that month. In the course of the visits, Stanford read Johnson's correspondence with his wife, and he did not hesitate to comment sharply about her having included mundane reports about the livestock on their upstate farm. Her letter, he commented, "exhibits either a great want of feeling or education," and he reprinted the whole for his readers to judge. Perhaps Stanford was also annoyed because in the course of the letter she and her daughter advised Johnson to guard his silence and not to confess to Stanford, or to anyone else.

> The people say that come up from New York, that you are going to write your life, but dear father there are more of writing going than you could think of. I hope God will have a little more guide in your hand than for to let you write anything about your life. It is bad enough now, don't let them have any speech nor any life to have printed in books when you are dead. And you have so much printed now it would take half a day for to read it. Dear husband, make your prayer to God and die innocently, as I believe you are; and make none to the public for they cannot relieve your poor soul.[61]

Mrs. Johnson's extraordinary letter shows that she understood several important things. Writing up his life would not save Johnson's soul or protect his life history from misinterpretation. This capable woman, who managed the family farm and reported its finances quite precisely, made no mention of the profits to be derived from publication; all a printed confession would do was prolong Johnson's notoriety and the family's shame. Johnson told her she was wrong to suppose that "if he said nothing either in prison or at the place of execution, the printers would not print anything respecting him, or have a picture of him hanging in the gallows." He knew that "whether he said any thing or not, the printers would circulate a pamphlet concerning him."[62]

Johnson chose as his public spokesman not John Stanford, who as state-appointed minister to the incarcerated claimed an official right to his story, but James G. Ogilvie, a Presbyterian minister with a church down the block from another New York printer, a French immigrant named Joseph Desnoues. Johnson gave Ogilvie his life story and "in his handwriting a certificate; the following is a copy: 'As a dying man, I certify that what the Rev. Mr. Ogilvie has read to me, is the truth and history of my

FIGURE 9 "Order of Procession" (from *A True Account of the Confessions and Contra Confessions of John Johnson*). Collection of the New-York Historical Society.

life.'" Ogilvie, not Stanford, had the document the prisoner had approved. Ogilvie and Desnoues recognized that the cooperation of the condemned made their pamphlet particularly valuable, and to validate their contentions, they reprinted the certificate from Johnson.[63] The testimony of a convicted criminal, rather than the testimony of "distinguished men," assured readers that the pamphlet told the "truth."

It is little wonder that Stanford, faced both with an uncooperative family and a rival minister and printer, needed the occasion of Johnson's execution to launch his own pamphlet. Stanford turned Johnson's silence—soon to become the silence of death—into material for publication, but even as he did so, he gave the condemned man an oddly heroic cast.

Johnson's execution was a great public event. He was escorted to the gallows by members of the cavalry, the infantry, and the clergy. According to one chronicler, a crowd of fifty thousand (nearly half the population of New York City) showed up at Thirteenth Street and Second Avenue and filled the park "to a degree that was never before witnessed. It presented as it were a solid mass of living flesh—men, women and children of all colours and descriptions." Here was the early-nineteenth-century executioner's nightmare—a mixed crowd (including enough pickpockets to produce dozens of complaints) and a sullen, uncooperative prisoner. Even on the scaffold, Johnson continued to resist pressure to confess to murder and went so far as to refuse to allow a clergyman to make a speech. (Stanford, nevertheless, felt it to be "his duty" to offer up a public prayer.)

After his execution, Johnson's body was given to surgeons, who wired it to a voltaic battery "of greater force than is anywhere else recorded. (328 pairs of plates of 4 inches)." In the theater of the College of Physicians and Surgeons, doctors made a play of the dead man's muscles. They not only reproduced the "results of Dr. Ure in Glasgow," they also produced a "nervous twitching of the mouth" and made the muscles of his heart contract. So the "strangely unfeeling and contradictory" man who had long refused to confess in public and held heart and voice apart from the city's commercial culture had his muscles of speech and sentiment manipulated when all his will was absent.[64]

Johnson lost the contest for power played out around the gallows where he died. His defeat reminds us how difficult it could be to control a story. Johnson, Murray, Stanford, Brown, Ogilvie, and Desnoues helped usher in the world where readers would purchase millions of words by and about notorious criminals. To many of these stories, readers would respond with a shudder reminiscent of Johnson's twitching body wired to its voltaic battery. Indeed, some publishers made the power of sensory connection explicit. An editor who joined a crowd at a murder scene of a murder noted that "one shudder of horror shook the hearts of the spectators of this direful scene with an electric spasm."[65]

The market for sensational tales of horror and violence was a good one. Even as readers turned to such stories to learn the dangers of a wayward life or to indulge passions forbidden in a public culture based on liberal humanitarianism, they promoted a market where a confession could be exchanged for food, comfort, or a gravestone.

The market for tales of suffering was more fickle. In the 1830s another group of powerless and sometimes illiterate narrators made their way onto the margins of print culture. Men and women who escaped from southern slavery addressed in print a northern audience learning to respond to suffering set down as story. To get what they wanted with their stories, fugitives adopted many of the strategies that served beggars and convicts. They, too, needed to persuade readers to believe their stories. They, too, needed readers to act to complete their tales. They, too, wrote as narrators who merely described their experiences. They too claimed they were willing to abase themselves before those who would present and ratify their accounts. Although we have come to accord slave narratives a central place in our cultural heritage, it was not always so. In many cases, it was easier for felons to profit from true stories told from prison than it was for fugitives to have their stories believed. Slaves testified in texts, as they did in court, under a cloud. Value was easily accorded to confessions of the condemned, for the condemned had already been convicted of the deeds they described. They could also be made to stand as witnesses to their own moral depravity, to utter the truths that naturally and unquestionably fell from the lips of those on the verge of death.

The indictments of society implicit in slave testimony were more difficult for many early-nineteenth-century white Americans to accept. Whereas those on the brink of death were presumed honest, slaves often were presumed dishonest. It was not easy to persuade readers—even sympathetic abolitionists—that the testimony of former slaves was true. To read fugitive narratives alongside stories peddled by others without social, cultural, or even legal standing reminds us how difficult it was for those without power or property to tell their stories when, where, and how they wanted.

✣

CHAPTER THREE

Slaves

The earnest wish to lay this narrative before my friends as an impartial statement of facts has led me to develope some parts of my conduct, which I now deeply deplore. The ignorance in which poor slaves are kept by their masters, preclude almost the possibility of their being alive to any moral duties.

Moses Roper,
A Narrative of the Adventures and Escape of Moses Roper from American Slavery (1840)

The facts in this case are my private property.

James Pennington,
The Fugitive Blacksmith; or Events in the History of James W. C. Pennington (1849)

JAMES WILLIAMS, AN AMERICAN SLAVE

On January 4, 1838, the Executive Committee of the American Anti-Slavery Society authorized the poet John Greenleaf Whittier to "write a narrative of the life and escape of a fugitive slave now in this neighborhood, & that the same be published under direction of the Publishing Committee, with a portrait and other embellishments."[1] *Narrative of James*

Williams, an American Slave was the first story of a fugitive slave to appear under the official auspices of organized abolition, and the small book about James Williams took its place in a growing library of antislavery publications. When the abolitionist James Birney took a count later that year, he found that the society had produced 47,250 tracts and pamphlets, 4,100 circulars, 10,490 prints, several hundred thousand periodicals, and 7,877 bound volumes. "Our publications," he added, "cannot be classed according to any particular style of quality of composition. They may be characterized generally, as well suited to affect the public mind—to rouse into healthful activity the conscience of this nation, stupefied, torpid, almost dead, in relation to Human Rights, the high theme of which they treat."[2]

For organized abolition, a library of publications served several purposes. At a most basic level, the sale of printed documents helped to underwrite the lecture tours of abolitionist speakers, both fugitive slaves and activists, black and white. By the late 1830s, "true stories" of slavery also helped to counter increasingly vocal slaveholders, who defended their practices not only as right but as positively beneficial to slaves and society. Dramatic tales added life to moral and philosophical debates over slavery, attracting audiences schooled in the emotional responses demanded of those who read novels. And common readings helped members of an extended movement to imagine themselves as a community of like-minded workers. Texts urged readers to envision the United States as a country without slaves.

The collaboration between Whittier and Williams illuminates just how complicated it was to launch a work designed to address such an agenda. The book that Whittier made out of Williams's story addressed the "high theme of human rights" by describing the experiences of a man who had been first a house servant in Virginia and subsequently a driver on a cotton plantation in Alabama. The 108-page book opened with a portrait of Williams engraved by Patrick Reason, an African American artist working in New York City. In an unsigned preface, Whittier condemned the hypocrisy of American slaveholders who were able to live with the

FIGURE 10   James Williams, from *Narrative of James Williams*. Courtesy of the American Antiquarian Society.

"hideous anomaly of a code of laws, beginning with the emphatic declaration of the inalienable rights of all men to life, liberty and the pursuit of happiness, and closing with a deliberate and systematic denial of those rights in respect to a large portion of their countrymen."[3]

However strict the official code, individual masters were far worse. Whittier reminded readers of this fact and detailed the measures slaveholders employed to keep "people in strict *subordination*." As though to bring slaveholders forward as witnesses to their own brutality, Whittier included in his preface several advertisements for runaway slaves. In each, he set in italics the scars that instruments of torture—whips, buckshot, dogs, branding irons, and iron collars—had left on the bodies of slaves. "Such testimony," he concluded, "must, in the nature of things, be partial and incomplete. . . . [F]or a full revelation of the secrets of the prison-house we must look to the slave himself." In other words, Whittier looked to Williams to read the scars, to tell the stories of pain, suffering and torture contained in each lash mark on a slave's back.[4]

In a first attempt to authenticate the document, Whittier contended that he had gathered the pieces of a "simple and unvarnished story" just as they had fallen "from the lips of the narrator." He urged the slave's story on readers with a sequence of sentences attesting to its visceral appeal. In Williams's story, Whittier said, "we hear," "we see," and "we look" on the suffering slave. As had the man who edited the story of the illiterate sailor Robert Adams, Whittier employed one of the key devices of authenticity: he assured readers that Williams had successfully repeated the events of his life on several occasions, and he listed in a footnote the names of "gentlemen, who have heard the whole, or a part of his story, from his own lips." To augment Whittier's assurances, the advertisements for the narrative claimed "the perfect accordance of his statements (made at different times and to different individuals) one with another, as well as those statements themselves, all afford strong confirmation of the truth and accuracy of his story."[5]

Using the first-person singular and his own writerly diction and language, Whittier presented Williams's "true" story. Clearly the words were Whittier's even if the experiences belonged to Williams, and we have entered a murky area of authorial collaboration, one marked by a distinctive mix of truth and invention. Like most slave narrators, Williams began with his place of birth. "I was born in Powhatan County, Virginia[,] on the plantation of George Larrimore, sen., at a place called Mount Pleasant, on the 16th of May, 1805." Williams's experience of slavery in Virginia was relatively benign, but he used the opening pages of his story to cite by name seventeen slaveholders, who thus fell under the book's general indictment of all slaveholders as cruel hypocrites.

The Virginia idyll was shattered when Williams's master married an ill-tempered French woman from New Orleans and settled with her, his 214 slaves, and an evil overseer named Huckstep on a plantation in Alabama. Williams detailed for readers the daily life of slaves, describing what they ate, where they lived, and how they worked. But the dramatic thrust of the story hardly lay in the details of life and labor; it lay rather in details of punishment. From Williams, readers learned how slave-holders disciplined a labor force: in Williams's particular case, the instruments of torture, rarely employed in Virginia, saw constant use in Alabama.[6]

Although he tried to cultivate sympathy for the enslaved, Williams did not describe himself as the victim of the tortures he detailed. Williams told Whittier he finally determined to escape the plantation after he had been asked to prepare a "burning solution," a wash of salt and pepper, "to bathe" the lacerations on the back of a flogged slave. "Sleeping . . . by day and travelling by night in a direction towards the North Star," he managed after several months to reach the house of friends in Richmond. With the help of his Virginia friends, he continued on to Philadelphia, where "benevolent" Quakers (like Whittier himself) sent him on to New York.[7]

The *Narrative of James Williams* concluded with a "Note by the Editor," which informed readers that James Williams, certain that he "would not be safe in any part of the United States" and wary of the "unsettled state of the Canadas," had sailed for Liverpool. Instead of selling his body, James Williams sold his story and took off for England. The editor appended the testimony of several "gentlemen," whose stories corroborated in a general sense the "facts stated by James Williams."[8] In its details and in its structure, Williams's story differed little from the classic slave narratives that were to play so important a part in the organized antislavery movement of the 1840s and 1850s. But when Williams left for England, his story ran into trouble.

Within a few months of its publication Whittier's neatly packaged project began to fall apart. Several parties, as we shall see, had an interest in whether James Williams had told a "true" story, and their interests, although sometimes complementary, were more often at odds. Defending his slaveholding readers, an Alabama editor challenged the truth of the *Narrative of James Williams*. In response, some abolitionists defended the honesty of the man and the power of his story and urged readers to ignore any questionable details and accept the narrative as a true portrait of slaves' suffering. Other abolitionists thought it better to hold slave narrators to strict standards of accuracy and recommended that a story that could not be presented as fact be withdrawn from circulation. The controversy around James Williams and his narrative reminds us how difficult it was in the late 1830s to incorporate the testimony of slaves into the cultural fabric of the antebellum North.

Although fugitives' narratives certainly depicted the pain and suffering of slaves, the political power of portraits of suffering depended on their being taken by readers and listeners as "true." When the board of the American Anti-Slavery Society approved Whittier's project, it was not altogether clear what the standards of truth were to be. Like their contemporaries in the press who worked out the conventions of "objective" journalism, abolitionists and fugitive narrators constructed workable compromises between the emotional pull of an individual story and the intellectual demands of a true one. Why did it matter whether James Williams invented the details of his story? To be embraced by abolitionist readers, how closely did a story have to stick to the facts? What was necessary to convince audiences and readers that former slaves, so notorious in bondage as skilled liars, had been converted in freedom to tellers of truths?[9]

The discussion that follows uses the slaves' narratives to explore changing ideas about truth in a society that was simultaneously democratic, slaveholding, market-oriented, and built on contractual relations. To understand the narratives produced by fugitives, we need to look to the texts themselves, to the abolitionist devices that framed them, and to the lecture platforms where former slaves described experiences and then answered questions about themselves and their stories. The controversy over James Williams and his story makes most sense if we see it as part of the process that turned slaves who "by nature lied" into freemen who by obligation told the truth and kept their word. By leaving the country, James Williams left the process unfinished. The printed page alone was not enough to convert slaves to truth tellers in the eyes of their audiences; the former slaves had to do more. Many had to present themselves for interrogation. Apparently, the further one descended the social scale in antebellum America, the more embodied and specific a tale had to be to be taken as true.

We have often looked on slave narratives as documents that tell a story of liberation, as if the narratives mapped the moves from bondage to freedom. And yet the stories told by former slaves did not always end with the narrators' incorporation into a free society; they ended with narrators on the lecture circuit—no longer enslaved, to be sure, but suspended somewhere between slavery and freedom.[10] Such unfinished stories made good literature for a political movement, because they encouraged those who heard and read them to take action to complete the tales. (This was a common tactic of poor people trying to use stories to accomplish something in the world. Take, for example, the cooper we met in the first chapter who asked readers to complete the plot of his misadventure and right the wrongs he had suffered.) Fugitives who appeared on the lecture circuit could also verify the tales they told. From the troubled history of James Williams, both fugitives and abolitionists learned the importance of allowing audiences to watch and question fugitive narrators. Set down in print, like the scenes of transfer so important to criminal confession, scenes of interrogation reminded readers that a story had passed a test of authenticity. But even though fugitives on the stage answered the questions about authenticity asked by abolitionist audiences, the figure of the fugitive on the stage left uncertain the social and economic futures of former slaves.

In their stories and in answering questions about them, fugitive narrators displayed their capacity to recognize the difference between truth and lies, between fact and fiction, and between experience and invention. An ability to lie may have been an asset to the slave, but in abolitionist circles it was a liability. To better suit the work of white abolitionists, fugitive narrators used stories to present themselves as individuals who possessed the moral capacity to tell the truth, give their word, keep their promises, and ultimately become free laborers. Stories enacted a form of conversion, but they also answered the concern that slaves were incapable of self-government because they were, to borrow the historian Eric Foner's characterization of southern fears, unable to "subordinate their passions to rational self-discipline."[11]

To best display their conversions to conscientious honesty, fugitive narrators had to remain on the abolitionist lecture circuit, and there the stories they told remained mere documents of promise. Like all personal narratives written not as worked memoirs but as means to a current goal, fugitive narratives told of lives still incomplete—mere promises, so to speak. While stories displayed narrators as individuals capable of keeping promises—to readers and to employers—they set those promises in a society where freedom had yet to be realized.[12]

Evidence of the unfinished nature of freedom is present in *The Life of William Grimes, the Runaway Slave* (1825), the first fugitive slave narrative published in the United States, which appeared in print more than a decade before organized abolition began to make use of slave narratives. Grimes published his book to make money: he paid for its printing, secured its copyright, and promised readers that his book would entertain, allow them to exercise sympathy, and satisfy their curiosity about "Old Grimes." He ended his preface with this appeal:

> To those who still think the book promises no entertainment, he begs leave to suggest another motive why they should purchase it. To him who has feeling, the condition of a slave, under any possible circumstances, is painful and unfortunate, and will excite sympathy of all who have any. Such was my condition for more than thirty years, and in circumstances not only painful, but often intolerable. But after having tasted the sweets of liberty, (embittered, indeed, with constant apprehension,) and after having, by eight years' labor and exertion, accumulated about a thousand dollars, then to be stripped of all these hard earnings and turned pennyless upon the world with a family, and to purchase freedom, this gives me a claim upon charity, which, I presume, few possess, and I think none will deny.[13]

Grimes worked out these multiple claims upon the public—that his story was entertaining, that he deserved sympathy, and that he had earned charity—by describing his life as a slave in Georgia and as a hard-working free man in Connecticut. He had escaped with the help of sympathetic sailors who helped him hide in a cotton bale that had been shipped to New York. Once north, he married a free woman and supported her and their many children by working odd jobs—cutting wood for a dollar a day, husking corn for fifty cents a day, tending horses, and selling groceries. Eventually, he established himself as a barber and clothes cleaner, catering, at various times, to the needs of students at Yale (where in six months he earned fifty dollars) and at the Connecticut Law School in Litchfield (where, with a more prosperous clientele and a business that some complained included "keeping a bad house," he earned between fifty and sixty dollars a month). Grimes was conscientious about saving his money, but his nest egg was wiped out at least once when he was forced to pay a former master the price he asked for him. In his old age, finished with slave catchers and college students, he took financial skills into his own community and opened a "brokerage business" for lottery tickets. "I would often have dreams," he wrote, "and of course I told my friends of them, and then they would greedily seize the lucky numbers, and be *almost* sure to get a prize."[14]

When Grimes published a second version of his life in 1855, he was a famous man, "one of the most remarkable personages of modern times," a "fixed institution" in New Haven, and he wrote to "gratify the laudable curiosity which so many of my friends have exhibited to procure a true and perfect Life of 'Old Grimes.'"[15] Unlike fugitive narrators more fully incorporated into abolitionist projects, Grimes did not appear on the lecture stage, nor did he spare the North a scathing indictment. Whereas other fugitives displayed scarred bodies to back up accusations of cruelty; Grimes considered offering his flesh as material for a bookbinder, making a striking association of a slave's bondage and the American Constitution. The last paragraph of his book reads: "I hope some will buy my books from charity, but I am no beggar. I am now entirely destitute of property; where and how I shall live I don't know, but I hope I may be prepared. If it were not for the stripes on my back which were made while I was a slave,

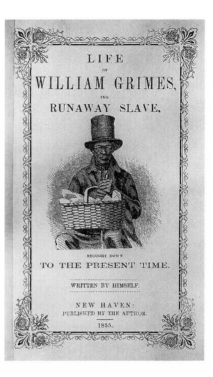

FIGURE 11 *Life of William Grimes, the Runaway Slave.* Courtesy of the American Antiquarian Society.

I would in my will, leave my skin a legacy to the government, desiring that it might be taken off and made into parchment, and then bind the Constitution of glorious happy *and free* America. Let the skin of an American slave bind the charter of American liberty."[16]

No one rose to challenge the truth of Grimes's allegations, for he spoke as "Old Grimes," a celebrity of sorts, an eccentric old man with a tale to tell. He did not invoke the rules of evidence, which would have lead readers to expect a tale that perfectly matched some legal standard. He did not doubt the market value of his story. Nor did he compromise what he saw as the truth to satisfy abolitionists who sought persuasive narrators. All this helps us understand why his story met with a better fate than that of James Williams.

THE TROUBLE WITH JAMES WILLIAMS

Although James Birney may have counted copies of James Williams's story in his census of antislavery publications, the book was hardly destined to play a major role in the abolitionist publishing project. Doubts about the veracity of Williams and the accuracy of his narrative began to appear within months of its publication. Although the Fifth Annual Report of the American Anti-Slavery Society, published in May 1838, cited the narrative as a "publication of much interest," the executive committee put forward a logical rather than an empirical argument for the truth of Williams's story. That the committee's logic was deeply racist is not surprising. The committee deemed the narrative "within the bounds of probability," pointing out that "there could be no imposition in the story without attributing to its author such powers of mind, as few men, either white or black, could justly lay claim to." The editor of the *Herald of Freedom* expressed similar sentiments, suggesting that if Williams invented the facts of his story, he was "a dabster at invention, for an 'inferior race,' and in time will be sharp enough for freedom, if he keeps on."[17]

But J. B. Rittenhouse, the editor of the Greensborough, Alabama, *Beacon*, was not entertained by listening to this "dabster at invention." If Williams told the truth, then he made liars out of slaveholders who defended their practices as good for slaves and country. Although we often think of slave narratives as addressed to northern audiences, Birney explained that the committee had sent the story south as deliberate provocation and, at first, the abolitionists welcomed the challenge from slaveholders.[18] Rittenhouse rejected the racist logic that made the complexity of the story a sign of its truth and dismissed the whole as a complete fabrication. The newspaperman could find neither the people nor the plantations mentioned by Williams, and he published his own letters from "gentlemen" who deemed the story a *"foul fester of falsehood,"* precisely what the editor and his correspondent expected of a lying slave. In the paper's opinion, the abolitionists had practiced a "notorious libel upon our country" by using the character of the fugitive as a mouthpiece. The editor answered the libel not by refuting it point by point but by printing a letter he had received from Geo. T. F. Larimer, whose name was similar to that of a man Williams had named as an owner.

Larimer countered Williams's story with his own sensational version of the slave's past. From the engraved portrait, he claimed he recognized Williams as a coachman named Shadrach Wilkins who was wanted in connection with an attempt to poison "Dr. Roy and his family." If allegation of attempted murder was not enough to brand Williams as an unreliable narrator, Larimer went on to detail Williams's escape from Alabama with a scheming abolitionist who financed their trip north by selling Williams to unsuspecting slaveholders, stealing him, and selling him again. Williams had tricked abolitionists with a fabricated story just as he had gulled unsuspecting slaveholders with counterfeit sales.[19]

Such a plot would have been familiar to readers who had followed the widely publicized adventures of John Murrell, bandit and slavestealer.[20] But Larimer's calling Williams a liar would also have sounded familiar to readers. For Williams, for all slaves for that matter, lying was a good means to resist slaveholders. But for Larimer, Williams's behavior merely illustrated an assumption common among slaveowners: "That the negro, as a general rule, is mendacious, is a fact too well established to require the production of proof, either from history, travels, or craniology." In effect, to have challenged individual allegations within the story would have been to admit the possibility that some of Williams's claims were true. Better to find the entire story false.[21]

According to Larimer, Rittenhouse, and all those who accepted their version of the events, Williams's appearance in print did not mark him as a new and free man; it was rather a continuation of slavish behavior in another venue, proof that slaveholders were right to refuse to accept the testimony of slaves. Critics of Williams's story suggested that an individual so schooled in falsehood could never be trusted to tell the truth.[22] Even though it is commonly understood that producing a book was for slaves a step toward freedom, the controversy over Williams's book reminds us how difficult such steps could be. For slaves, reading and writing could correspond with migration north and, in most cases, a move north was at least a partial move toward freedom; but if Williams learned in England the fate of his book, he probably noticed that a fugitive telling a story did not do so as an entirely free man. Like poor and propertyless beggars, like incarcerated convicts, an illiterate fugitive like Williams had to allow his story to be run through a gauntlet of authentication. And like so much else in the antebellum United States, this cultural process was skewed by chattel slavery. Technologies of reading and writing and publishing worked differently for free white northerners than they did for fugitive slaves.

Historians who have studied societies based on a code of honor have argued that in such societies telling the truth is the prerogative of gentlemen. The concept of honor that governed the social life of the South was enacted in careful distinctions about who could and who could not tell the truth. As the historian Kenneth Greenberg puts it, "Masters repeatedly expressed exasperation about the deceitful behavior of their slaves. But in another sense, masters welcomed the chance to catch their slaves in lies. Their own honor and the respect accorded their words could then stand in favorable contrast to the dishonored condition of slaves." It was not that masters could not lie, but that they could not, without losing face, be caught in a lie.[23]

Williams tried to expose the lies of slaveholders, the cruelty and false promises of his master; but he too was vulnerable to exposure, and his story was too weak to work as an indictment of slaveowners. It was, from the start, an unequal contest. Rittenhouse and Larimer exercised in print the power to unmask Williams and to expose his abolitionist friends. Eventually, after a set of conventional safeguards had been put in place, northern audiences would give credit to fugitive narrators, but Rittenhouse and Larimer, representing slaveholders, won the first round. This early fiasco probably accounts for the later, sometimes obsessive seeming emphasis on verifiability of fugitive narratives and the literacy of their authors.[24]

In response to the challenge from the South, the executive committee of the American Anti-Slavery Society directed New Yorkers James Birney and Lewis Tappan to investigate the matter and produce a "statement for publication." Although northerners were by no means immune to the notion that slaves were liars, the executive committee declared themselves predisposed to accept Williams's version of the events. "After all the fraud and trickery of the slaveholders and their abettors, to cover up their shameful deeds, the friends of the slave know full well the injustice of setting down as undeniably true all the oppressor says in his own favor, and as undeniably false, or doubtful, all that the victim relates concerning his own sufferings."[25]

By early fall, however, answers to the letters of inquiry Birney and Tappan sent south forced them to conclude that "many of the statements made in the said Narrative were false," and although they hesitated "to decide of *course*, or hastily, against a *black*, where the testimony was contradicted by a *white*," they found they could not "ask for the confidence of the community in any of the statements contained in the Narrative." And in October, the executive committee directed the publishing agent "to discontinue the sale of the work."[26]

Birney and Tappan tried hard to find the means to verify Williams's story. They employed in their report the language of the law, setting themselves up as an impartial jury convened to weigh the testimony of a man who had been silenced by the laws of slavery. They listened to those who questioned Williams's version of his life, sitting as "the tribunal before which this matter is litigated; yet are they, in absence from the country of one of the parties, and in his weakness, (if he were here) when compared with his adversaries, endeavoring by all means in their power, to obtain such testimony as will convince all impartial and candid persons that *justice* has been done in the premises." Should the narrative prove untrue, Birney concluded, "it will present one of the most extraordinary cases of conflicting circumstantial testimony that has any time occurred in this country."[27]

Williams seemed to them an honest man. "He was intelligent, far beyond what slaves usually are. His account of himself, and of what he had seen, whether true or false, proves this. His wardrobe was but indifferently supplied—yet he seemed careless about replenishing it with more than was necessary for his actual comfort. He had no money—and he asked for none." He was not, in other words, a man who set out to profit by selling his story. "From first to last he seemed to have no idea of deriving any pecuniary benefit from the publication, in any form, of his sufferings in slavery, or from the sympathy he had excited in those to whom they were rehearsed."[28]

Or so they thought. Williams certainly bartered his story for at least enough money to pay his passage to England. For all we know, Williams may have been a confidence man, trading on northern interest in stories told by fugitives and happy to find the means to put an ocean between himself and his pursuers.

In the meantime, the executive committee had to figure out what to do about James Williams. He could not be called upon to support his story by displaying a scarred body and demonstrating his "artless" candor. Writing to Angelina Grimké in December 1838, Lydia Maria Child asked, "Where *is* James Williams? Can he not be found and cross examined?" Child believed Williams's story, "except that he had resorted to common artfulness of a slave, with regard to *names*."

What Child meant by *artfulness* is not entirely clear. It is possible that Williams simply exercised a right of authorship and made up the names of the several slaveholders who people his story. Williams opened the book with a veritable "nominating frenzy," listing by name seventeen Virginia slaveholders.[29] Like other fugitives, he may have deliberately disguised the names of owners to protect himself from capture. An aged Charles Ball, for example, acknowledged that he "might even yet be deemed of sufficient value to be worth pursuing," and he followed the advice of those "whom I believe to be my friends, not to disclose the true names of any of those families in which I was a slave, in Carolina or Georgia, lest this narrative should meet their eyes, and in some way lead them to a discovery of my retreat."[30] Reminiscing about his days with the underground railroad, Levi Coffin recalled that fugitives "were generally unwilling to tell their stories, or let us know what part of the South they came from. They would not give their names, or the names of their masters, correctly, fearing they would be betrayed."[31]

Of course, it is also possible that Whittier misspelled names that Williams, a man who made no pretense to literacy, had never seen written down and that slaveholders chose to read an innocent error in transcription as deliberate provocation. The tenor of slaveholder response, however, suggests that whether Williams used names as art or accusation, as invention or as libel, it was a significant move for a silenced slave finally to name names.

Williams found it safest to make his accusations and leave the country, but his absence meant that there was no one to bear witness to his story. He failed to complete the compromise that allowed fugitives from slavery to appear before the public and gain what they could by telling and selling their stories. The controversy over Williams and his story reveals the patterns of authorship that many scholars have found peculiar to slave narratives. As the literary scholar Karen Sánchez-Eppler has written, "the position of author gains its privilege, precisely because the text produced occludes the specific physical body of the person who produced it. Inverting this pattern, slave narratives, and perhaps all confessional or testimonial genres, rhetorically create an authorial body. Rather than attempt to assert the incorporeality of authorship, testimonial writing inscribes the author's bodily existence and experience."[32] For a fugitive like Williams, bodily inscription could not be accomplished with rhetoric alone. When Williams disappeared, removing his body from the abolitionist conversation, all the verbal art in the world could not dispel doubts about the veracity of his story: a rhetorical body was just not enough.

The debate about Williams, Child continued in her letter, "has a very bad effect on the numerous class who do not look below the surface into the principles of things." A few days later she returned to the subject, explaining to Theodore Weld that "to you and I, who look on the *foundations* upon which slavery rests, it is not slightest consequence whether James Williams told the truth or not; yet the doubt thrown on his narrative is doing incalculable mischief."[33] At home with arguments designed to appeal as much to the emotions as to the intellect, Child, like many reformers of her generation, read as "true" the stories that moved her. "In the evangelical framework," the legal historian Elizabeth Clark has written, "the measure of authenticity lay in the feelings, not the intellect; the most striking oral and written testimony was the eyewitness account, which put the reader as close as possible to the slave's pain." "By the 1830s," she continued, "many Americans turned for guidance to the emotions over the intellect, identifying the moral sense more with feeling than with rational thought."[34]

The controversy around the story of James Williams reminds us that in the late 1830s it was difficult to circulate a tale that drew on both emotion and intellect, feeling and rational thought. Although students of nineteenth-century American literature have placed slave narratives in the pantheon of sentimental culture, the vigilance organized abolition exercised over stories and storytellers (after the controversy around Williams subsided) suggests that fugitive narratives belonged to the head as well as to the heart. Perhaps if Williams and Whittier had not begun by naming names, their story would have fit easily in a canon of sentimental literature. To be sure, stories like that of James Williams were meant to appeal to the emotions, but an abolitionist imprint guaranteed that the books published after Williams's conformed as well to rules designed to establish "facts."[35]

Like their Boston colleagues, Birney and Tappan recognized that depictions of suffering had strategic value for organized abolition, and they did not dismiss the power of an eyewitness or the pull of the emotions. And yet, giving voice to a common-sense strain deep-seated in American thought, they concluded that testimony more closely akin to empirical truth would better turn slave narratives into political propaganda. To this end, they employed the methods and metaphors of the courtroom, constructing slave testimony not as the testimony of evangelical witness, but as the testimony of instructed legal witness.[36]

With New York evangelicals such as Birney and Tappan on one side and Boston radicals such as William Lloyd Garrison, Child, and Whittier on the other, the controversy over Williams's narrative can be read as a small skirmish amid the larger disputes that would soon separate the New York abolitionists from their Boston colleagues. Conflicts over political strategies, social institutions, and the role of women in the antislavery movement would cause more significant divisions between the abolitionist groups, but the story of James Williams suggests that there were also small intellectual differences between the New Yorkers and Bostonians. They differed on the question of how the truth of a slave narrative could best be established for white northern readers.[37] Whittier and Child implied that they had tested the man and, even if he had changed the details of his story, found him a believable narrator. Birney and Tappan, men with strong faith in the importance of institutions and organizations, insisted that they test the tale as well.

Birney was probably not surprised to find in Whittier a man whose standards of truth differed from his own. In August 1837, he had received from his colleague Henry B. Stanton a letter that candidly assessed Whittier and his abilities. "He makes a pretty good Secretary," Stanton wrote, "is quite good at executing a plan after it is laid out to his hands, but has no power of originating,—is rather poetical in his temper i.e. *unstable*, subject to low spirits, hypo, etc.—is a Quaker from head to foot,—is rather careless in his business habits,—in a word needs as much supervision as to details, as a clerk." And Birney himself had once described Whittier as a poet who addressed himself "powerfully to the imagination and feelings" of readers.[38]

For Lewis Tappan, the problems posed by James Williams and his story probably had particular resonance. In the aftermath of the Panic of 1837, the silk firm that Tappan ran with his brother was barely able to meet its financial obligations, let alone continue to underwrite the work of the American Anti-Slavery Society. He knew from personal experience the costs of dealing with careless strangers, with men who ignored the details of agreements to pay and were less than scrupulous about keeping their word. As Tappan's biographer Bertram Wyatt-Brown puts it, Lewis and Arthur Tappan were experts in all the "methods of evasion and fraud that country traders used to escape their liabilities." In 1838, hoping to bring order to business transactions, Lewis Tappan opened a service he called the Mercantile Agency, an organization funded by subscribers anxious about the financial standing of those who came to trade in New York. A network of correspondents composed of Christian abolitionists, lawyers, and ministers described for subscribers the financial worth, honesty, reliability, and sobriety of those with whom subscribing city merchants dealt. Despite the fact that some in the New York business community dismissed Tappan as a meddlesome reformer and many in the South saw him as an abolitionist spy, the agency succeeded.

According to Wyatt-Brown, the Mercantile Agency sometimes produced a social benefit in the process of offering financial service. "It must have occurred to Tappan that his business was rather useful as a means of social control in the hinterlands. The drinker or the philanderer who traded in New York goods might find his credit had disappeared because of an unfavorable report made out by a pious bank cashier or a teetotaling attorney."[39] Tappan apparently extended this faith in investigation to fugitives who asked listeners to credit their stories. Supporting Williams, even if he lied, entailed no great financial risk, but his story raised the troubling possibility that fugitives, like country merchants, imposed on the unsuspecting abolitionists who were so anxious to hear their stories. The best Birney and Tappan could do to protect against such imposition was to write to men they knew who might have known the fugitive slave and ask them to assess Williams and his tale, just as they would if Williams had asked for credit. As they had applied the lessons of organized reform to the marketplace, so they applied the lessons of the market to abolitionist publication.

With the publication of Birney and Tappan's report, the more conservative members of the New York branch of the American Anti-Slavery Society committed themselves to literalism and verifiability in slave narratives. In the future, the stories published by the American Anti-Slavery Society were to be the product of storytellers who met abolitionist criteria for transparent honesty, people who, in other words, gave literal, verifiable descriptions of their experiences. And here we find the same features that appeared in the frames of the tales told and sold by many poor men and women. The devices of honesty so familiar to readers of slave narratives included the assertion, most often found in a preface, that a tale had been repeated on several occasions without alteration to "gentlemen." But slave narrators were not entirely dependent on external ratification by white gentlemen. The "truth" of slave narratives was also asserted in descriptions of fugitive narrators answering questions on the lecture circuit. It was asserted in displays of conscience by slaves who admitted that they had learned in freedom the significance of telling the truth and now forswore the clever lies that had helped them to survive as slaves and to elude pursuers during escape. And it was asserted in portraits of slaveholders who called themselves honest men but regularly broke their promises to slaves and, in bringing human chattel to market, engaged in deceitful practices that differed little from those of the Yankee traders they so disdained.[40]

In abolitionist debates over how best to read the slave narratives, we are reminded that truth is a social convention, the product of agreements among people. What good are the "facts" of the story if no one believes them? Facts are things that must be set down in words, but the words of former slaves circulated within a world where audiences scrutinized the teller and not just the tale.

A pledge to hold slave narrators to the facts was a mixed blessing. To hold them to the facts and nothing but the facts sometimes stripped from narrators the right to interpret their stories and artfully embellish their experiences. But it certainly helped to make their stories effective pieces in an abolitionist arsenal, and it illustrated for northern readers that the men and women whom slaveholders had marked as notorious liars had been converted in freedom to tellers of truths. In effect, scenes in which former slaves discussed their growing awareness of the differences between telling the truth and inventing a lie allowed them to express a willingness to abide by the moral principles that governed the contractual relations of a free-labor society. The story of James Williams reminds us that the narratives were not mere descriptions of change; published stories in which fugitives kept promises to tell the truth to readers were themselves instruments in the former slaves' transformation into individuals capable of abiding by the rules of the society they now entered. In telling true stories, fugitive narrators demonstrated that they were bound by words, not by a master's chains.

In 1861 the legal historian Henry Sumner Maine wrote, "There are few general propositions concerning the age to which we belong which seem at first sight likely to be received with readier concurrence than the assertion that the society of our day is mainly distinguished from that of preceding generations by the largeness of the sphere which is occupied in it by Contract." And he made explicit the connection between the growth of contractual relations and the decline of those such as slavery, which were based on status. "The point, for instance, which is really debated in the vigorous controversy still carried on upon the subject of negro servitude, is whether the status of the slave does not belong to by-gone institutions, and whether the only relation between employer and labourer which commends itself to modern morality be not a relation determined exclusively by contract."[41]

For contractual relations to work, all parties must keep the promises they make. As the literary historian Brook Thomas wrote, the "association between promising and contract gives a contractual society a moral foundation that results not from preconceived notions of status but from the duties and obligations that individuals impose on themselves in their dealings with other members of society."[42] In distinguishing between the true and the false, on stage and in print, stories put the consciences of fugitive narrators on display. Such display was instrumental in inducting former slaves into the limited freedoms afforded by the contractual society of the North, where the whip was replaced with "the compulsory contract and the collar with the guilty conscience."[43] For Birney and Tappan, it was not enough for James Williams to move readers with a display of suffering; he had to move them by a display of conscience and by demonstrating his willingness to respond to interrogation by curious, doubtful, sympathetic, hostile, and helpful audiences.

In the abolitionist press, in books themselves, and—most importantly—on the lecture circuit, storytelling fugitives and abolitionist sponsors worked out the rules that brought inventive slaves before a white northern public hungry for the literal truths of bondage but reluctant to accord to slaves a license to describe in any way they pleased all that they had seen, heard, and suffered. Nor did northern audiences want to hear about the former slaves' experiences of "the quasi-freedom of inequality" once they had made their way north.[44] Instead, many readers accepted the quasi-truths provided by fugitive narrators, acknowledging their pledge to keep their cultural contributions to those things they could be said to have seen and heard. Licenses to invent would be long in coming.

It is clear from the case of James Williams and his story that it meant one thing for a slave to lie to slaveholders in the South and it meant another for a former slave to lie about slaveholders to white northerners. It also meant one thing for James Williams to give his word and forego his right to lie as a freeman contracting to sell his labor, and it meant quite another for him to forswear a capacity for invention as a writer or artist contracting to sell a story.

In the end, even the abolitionists, who had agreed to adhere to the most scrupulous standards of fact, proved willing to compromise. Months after *The Narrative of James Williams* had been challenged and found wanting, the book continued to appear on lists of antislavery publications available through abolitionist societies. It is possible that the American Anti-Slavery Society, pressed for cash in the hard times of the late 1830s, opted for expediency and continued to sell a book that the society had already paid to produce. Writing to Arnold Buffum on November 8, 1839, James Birney acknowledged that the movement felt a financial pinch. "You have doubtless, noticed in the Emancipator how meager have been the money receipts for a long time past. The main cause of this is the sudden and unexampled embarrassment into which the whole country have been brought, involving our anti slavery friends as well as others." Although revenue from the sale of books and pamphlets could hardly make up the deficit left when the Tappans and other large donors cut back their support for antislavery societies, sales of publications did help support the local societies that sustained the movement through the 1840s.[45]

In "embarrassed" circumstances, both abolitionists and former slaves cultivated the market for stories. Perhaps some of those who followed the controversy about James Williams and his story bought his book to see if they could decide for themselves whether he told the truth. In doing so, they would have been acting no differently than their contemporaries who were drawn to the clever frauds P. T. Barnum displayed. Barnum's appeal, historians have suggested, was based in part on invitations he offered patrons to see and to judge for themselves the exhibits he put on display.[46]

Perhaps in this sense the antislavery movement, so full of high purpose, also offered entertainment. Former slaves who told their stories attracted crowds. As John Collins, the general agent of the Massachusetts Anti-Slavery Society, wrote to William Lloyd Garrison in 1842: "The public have itching ears to hear a colored man speak, and particularly a *slave*. Multitudes will flock to hear one of his class." The fugitive presence on the lecture platform offered abolitionists a means to make compelling the oft-rehearsed moral, religious, legal, and philosophical arguments against slavery, but it also gave fugitives an opportunity to turn a profit on their experience, and many fugitives chose for themselves careers as antislavery activists. According to historian Marion Starling, "Except in Canada, where the fugitives settled down into more or less normal pursuits to earn their livelihood, lecturing seemed to be the chief means of subsistence that came into the fugitive's mind, whether or not he had ever heard a lecture in his life before."[47] Though Starling did not specify the numbers she had in mind, several dozen fugitives became professional lecturers. Many supported themselves and funded their lecture tours by selling printed versions of their lives. Just as the success of publication came to depend on former slaves appearing on the lecture circuit, so the efficacy of an antislavery lecture came to depend on the ability of former slaves and their audiences to conjure antislavery arguments out of personal experiences.[48]

TELLING AND SELLING A STORY

Although Birney found virtue in the fact that James Williams told his story without asking for money or clothes, many slave narrators found it necessary to barter their tales for food, shelter, clothing, and cash. Exchange of a tale did not necessarily involve publication; fugitives, like the penniless beggars who had nothing but an ability to tell a tale, were often obliged to give an account of themselves to get the sustenance they needed. Men and women running from slavery encountered slave catchers to whom they lied. They stopped at farms and plantations and, under various pretenses, begged food and shelter from those they met.

In the true stories they produced in freedom, former slaves frequently recounted the inventions that had facilitated their escapes. Some used accounts of storytelling to denounce their old gifts for the lie, marking the moral distance they had traveled from slavery. For others, accounts of storytelling offered prior evidence of the skills they now needed to support themselves; according to Marion Starling, many who fled slavery and arrived in the North after 1840 often found it as easy to sell a story as to sell their labor.

But for those who had run from slavery, the revelation to white northern audiences of almost any aspect of a past life was always vexed, especially after the passage of the Fugitive Slave Act in 1850. As Frederick Douglass recognized, "A colored man was deemed a fool who confessed himself a runaway slave, not only because of the danger to which he exposed himself of being retaken, but because it was a confession of very *low* origin!" For all the similarity of their stories, fugitive narrators solved the problems involved in revealing their histories in different ways.[49]

William Green and his friends, for example, reached a moment of desperation. "At the end of two weeks our funds became so reduced that we hardly knew what scheme to fall upon in order to make our ends meet and pay our board. After consulting awhile we concluded to throw ourselves upon the mercy of our landlady, and tell her our condition, and see if she would be lenient with us for a short time, until we could look round us and see what we were to do."[50]

Similarly, Henry Watson, a Mississippi man whose narrative was published in Boston in 1848, remembered hiding for three weeks before he "ventured out, and my case became known among people of color." He told his history to William Lloyd Garrison. "[A]fter giving me pecuniary assistance, [Garrison] advised me to leave the country and go to Canada, or England." Watson sailed for England, but returned to the United States to work as an antislavery lecturer. The book he produced had the common virtues of a true story of a suffering slave, but he also pointed out the special value of its Mississippi setting, "the narratives of other fugitives having for their scenes other States."[51]

It is possible that Watson learned in England the importance of distinguishing his story from all others. By the early 1850s, fugitive slaves who journeyed to England found little employment. In 1853, a columnist in the *Anti-Slavery Advocate* warned would-be migrants that African Americans were living in Great Britain as beggars and tramps. Refugees from North American slavery competed for cash and sympathy with refugees from the continental revolutions of 1848. Without some special talent, fugitives found it difficult to sustain themselves on the British lecture circuit. In July 1851, Garrison published a letter from William Wells Brown cautioning his "fugitive brethren" against a too easy confidence in marketing their stories in England.

> Too many of our fugitive brethren are of the opinion that because they can tell, by the fireside, the wrongs they have suffered in the prison house of slavery, that they are prepared to take to the field as lecturers. And this being the fact, there are numbers here [in London], who have set themselves up as lecturers, and who are, in fact, little less than beggars. . . . I would say to our fugitive brethren, if you don't want to become beggars, don't come to England.[52]

Watson had confidence in the American market. As he told Garrison, the "narrative of my life and sufferings in the prisonhouse of liberty is nearly ready for distribution. And will, I trust, yield a sufficient return to maintain myself and my family for some time longer, and enable to plead the cause of 'the brethren' I left behind."[53]

Differences between making up a story in the South and making a market for a story in the North appear in the tale of Moses Roper, whose narrative appeared in an American edition shortly after James Williams's. Roper fled his miserable life in the South in 1834, and like most fugitives he told stories about himself as a means of escape. In fact, as Henry Watson reminded readers, running slaves had little choice but to offer some account of themselves. Watson reprinted excerpts from slave codes, including the following from a South Carolina statute of 1740:

> If any slave who shall be out of the house or the plantation where such slave shall live, or shall be usually employed, or without some white person in company with such slave, shall *refuse to submit* to undergo the examination of *any white* person, it shall be lawful for such white person to pursue, apprehend, and moderately correct such slave; and if such slave shall assault and strike such white person, such slave may be *lawfully killed!!*

In such circumstances, Watson implied, the only question was what to invent.[54]

Roper spent his first night as a runaway in a barn. An overseer woke him in the morning and asked him who he was. At first, Roper said nothing. "On my way to his house, however, I made up the following story." He told the overseer that he had been bound to a cruel master as a little boy and that he had just run away to see his mother. "This statement," he explained to readers, "may appear to some to be untrue, but as I understood the word *bound*, I considered it to apply to my case, having been sold to him, and thereby bound to serve him." Acknowledging that his case was perhaps a weak one, Roper confessed that he did not then know "the sin of lying."[55]

Roper's first story was persuasive enough to earn him a glass of buttermilk and something to eat. The overseer's wife took him for a white man and sent him on his way. This was merely the first of many occasions on which people called upon the fugitive to give an account of himself. Roper was a deft dissembler, pretending in one instance to be part of a group returning from market and in another to be on his way to rejoin his master in Tallahassee. He passed for a white apprentice, an American Indian, and a "free coloured person." He tricked a boy, two drovers, and a rich cotton merchant into writing a passport for him. He finally made it to New York and then to England, where he again gave account of himself, this time convincing abolitionist sponsors that his story was the "artless narrative" of an honest man.[56] Although Roper had proved himself adept at trading fabrications for food, information, and shelter, his simple apology served to cleanse him of his lies. His acknowledgment that as a slave he did not know the "sin of lying" called attention to the moral differences between Roper, the clever slave, and Roper, the honest freeman. His editor also called attention to his religious profession, sobriety, honesty, intelligence, and reticence. Better still, Roper wrote to raise money to fund his own education and to support his missionary activities in the West Indies. Sale of the narrative would provide the seed money to render him "independent of eleemosynary support." A reviewer for *The London Christian Advocate* added that Roper sold his story out of a "manly and benevolent desire of realising thereby the means of educating his own emancipated mind, that he may become the instrument of emancipating the minds of his 'kinsmen according to the flesh.' "[57]

Some who bought Roper's book no doubt did so as an act of charity, more from a wish to benefit Mr. Roper and his kin "than from a desire to obtain such a book" (as the Reverend Michael Smith put it). But fugitive narrators who cultivated a charitable impulse in readers acknowledged that curiosity about the experience of slavery helped make the market for their tales. Those who revealed too much on the lecture circuit, however, risked reducing the cash value of their stories. Henry Bibb, a successful antislavery lecturer who began work among Michigan abolitionists in 1844, addressed this issue. In a preface, his editor promised a narrative "equally distinguished as a revolting portrait of the hideous slave system, a thrilling narrative of individual suffering, and a triumphant vindication of the slave's manhood and mental dignity. And all this is associated with unmistakable traces of originality and truthfulness." But Bibb himself wondered in type why he should publish his narrative after having "told it publically all through New England and the Western States to multiplied thousands." His gesture at satisfied audiences, of course, served to emphasize the fact that no one had challenged his story's truth. Lest the assertion crucial to establishing the story's truth undercut the tale's market value, he added "that in no place have I given orally the detail of my narrative; and some of the most interesting events of my life have never reached the public ear."[58]

Fugitives understood that it was difficult to create the market for their stories and difficult to maintain it. Andrew Jackson, a man from Kentucky, kept a journal in which he described life on a backwater lecture circuit where lesser fugitives supported themselves and the work of abolition by telling and selling stories. For fourteen months in 1846 and 1847, Jackson entertained crowds in upstate New York. Night after night, in school houses and churches, before audiences rough and respectable, he linked the twin sins of slaveholding and intemperance. He talked, he sang, he entertained, and he peddled his book. Like the fugitives Lewis and Milton Clarke, who reprinted for readers a list of the questions audiences frequently asked, Jackson sparred with his audiences, teasing them with his learning.[59] He also had to defend himself against accusations of fraud. He remembered drawing a "good congregation" one night in "the Merwin district" when it was "announced that a lady was going to be present and prove me an imposter." The lady never came forward with her challenge, but Jackson told his story, presenting a "true history of facts, to show from what source I had received my instruction."[60]

Jackson described a pattern of audience banter that conveyed his mastery of the antislavery performance. In contrast, *A Narrative of the Life of the Rev. Noah Davis* documents the process of learning the art of the artless performance. Davis had his narrative published in Baltimore in 1859, the only slave narrative printed in a slave-holding state. By the time he published his book, he had already raised enough money to purchase his wife and five of his seven children, and he hoped with proceeds from its sale to purchase the last two. In the book, he described how he learned to market his story. He set out first to find the funds to purchase himself. In June 1845, with his master's permission, he left for the North to "find friends who would give me money." For four months, he wandered the streets in Philadelphia, Boston, and New York, looking for sympathetic listeners. He raised only 180 dollars and returned "disheartened" to Virginia. He said that he had failed in his attempt because he was "unaccustomed to addressing large congregations of strangers; and often, when I was favored with an opportunity of presenting my case to the people I would feel such an embarrassment that I could scarcely say anything." Like Frederick Douglass, he also encountered those who were unwilling to subsidize slaveholders by providing the funds to purchase fugitives. "I confess this was new to me, and would cut me down much in my spirits—still I found generous and noble-hearted friends, who treated me with every mark of kindness." On subsequent trips, Davis had greater success, particularly when one Baptist congregation would recommend him to another, and he finally raised the cash to buy the last of his children.[61]

MINSTRELSY

What then was an antislavery performance? Successful fugitives mastered something that audiences saw as an artless performance; they performed and published stories believed to be authentic accounts of experience. Frederick Douglass understood that authenticity was manufactured by a kind of artifice and that northern audiences had particular notions about what constituted an authentic tale of slavery. Douglass knew that a tale of experience would help confirm his identity as a fugitive slave, but he also recognized that fugitives who revealed too many specific details about their lives in bondage risked capture and return to slavery. As we will see, Douglass had many reasons to keep the details of his life to himself, but when he refused to recount the "story of his experience" some began to wonder whether he had ever really been a slave at all. Douglass was reticent about himself, and worse, when he did talk, some said he did not sound like a slave. Apparently, an "authentic" slave performance included dialect speech and "slavish" behavior. As Douglass remembered, "It was said to me, 'Better have a *little* of the plantation manner of speech than not; 'tis not best that you seem too learned.'" Audiences, he learned, "said I did not talk like a slave, look like a slave, nor act like a slave, and that they believed I had never been south of Mason and Dixon's line."[62]

What did northern audiences expect from an "authentic" slave? Surely some learned the speech, appearance, and gestures of slaves from hearing them lecture, reading their prose, and visiting the South. But Douglass's anger suggests that some also learned about slavery from blackface performers. In a sense, fugitive lecturers and blackface performers staged competing versions of slavery. Although abolition may have "supplemented minstrelsy's range of darky fare," to borrow a stark phrase from Saidiya Hartman, fugitive lecturers and narrators pointedly refused to behave like their counterparts on the minstrel boards.[63] The grinning degradation of blackface performance was probably horrible for fugitive slaves to contemplate. Even if minstrel performers played on a certain sympathy for slaves that lingered in the northern white working class, the blackface figures of minstrelsy (happy, grinning, singing jokesters) were precisely what writing fugitives were not. Nevertheless, minstrelsy shaped the stories of fugitives, and just as white audiences for minstrel shows felt contradictory pulls of romance and repulsion for the blackfaced figures they watched, so perhaps audiences for slave narratives felt contradictory pulls of personal sympathy and impersonal horror for the displays of suffering they witnessed. It was, in part, against a background of minstrelsy that the truth of fugitive narratives was constructed, because it was the artful performances of blackface minstrelsy that helped to make slave narratives seem documents of artless candor.[64]

In the 1840s, as blackface performers entertained audiences composed largely of working-class white men in cities and fugitive lecturers instructed middle-class men and women at antislavery meetings, observers hailed both minstrel songs and slave narratives as expressions of genuine American art. Writing for the *Christian Examiner* in 1849, the Reverend Ephraim Peabody described narratives of fugitive slaves as "the most remarkable productions of the age" and America's contribution to the "literature of civilization." He constructed for slave autobiographies an impeccable cultural pedigree, finding in them both a "whole Iliad of woes" and adventure sufficient to "write a modern Odyssey."[65]

Peabody was not alone in thinking he had located an American contribution to the history of civilization, nor in turning to the Greeks to explain the importance of the cultural form he described. In a preface to *Christy's Plantation Melodies No. 4*, the publisher asserted that E. P. Christy's blackface performances expressed America's "native genius" in music. Christy was "a triumphant vindicating APOLLO[,] . . . the first to catch our *native airs* as they floated wildly, or hummed in the balmy breezes of the sunny south."[66]

In the 1840s and 1850s writers, musicians, editors, and abolitionists offered competing black performances to large, and largely white, audiences. Whereas some scholars have found in the minstrel performances based on *Uncle Tom's Cabin* elements of an antislavery blackface, others insist that every moment of sympathetic identification made possible by such melodramas was, in fact, based on the subjection and degradation of black men and women.[67] Slave narratives certainly mobilized sympathy and staged scenes of degradation, but degradation was not the entire story. Gesturing at artlessness and authenticity, fugitive narrators used stories to their own ends. They did this in part by working through a language of artlessness that distinguished them from blackface minstrel performances.

Although an individual with the generous cultural sensibilities of Walt Whitman may have been capable of espousing antislavery politics and appreciating minstrel performance, in general audiences for the two kinds of representations divided along lines of gender, class, and politics. Minstrel performers had close ties to northern Democrats, and performances cultivated in white workers nostalgia for a premodern agrarian life on the plantation and sympathy for slaveholders. Minstrels performed black characters who were illiterate, inarticulate, lazy, content, and highly sexual.[68]

Those who narrated fugitive autobiographies were in many ways the precise opposites of such characters, and the audiences who attended to these autobiographies expressed a different set of cultural and political allegiances than those who attended minstrel performances. Audiences for antislavery performances were black and white, male and female, and likely to be interested in the social reforms that helped to define the middle class. Their emotional sympathies lay with suffering slaves, not with slaveholders, and their political sympathies led them into the Liberty and then Republican parties. In fugitive autobiographies, African American characters were literate, articulate, hardworking, and deeply discontent at their lack of liberty. The plantation was a torture chamber rather than the lost site of racial harmony. And the most highly sexualized figures were slaveholders, not slaves. When abolitionists insisted that fugitive narrators appear beside their stories, they emphasized just how much such stories differed from blackface performances.[69]

The two kinds of performances, embodying distinct class projections, ran on very different tracks though the cultural landscape of the antebellum North. Minstrel circuits connected the urban theaters of the Northeast and the far West, whereas slave narrators performed on the lecture circuits of organized reform, talking to audiences as interested in temperance and religion as in abolition. Fugitives addressed men and women accustomed to lyceum lectures and peddled their books among those they had first persuaded to accept their stories as true and authentic accounts of experience by appearing before them as speakers.[70]

It is sometimes difficult to think about minstrelsy and slave narratives together because the two have left us such very different cultural legacies. It is true that imagery drawn from blackface minstrelsy has been used to support racism, giving white mobs, particularly in the Jim Crow South, targets for violence. But it is also true that memories of antebellum minstrel performances made it easier for some African American artists to take to the stage after the Civil War, opening for them careers that might otherwise have been closed. Slave narratives, too, began in the world of antebellum performance, but when narrators wrote down their experiences, they provided a foundation for subsequent African American literary production. According to the legal historian Elizabeth Clark, writings of fugitives also provided a residue of humanitarian rhetoric, a cultural base for legal claims to individual rights.[71]

Scholars have made much of the fact that antebellum white performers justified their theft of black music by pretending that the music made by slaves was a mere emanation of nature and not the complex product of the human imagination.[72] Although their intentions were different and they aspired to honesty rather than entertainment, the white writers who presented slave autobiographies similarly stripped art from African American writers. Their stories, presenters said, were plain, unvarnished tales, literal and true renditions of experience rather than lies or works of imagination, art, or philosophy. The literal would come to grate on Frederick Douglass, who remembered bitterly the abolitionist John Collins's injunction to "'give us the facts'" and "'we will take care of the philosophy.' Just here arose some embarrassment," Douglass continued. "It was impossible for me to repeat the same old story month after month, and to keep up my interest in it. It was new to the people, it is true, but it was an old story to me; and to go through with it night after night, was a task altogether too mechanical for my nature." But, as any reader of Douglass might suspect, something more complicated than boredom lay behind his complaint.[73]

SYMPATHY AND CURIOSITY

Many students of Frederick Douglass have noticed his extraordinary ability to resist white handlers, and they have suggested that the relationship between Douglass's autobiographies and their framing documents differs from that of other slave narratives.[74] Coming to Douglass by way of the beggars' stories that introduced this study and the minstrel performances that entertained his contemporaries calls our attention to two distinct aspects of that difference. Douglass did not need white abolitionists to cleanse his tale of lies, and Douglass himself understood the play of sympathy and curiosity so crucial to pulling readers into narratives of personal experience.

Like the begging sailor Robert Adams and other captives, converts, and criminals who turned their stories into successful narratives, Douglass allowed figures of standing to introduce his book into the marketplace. But Douglass did not need these figures to defend him as an artless writer. Unlike Moses Roper, who celebrated his accomplishments as a dissembler, Douglass seems to have gone out of his way to avoid describing himself as lying. In situations when he might have been called upon to invent a story, he stepped gingerly around the verbal lie, often with phrasing worthy of a prudent lawyer. Take his description of an early escape plan. "On the water, we had a chance of being regarded as fishermen, in the service of a master. On the other hand, by taking the land route, through the counties adjoining Delaware, we should be subjected to all manner of interruptions, and many very disagreeable questions, which might give us serious trouble." What appears here as expedient for the slave, is, in fact, also wise policy for the slave narrator. The water route required no dissembling on the part of fugitives; it left conjecture to those who saw them.

Douglass could not always avoid lying, but his preferred tactic as a slave was to "own nothing." (What, after all, could a slave own?) When caught with forged documents, Douglass chose to remain silent, to burn or swallow the evidence of his lies rather than compound them with invented explanations that might have seemed to compromise the truthful narrator he presented himself to be.

"A still tongue," as he put it elsewhere, "makes a wise head." Slaves, he acknowledged,

> suppress the truth rather than take the consequences of telling it, and in so doing prove themselves a part of the human family. If they have any thing to say of their masters, it is generally in the masters' favor, especially when speaking to an untried man. I have been frequently asked, when a slave, if I had a kind master, and do not remember ever to have given a negative answer; nor did I, in pursuing this course, consider myself as uttering what was absolutely false; for I always measured the kindness of my master by the standard of kindness set up among slaveholders around us.[75]

Even when captured, Douglass and his fellow conspirators did not invent a story: they denied that they had intended to run away, but denial is not fabrication. And it would have been in keeping with Douglass's logic to have abandoned plans to run away when capture appeared imminent. Douglass's way with scenes in which he might have depicted himself in a lie thus diminished his need for an abolitionist preface to return him to the moral fold of artless truth tellers: by refusing to describe himself as ever having been an artful liar, Douglass maintained his access to art, his right to move beyond a simple account of his experience. He preserved his story for his own uses.

Compare, for example, scenes of interrogation in *The Fugitive Blacksmith; or, Events in the History of James W. C. Pennington* (1849) and *Life and Times of Frederick Douglass* (1881), the last of Douglass's autobiographies and the one in which he finally gave his readers the long-withheld account of his escape. Pennington, who fled a Maryland master, described the following conversation with a young man he met on the road. "'Are you free?'" the man asked. "'Yes, sir,'" was Pennington's simple reply. When apprehended, he invented an interesting story about having been part of a gang of slaves decimated by smallpox. The story of a gang lost to disease not only accounted for his appearance, alone and unsupervised, but also prompted several of his would-be captors to withdraw. The incident led him into a meditation on truth and falsehood.

The facts here demanded were in my breast. I knew according to the law of slavery, who I belonged to and where I came from, and I must now do one of three things—I must refuse to speak at all, or I must communicate the fact, or I must tell an untruth. How would an untutored slave, who had never heard of such a writer as Archdeacon Paley, be likely to act in such a dilemma? The first point decided was, the facts in this case are my private property. These men have no more right to them than a highway robber has to my purse.[76]

Pennington found in the idea of property rights a way out of his moral dilemma. His story gave him the means of fashioning self-possession, of holding a proprietary interest in himself. Through his story, Pennington came into his own: he became a free man, the "proprietor of his person and his capacities." But to do so, he had first to assert a property right in his story, to turn it into a commodity he would surrender only when he willed to do so.[77]

Although the slave catchers may have seen Pennington as a prize of dubious value (a danger, likely to spread infection among them), he presented himself to abolitionist audiences as a man ready to enjoy the privileges of self-possession. He concluded his account of escape by asking readers not to admire his "fabrications," but to see in his "history of events of the day . . . the impediments that often fall into the pathway of the flying bondman." It is most telling that to justify his lie, Pennington turned to a commercial metaphor—the facts of his life were his private property—instead of insisting, as even Cicero would have allowed, that there was nothing morally wrong with a lie told to save his life.[78] Pennington thus showed himself to be a man who had adopted the cognitive style of those who read his story, a man ready to join a community of those who gave their word to act as agents freely contracting to sell their labor.

When Douglass recalled his escape, he revealed himself a different sort of man. Like beggars, Douglass understood the play of sympathy and curiosity that shaped the appeals of the very poor, and he used his art to balance the competing pulls of these two responses. He warned readers that his story was neither particularly heroic nor thrilling and that he must attribute his success in fleeing slavery more to bearing and good luck than to courage and bravery. Success also depended on avoiding scrutiny; in avoiding scrutiny, he avoided the bold lie. Dressed as a sailor (a disguise, to be sure, but for a writer of books something less than a verbal lie), Douglass boarded a train headed from Baltimore to Philadelphia. He escaped examination by the railroad official by arranging to arrive just as the train was leaving the station. A conductor reached him on the train; "'I suppose you have your free papers?'" the conductor asked. "'No, sir; I never carry my free papers to sea with me,'" was Douglass's response—a completely truthful albeit obfuscatory answer that concealed the fact that he lacked any such papers. "'But you have something to show that you are a free man, have you not?'" the conductor continued. To this Douglass could answer a truthful yes, for he had just such a thing—a sailor's protection, a document that indeed "showed" him to be free. It finally matters little whether or not the exchange on the train happened just as Douglass set it down. His description of himself as a man who did not lie helped establish the voice in which he told his tale as a truthful one.[79]

Douglass thus negotiated a territory treacherous for fugitives and for fugitive storytellers. He eluded the slave catcher and he avoided the verbal lie. By the time he told the tale of his escape, however, the stakes in the game had changed. He no longer risked recapture as a fugitive, and he no longer needed to keep a route of escape secret from slaveholders. Explaining his long silence about his escape, Douglass talked about sympathy and curiosity. In *My Bondage and My Freedom* (1855), he acknowledged that an account of his escape "would materially add to the interest of my story, were I at liberty to gratify a curiosity which I know to exist in the minds of many." But gratification was not the only issue: as Douglass acknowledged, an account of escape served to ratify the tale and its teller. Depriving readers, he likewise deprived himself. "I would allow myself to suffer under the greatest imputations that evil-minded men might suggest, rather than exculpate myself by an explanation, and thereby run the hazard of closing the slightest avenue by which a brother in suffering might clear himself of the chains and fetters of slavery."[80]

And yet it is also true that in refusing to pen the details of his escape from slavery, Douglass escaped the confines of literal description. He knew that he had not achieved freedom merely by boarding a train bound north and that to tempt fellow slaves with the mere mechanics of flight would accomplish little. The lessons of freedom contained in his narrative were moral and philosophical (not merely legal and literal), and his flight to freedom began when he learned to read, years before he set foot on northern soil. As he had Mr. Auld repeat in his story, " 'Learning would *spoil* the best nigger in the world. Now,' he said, 'if you teach that nigger (speaking of myself) how to read, there would be no keeping him. It would forever unfit him to be a slave.' "[81]

Douglass reminded readers that as long as men and women were in chains, sympathy should trump curiosity, and former slaves should be accorded the privilege of silence—a privilege frequently denied them by slave codes. But Douglass also recognized that a poor and powerless writer held readers by appealing to both curiosity and sympathy. When he finally disclosed the manner of his escape, he expressed an almost perverse desire to tantalize readers and keep his secret. "I have sometimes thought it well enough to baffle curiosity by saying that while slavery existed there were good reasons for not telling the manner of my escape, and since slavery had ceased to exist there was no reason for telling it."[82] In this very different context, Douglass returned to James Pennington's sense that the facts of his life were his private property. When he needed to turn readers into antislavery activists, Douglass had to justify his silence. When he no longer needed to produce such sympathy, his refusal to gratify curiosity was a simple display of his power as a free artist.

Douglass had learned, however, that the value of his story was subject to severe fluctuation and that slave narratives did not always find eager listeners. As we shall see in the following chapter, some of those whose ears had once itched for tales of slavery turned their attention to the stories of northern soldiers who had been captured by the Confederacy and who turned to their own ends the methods and metaphors so carefully worked out in the stories told by fugitive slaves.

CHAPTER FOUR

❀

Prisoners of War

Every returned prisoner has brought his tale of suffering, astonishing his neighborhood with accounts of cruelty and barbarity
on the part of the enemy. Innumerable narratives have been published.

> United States Sanitary Commission, *Narrative of Privations
> and Sufferings of United States Officers and Soldiers while
> Prisoners of War in the Hands of Rebel Authorities* (1864)

Without any aspirations whatever to literary notoriety, I have endeavored to give a plain, unvarnished narrative of facts and incidents of prison life, as they occurred, under my observation, during twenty-two months in various rebel prisons. I have added,
also, the statements of several other Union prisoners, who stand
ready to vouch for the same with their affidavits.

> Lt. A. C. Roach, *The Prisoner of War and How Treated* (1865)

MR. ABBOTT'S QUESTIONS

In 1865, Mr. A. O. Abbott, a lieutenant in the First New York Dragoons,
published his *Prison Life in the South*. He wrote, he said, to "throw some
light upon the barbarous treatment we received at the hands of Rebels."

But, he added quickly, "Should these pages serve to throw any light upon the question 'What shall we do with the Negro?' I shall feel that my labor has not been in vain."[1] Abbott said little that could be read as a direct answer to his second question, but by posing it in his preface, he placed his whole book in service of an issue that preoccupied many of his contemporaries, black and white. About the "barbarous treatment" he had received, he was more forthcoming.[2]

Most historians who have studied books like Abbott's have turned to them for descriptions of conditions, physical and psychological, in southern prisons. And indeed, they offer much information on the poor sanitary conditions, meager diet, hard daily life, and physical sufferings of prisoners of war.[3] Following Abbott's suggestion, students of the African American experience of the Civil War have found in them a second story, because most such books reveal a great deal about former slaves' contributions to the Union war effort. The historian Leon Litwack found the literature by prisoners "replete . . . with stories of how slaves and free blacks rendered invaluable assistance to Union soldiers who had escaped from Confederate prisons."[4] To describe the contributions of the freedpeople was, Abbott sensed, one way to think about the part former slaves would take in postwar America. In fact, stories of suffering soldiers and helpful slaves are significantly entwined. But not always in the ways scholars have imagined.

To describe their confinement, white prisoners borrowed descriptions of slavery. It is not surprising that antebellum Americans deprived of freedom thought first of slavery. Many white soldiers characterized even the discipline and subordination of military life as a kind of slavery.[5] But the discomforts of the military were compounded in prison camps, and soldiers who might once have described themselves as "slaves" of military regulation and strict discipline now saw themselves supervised by men accustomed to disciplining slaves. What little freedom they retained in northern armies vanished in southern prisons. Several soldiers who published books and pamphlets recounting their experiences as prisoners of war also described themselves in confinement as "blackened" by filth. In their personal narratives, prisoners took on both the legal status of slaves and the racial characteristics of African Americans. In the period following emancipation, such double borrowings could be consequential for all who were trying to reimagine the United States as a country without slaves. Prisoners' stories became pieces in the war's official history, but as chapters in that history, they told stories of racial difference that helped reconstruct racism for postwar white Americans.

Some white prisoners sympathized with slaves, and those who escaped usually acknowledged the help they received in flight from communities of freedpeople. But sympathy and gratitude were both undermined by the ways former prisoners told their stories. White soldiers were the actors in these stories, the agents who made history and deserved recognition and reward.[6] Even when prisoners recognized the help given them by former slaves, they managed to belittle that help, describing a people blessed with an abundance of food and given to expressing themselves like comic characters on a minstrel stage. In the high tone of heroic suffering adopted by most prisoners, the contrast between former slaves and white soldiers is striking. In stories told from Rebel prisons, former slaves appear as a passive and docile people whose painless contributions to the war effort little deserve an honored place in official public memory. Former prisoners, in contrast, took pride of place in memorials to wartime suffering. Those who wrote their narratives to gain pensions from the government paid little heed to the fact that few of the material rewards for wartime sacrifice were going to former slaves. In fact, the wide circulation of prisoners' accounts may have helped push to the margins the claims of freedpeople.[7]

In the years following the war, African Americans recognized the high cost of their exclusion from official wartime memories. Throughout the 1880s, Frederick Douglass worked to remind Americans, who were bent on forgetting wartime differences, that the war had been fought over differences worth remembering. To ignore the significance of the struggle over slavery was to erase a national obligation to the freedpeople. "Well the nation may forget," Douglass declaimed in 1888, "it may shut its eyes to the past, and frown upon any who do otherwise, but the colored people of this country are bound to keep the past in lively memory till justice shall be done them."[8]

To read accounts left by Union prisoners is to be reminded that racism is neither immune to change nor without history. Prisoners' stories can be read as artifacts of racism's history, one of the places where racism was reproduced in a post-emancipation society. Specifically, prisoners' stories incorporated imagery borrowed from slave narratives, recycled blackface caricatures of freedpeople, and staged a contest in suffering between prisoners and slaves. The prisoners' victory, we will see, helped translate the double dialectic of condition and race—slavery and freedom, black and white—into a dialectic of race alone, thereby easing the white nation toward an indifference to the lives and labor of former slaves. The role of published tales may have been small, but as the historian Thomas Holt reminds us, the "everyday acts of name calling and petty exclusions are minor links in a larger historical chain of events, structures, and transformations anchored in slavery and the slave trade."[9]

Abbott saw that his account of experience, the story of an ordinary man caught in extraordinary circumstances, might play a role in remaking the postwar nation. But first, like all poor storytellers who made claims based on experiential knowledge, he had to get his story out, get it printed and into the hands of readers, and have it validated as true.

PRISON NARRATIVES

Only a small fraction of the 188,145 Union prisoners held by the Confederacy published accounts of their captivity. Nonetheless, according to the historian of the Sanitary Commission, Charles Stillé, prisoners' stories "roused most deeply, public indignation during the war."[10] At the prompting of family, friends, government committees, members of the Sanitary Commission, and fellow soldiers, former prisoners molded experiences into published stories. Some wrote stories during the war and let them serve as propaganda; others set down their accounts after the war to document the patriotism of captured soldiers; some wrote for commercial markets; others (like old Israel Potter) sought from readers the compensation that had been denied them by pension agents. Although a few prisoners' stories were produced by New York houses such as Harper and Brothers, more were the work of hometown presses and newspaper printing offices—outfits like the Methodist Book Concern of Cincinnati, the Railroad City Publishing House of Indianapolis, or Daily Wisconsin Printing House in Milwaukee. Narratives by former prisoners appeared in congressional reports, magazines, straightforward commercial publications, gift books, bound journalism, subscription volumes, and cheap pamphlets.[11]

Most stories came out during or immediately after the war, when tales of Confederate villainy had the greatest appeal for northern readers. Nineteen separately published accounts of prisoners' experiences appeared in 1865 alone; another seven appeared in 1866. Production slowed in the 1870s, particularly after members of a congressional committee published extracts from testimony of some three thousand former prisoners. Committee members concluded that mistreatment of prisoners was part of a deliberate Southern policy, and their published findings quieted public discussion of prison life.[12]

In the mid 1880s, enlisted men who had been held in Confederate prisons turned to publication when they could not find the officer or two comrades whose testimony was necessary to prove that a pension-securing disability had been contracted during confinement.[13] Public interest in war stories was renewed by the debates over pension legislation, and writers in search of pensions took advantage of that interest. Among these writers was the soldier John Ransom, who in 1881 published a book that he claimed was based on a diary he had kept while a prisoner in Andersonville. The book is a testament to Ransom's good nature and a tribute to the cooperation among soldiers that helped some avoid death in confinement. However, according to the historian William Marvel, Ransom had more immediate motives in mind: he wrote because he had lost his teeth and thought himself entitled to a government pension. His dental problems, Ransom contended, all began when he contracted scurvy in prison, and he presented a fabricated prison diary as evidence for a history of disease.[14]

Ransom urged Congress to heed the appeals of the "National Ex-Prisoners of War Association" to expand the ranks of those eligible for pensions by including every soldier "on record or [who has] other proof of confinement in a confederate prison for a prescribed length of time." Former prisoners sometimes had a hard time collecting pensions because they could not readily produce the proof of disability required by the pension bureau. Prisoners who escaped and made their way to Union lines were often sent home immediately and then discharged from the army. No one bothered to record their diseases. Few of those who arrived home consulted doctors who would have documented their disabilities. Instead they sought "the kindly nursing of mother or wife and nourishing food," as one man remembered. Most also suffered from "General Debility," a collection of complaints not found on the specific lists of wounds and illnesses easily traced to military service. A published story constituted an alternative documentation, and publicity surrounding pension decisions prompted several men to write their histories. Hoping that Congress would recognize that confinement itself was sufficient to earn a pension, many appended to their stories lists of their comrades who had been imprisoned with them. The ghost of Israel Potter must have whispered to some that if appeals to the government failed, the market for little books might make up the difference.[15]

A third group of prison narratives appeared in *Century Magazine* between 1889 and 1891. The extraordinary success of *Century*'s series on *Battles and Leaders of the Civil War* (1885–1887) prompted the editors to publish more war-related material. Although recollections of prisoners did not necessarily promote the "intersectional reconciliation" behind *Century*'s project, writers and editors did their best to minimize recrimination and resentment in the stories they published.[16] When T. H. Mann wrote about his experiences at Andersonville, he admitted that he had revised his original manuscript, "leaving out much of its bitterness, and nearly all the explosive adjectives and personal opinions." To promote fraternal feelings among former combatants, he blamed mistreatment of prisoners on an incompetent home guard—on men who knew nothing of battlefield valor. "[D]uring our whole captivity we always experienced good usage from an old soldier—from all those who had fought and met us upon the many battlefields of the war."[17]

Although produced for different venues, prison narratives shared certain distinctive characteristics. They were above all modest stories produced by modest writers. Unlike middle-class autobiographers for whom experience in war became part of a life history, most common soldiers who wrote narratives based on prison experiences produced books largely limited to accounts of confinement.[18] Narrow focus was perhaps a marketing ploy, allowing former prisoners to distinguish themselves from the mass of soldier-memoirists, but it also gave them an arena of expertise. Concentrating on their sufferings in confinement, prisoners gave scant space either to the larger issues of the war or to their postwar lives. Prison experience gave them but a narrow purchase on expertise, and they left to others the task of producing the grand narrative of the war.[19]

Whether writing as propagandists, as petitioners for relief, or as warriors recalling their days of glory, soldiers promised to tell the "truth," assuring readers that they described experiences in honest, "unvarnished prose." Many apologized for writing, insisting that they appeared in print at the urgent "solicitation of friends," and described only what they had themselves seen, heard, or felt. As Lt. A. C. Roach put it, "Without any aspirations whatever to literary notoriety, I have endeavored to give a plain, unvarnished narrative of facts and incidents of prison life, as they occurred, under my observation, during twenty-two months in various rebel prisons."[20]

When possible, former prisoners framed their accounts with testimonials from comrades and commanding officers. One enterprising man solicited an endorsement from Ulysses Grant and embossed it on his book's cover—"Thrilling Account, Gen'l. U.S. Grant." An attentive reader would find that the words had been excerpted from a letter in which Grant thanked the soldier for sending him a copy of the narrative, promising to "take an early day to read over the thrilling account of your wanderings while escaping from a rebel prison."[21]

Several prisoners made the act of composition itself a sign of authenticity, describing in detail the diaries they kept while imprisoned, the pencil stubs they used to write them, the efforts they made to preserve them, and the ingenious schemes they used to smuggle them back to northern printers. Abbott's story is typical. He described himself in his "brush shanty sitting flat on the ground writing on my knee." The diary itself, he asserted, was smuggled through Confederate lines "secreted in the back of a coat."[22]

Composing a story was one thing; publishing it was another. A striking number of former prisoners who published their experiences had worked as reporters, ministers, and printers and so were familiar with the mechanisms of getting stories out as books. Portions of John Ransom's *Andersonville Diary* first appeared in the pages of the Jackson (Michigan) *Citizen*, the paper where he had "pulled a press" before the war. Eugene Forbes, a soldier who kept a diary as he starved to death in Florence, South Carolina, had been a printer's apprentice before the war. After his death, his printer friends published his book. And Lieutenant A. C. Roach wrote an account of his colonel's escape and his own imprisonment for the subscription house opened in Indianapolis by Colonel A. D. Streight, the man who had commanded his regiment.[23]

A few stories apparently sold well; others did not. In 1865, the subscription publishers of Robert Kellogg's book complained in the book itself that they were losing money. Calculating the costs of taxes, paper, binders' boards, binders' cloth, and gilding, the publishers figured that Kellogg's book should sell not for the $1.65 they had asked, but "at $2.50. We have lost $6,000 in the book business the past four or five years, besides our time, and the use of $10,000 to $15,000 on capital; yet we have not made $300 bad debts. We have sold books less than cost. This," the publisher concluded, "is the trouble."[24] It is difficult to know whether the publisher's unusual confession was meant to convince readers that they had made a good bargain in buying the book or to produce sympathy for businessmen struggling in war to balance patriotism and profit.

Some publishers found a good market for inexpensive prison stories. In the 1880s, W. H. Newlin's publisher promised a book set in large type and, like the dime novels and story papers so popular with postwar readers, "well adapted for reading while riding in a railway passenger coach." Newlin apparently made money with his story. He reprinted on the front cover a letter from a book agent in Anaconda, Montana. "I came here this A.M., and sold twenty-one copies of 'Prison Escape' at 35 cents each. Could have sold more, only it rained, and I had to quit work. I am glad your book sells so well. Send me 300 copies by freight, at once to Missoula, Missoula County, Montana."[25]

Those who purchased Newlin's book bought a good adventure. Others appended to their adventures a list of fellow prisoners. Although the stories themselves ended with freedom from captivity, with death or with a soldier's restoration to regiment or kin, many printed books ended with lists of prisoners of war—those who had survived and those who had died. In the earliest publications, such lists authenticated the experiences described. They substantiated southern cruelty, conjuring for readers the sheer mass of men held in close quarters. For prisoners seeking proof that they had been held captive, published lists offered evidence to support pension claims. But most important, lists of names turned tales of individual suffering into war memorials—verbal monuments to heroism and sacrifice.[26]

Some writers made explicit their memorial intentions. John McElroy asserted in the preface to his *Andersonville: A Story of Rebel Prisons*, a book published in 1879, that "his chief reward in writing the book is the thought that he may have been able by it to add a single leaf to the wreath of unfading glory with which history will decorate the brow of the noblest and bravest soldier who ever stood upon any field of battle—the American boy." In a different fashion, Robert Kellogg made his book into a war memorial, opening it with a typographical obelisk, a tribute to his fellow prisoners.[27]

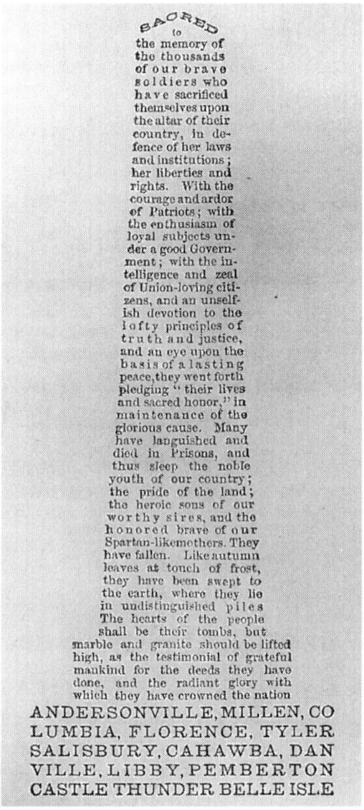

SACRED
to
the memory of
the thousands
of our brave
soldiers who
have sacrificed
themselves upon
the altar of their
country, in de-
fence of her laws
and institutions;
her liberties and
rights. With the
courage and ardor
of Patriots; with
the enthusiasm of
loyal subjects un-
der a good Govern-
ment; with the in-
telligence and zeal
of Union-loving citi-
zens, and an unself-
ish devotion to the
lofty principles of
truth and justice,
and an eye upon the
basis of a lasting
peace, they went forth
pledging "their lives
and sacred honor," in
maintenance of the
glorious cause. Many
have languished and
died in Prisons, and
thus sleep the noble
youth of our country;
the pride of the land;
the heroic sons of our
worthy sires, and the
honored brave of our
Spartan-like mothers. They
have fallen. Like autumn
leaves at touch of frost,
they have been swept to
the earth, where they lie
in undistinguished piles
The hearts of the people
shall be their tombs, but
marble and granite should be lifted
high, as the testimonial of grateful
mankind for the deeds they have
done, and the radiant glory with
which they have crowned the nation
ANDERSONVILLE, MILLEN, CO
LUMBIA, FLORENCE, TYLER
SALISBURY, CAHAWBA, DAN
VILLE, LIBBY, PEMBERTON
CASTLE THUNDER BELLE ISLE

FIGURE 12   "Sacred to the Memory"
(from Robert Kellogg, *Life and Death in Rebel Prisons*). Courtesy of the American Antiquarian Society.

"TRANSIENT AND SOMEWHAT FUGITIVE HISTORIES"

Prisoners worked to make their books, modest though they were, into monuments to suffering and sacrifice. When government authorities scrutinized prison tales and pronounced them authentic, they made the stories part of an official northern version of the war. Formal efforts to evaluate the truth of prisoners' reports began nearly a year before the war ended. A northern public, incensed by rumors of disease and starvation in Confederate prison camps, demanded an explanation for southern cruelty. The number of prisoners of war rose after the great battles of the summer and fall of 1863, and in the absence of a working agreement for the exchange of prisoners, tens of thousands of Union soldiers sickened and died in hastily constructed Confederate stockades. Informal battlefield exchanges continued, but the federal government's attempts to renew a formal exchange agreement failed when the Confederacy refused to treat soldiers captured from black regiments as prisoners of war.[28] In the summer of 1864, woodcuts of photographs of maimed and skeletal men released from confinement appeared in the illustrated press; in consequence, a "tidal wave of rage," as the historian James McPherson puts it, swept through the North.[29]

Suffering grew worse in the spring of 1864, when the Confederate command decided to move Union prisoners south from Virginia. The Confederacy massed prisoners far from the Union lines, near the small station of Anderson on the Georgia Central Railroad, located some sixty miles southeast of Macon. In February, the first prisoners arrived at Andersonville from Richmond; by August more than thirty-three thousand men were crowded onto twenty-six acres of bare red dirt. In large numbers, they suffered and often died from diarrhea, dysentery, and scurvy.

Although many northerners believed that prisoners were victims of a deliberate policy designed to kill captive soldiers by starvation, exposure, and disease, most historians have concluded that the high mortality rate in southern prisons is better explained by incompetence than by evil design.[30] Some defenders of the South, however, have claimed that the Confederacy was simply too poor to feed the captives that Lincoln, by refusing to accept an agreement on exchange, left to rot in southern hands. By 1864, the South's economy was in shambles, and the rail system was already hard-pressed to distribute food and supplies to both soldiers and civilians. Poor conditions in the prisons were exacerbated by inefficiency and bad planning: in the expectation of early exchange, Confederate authorities made no long-term arrangements to feed and house the men they captured.

Conditions common to all prisons were worse at Andersonville, where mobs of men lived on slight rations in the open air beside a stream choked with kitchen waste and human excrement. Pressing military needs for men and materiel left too few guards competent to supervise work details in the woods around the prison compound, too few axes for prisoners to cut logs, too few sawmills to make boards of trees that were cut, and too few nails to turn boards into shelter. And so, as James McPherson concluded, prisoners managed a poor existence as they "broiled in the sun and shivered in the rain."[31]

How were northern readers meant to respond to the awful stories that former prisoners told? What conclusions were they expected to draw? As we have seen, soldiers filled publications with words meant to serve ipso facto as warrantees for the truth of all they had written. They shied away from extensive interpretation, but they little doubted the significance of what they had witnessed. Robert Kellogg opened with the epigraph "We speak that we do know, and testify that we have seen." He quoted with approval the testimony of a Confederate sergeant:

> "It is true that a great part of the suffering in this present war, as in all wars, must remain forever with the secrets of *unwritten history*. A few who were themselves actors in the tragic scenes may rehearse the story of their individual experience, and thus furnish, as it were, a key to unlock the gates through which others may enter and take a look. This is the only way in which the people at large can become acquainted with this thrilling portion of the war, and authentic and reliable statements are therefore of deep interest and importance."[32]

As we have seen, prisoners presented their tales as "authentic" versions of experience. Like confessing criminals, they acknowledged the value of authenticity and employed the social and rhetorical devices designed to signal to readers that the story they held was a true one. Yet as beggars, convicts, and slaves all learned, the verbal assurances of marginal writers were rarely sufficient in themselves to guarantee that their stories would be accepted as true. Former prisoners too found powerful allies who turned discrete tales into authorized documents. According to members of the Sanitary Commission, some readers were skeptical about the prisoners' accounts, despite authors' promises to tell the truth. Two "authorized" bodies (composed of people like the middle-class friends and allies whom Henry Mayhew recruited to form his Mendacity Society)—the

Sanitary Commission and a congressional committee—sorted through the experiences of soldiers, offering readers a guarantee of their authenticity and sketching for them the meanings to be extracted from so many individual accounts.[33]

In 1864, when the United States Sanitary Commission set out to investigate the "privations and sufferings" of prisoners of war, commission members acknowledged the intellectual problems posed by an unorganized collection of tales of suffering. "Every returned prisoner has brought his tale of suffering, astonishing his neighborhood with accounts of cruelty and barbarity on the part of the enemy. Innumerable narratives have been published." The commissioners noticed that "the public have been made very uneasy by these reports. One class have accepted them as true; another felt them to be exaggerated; still another have pronounced them wholly false,—fictions purposely made and scattered abroad to inflame the people against their enemies, and doing great injustice to the South."[34]

The commission took depositions from former prisoners in order to ascertain the exact extent of their suffering. Commission members claimed to have heard from "every station in the distant South" identical stories of robbery, insult, starvation, exposure, "shootings without warning, of close and filthy rooms or unsheltered encampments, of disease without care or medical treatment, and of deaths without number." Acting as witnesses at one remove, they described what they had seen of the emaciated prisoners and heard of their stories. Commissioners "did not feel at liberty . . . to make any inferential statements," but the connections between "certain known effects" and "certain established causes" were inescapable.[35]

Employing yet another apparatus of "truth," they appended to their report engraved reproductions of four photographs of unnamed emaciated soldiers who had been held at Belle Isle. One image of a skeletal soldier posed with his back turned to the audience seemed designed to recall an image of the scarred back of Private Gordon, a widely circulated image of a slave who had escaped to the Union lines in Baton Rouge in 1863. An engraving of Gordon's scarred back was published as the central image of a

FIGURE 13 Soldier's Back (from U.S. Sanitary Commission, *Narrative of the privations and sufferings of the United States Officers and Soldiers*). Courtesy of the American Antiquarian Society).

tryptic in *Harper's Weekly* on July 4, 1863—Gordon in rags, Gordon stripped naked, and Gordon in uniform. In the summer of 1863, Gordon, the man and soldier, perhaps no longer needed the sympathy mobilized by the image of his furrowed back. Those who made pictures of returned prisoners appropriated the visual vocabulary designed for images of slavery, the ribs of the starving soldier replacing the lash marks on the slave's back. In the little world made from stories of suffering, the emaciated veteran upstaged the emancipated slave.[36]

To all the material they had collected, commission members encouraged readers to respond first through sympathy—"with a sorrow and indignation which words cannot speak, and which can only be expressed by tears, and sobs, and teeth set closely together"—and then through more

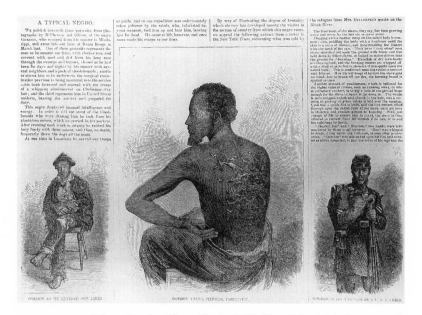

FIGURE 14   Private Gordon (from *Harper's Weekly*, 4 July 1863). Courtesy of the American Antiquarian Society.

rational inquiry to gain a "clear knowledge of the origin of these horrors." Although the abolitionists who had to decide what to do about James Williams's narrative divided over how best to assert the truth of his story, members of the Sanitary Commission were not averse to employing the sentimental appeals that reached audiences through their hearts—a response most often encouraged by those who composed personal narratives. They were also aware that they addressed some who preferred to respond through a scientific understanding of events—who preferred to listen to those who were "professionally competent to read the unerring testimony of nature in the physical condition of the men." Commission members crafted a sort of evidentiary pyramid, forming a sentimental base from prisoners' stories and then building on that base with material drawn from medical reports and from their own practiced observations; they thus constructed an argument better suited to the bureaucratic order of the postwar world. In doing so, they also solved the problem that had vexed abolitionists: sentimental truths could be incorporated into a properly ordered intellectual sequence.[37]

Similarly, in 1869 the Congressional Committee on the Treatment of Prisoners of War extracted from the "transient and somewhat fugitive histories based on personal experiences and observations of authors" "an enduring record, truthful and authentic, and stamped with the national authority." The committee invited written responses and sent out agents who combed the country, holding public hearings and collecting testimony from survivors sufficient to discount the eccentricities in any individual account. Some three thousand men sent letters to the committee, and the committee's agents in the field interviewed hundreds more. Under oath, soldiers described their experiences—things they had seen, heard, and felt—and the congressional publication molded firsthand testimony into an official record. Individual histories, the committee found, could

> hardly be trusted to convey to future generations in living and permanent form the horrors of southern prison life. Though to readers of the present day, to whom they are accessible, they furnish a startling tale of hitherto unknown suffering and brave endurance. But it may well be questioned whether these detached though numerous works are destined to live in the great future, or insure for themselves an extended historical reputation and existence. Their very number may hereafter serve to confuse the general reader searching for some comprehensive history of this great era, and finally banish most of them from the libraries of the people, when the personal suffering or individual heroism which now lends them their interest and popularity shall have faded from the memory of friends.[38]

Congressmen were not trained in literary analysis, but in framing prisoners' stories they described characteristics of many plebeian narratives. Committee members sensed that each individual story was a partial one and that the whole truth could only be established by a body capable of commenting from a distance. Soldier-narrators could comment with authority only on those things they had seen and heard. No single story could document a collective experience; no individual narrator could produce a true and enduring account of the experience of many. That was the task of the congressional committee, whose members had read and heard enough to separate facts from fantasy.

The written report nevertheless relied heavily on certain individual stories, particularly those published by Henry M. Davidson of Ohio and by Warren Lee Goss of Massachusetts. Stories told by Davidson and Goss thus appeared as particularly true, as synecdoches, after a fashion, standing for the whole confused collection of prison experiences. Ironically, the sacrifices and sufferings that soldiers described helped legitimize the kinds of authorities—experts, commissions, and committees—that now validated their stories. Professional interpreters—in this case, doctors, reformers, and politicians—emerged to validate and interpret the narrow empirical claims of prisoners' stories.[39]

The authority most common soldiers derived from their experiences was insufficient to allow them to generalize: to draw sweeping conclusions would violate the cultural logic that brought their stories forward in the first place. They operated in the tradition of the humble narrator who was the unwilling or accidental victim of experiences that transformed him (or her) into a cultural agent. In the past, such stories offered ground for the interpretive work of ministers, meshing easily with an evangelical faith in testimonies of personal conversion. In the increasingly bureaucratized society of the postwar world, men of the professions—doctors, lawyers, scientists, and professors—reserved for themselves the rights to establish facts and to draw conclusions from those facts. Prisoners' narratives document a chapter in the history of the American Civil War. We can also read them as a chapter in the history of "truth." Like beggars, convicts, and slaves, prisoners by themselves could not be trusted to produce the authoritative account of events. But prisoners did not call upon the same mediating authorities these other humble narrators used. Instead they turned to a government bureaucracy that in the course of the war had come to be accepted by the public as the ultimate arbiter. This bureaucracy collects,

verifies, and when necessary mediates among those men of the professions, all the voices of authority competing for the last word.[40]

The Sanitary Commission asked a group of doctors to corroborate the
suffering the soldiers described. The doctors produced a general tale from
the impartial and scientific evidence they extracted from soldiers' bodies.
But they could not explain why the prisoners had suffered so. The commissioners reserved for themselves the right to explain the enemy's motives and to interpret the soldiers' experiences. If storytelling prisoners
stood in the position of storytelling slaves, so the members of the Sanitary
Commission assumed the position of abolitionist sponsors. A powerful
state now stood behind the commissioners as they took upon themselves
the task of turning the fragments of individual experience to political ends:
in this case, into propaganda to maintain northern resolve in the last
months of the war. Unlike fugitives from slavery who found their stories
dismissed as "outdated curiosities" after the war, prisoners continued to
find readers.[41]

The congressional committee forged its report out of testimony, verbal
and written, as well as statistics and "official documents." After a brief description of the investigation's purpose and method, committee members
reviewed the history of the treatment of wartime prisoners. They described the mass of corroborative testimony extracted from 139 sworn witnesses and three thousand letters, but they saw fit to introduce contemporary testimony with a history of such "savage" practices as cannibalism
and deliberate human sacrifice. Confederate treatment of prisoners of war
thus appears little removed from behavior practiced most often in the "interior portions of Asia, Africa, and some of the islands." "Prisoners of war
among such nations or tribes are usually murdered as soon as captured, or
retained for a time for cruel exposition or brutal sacrifice, and are often
cooked and eaten by their captors, or sold in market like stock, and fed
and prepared for their fate."[42]

A trace of savage practice lurked beneath the civilized face of the
South, and in the committee's report, the Confederacy was Africanized.

Descriptions of savage warfare set the mood for the thousand pages of testimony that led the congressional committee to conclude that captive Union soldiers had been the victims of deliberate barbarity. But the invocation of Africa could work in a more complicated fashion. The association of savagery and cannibalism with Africa implied that slaveholders (turned prison keepers) had fallen under the influence of the African slaves they held. The origins of barbarity, like the origins of slavery, were to be found in Africa. This being the case, the report implied, the ultimate blame for the prisoners' sufferings perhaps should be laid at the feet of slaves.

Committee members acknowledged that their conclusions would have been impossible without the soldiers' observations that were incorporated into the report's discussions of suffering. In fact, as the former prisoner John Urban wrote, "It is only through the experience given to the public by the survivors, that this thrilling part of the history of the war can become known."[43] A congressional authority validated a version of the soldiers' experience, lending official support to the claims of truth and authenticity that framed prisoners' accounts of what had happened to them. But as Mr. Urban reminds us, we cannot discount the possibility that congressmen, like many readers who enjoyed the scenes of cruelty in Gothic fiction and in slave narratives, found the horror of prisoners' accounts titillating. Suffering was a "thrilling part" of the war's history. Sensation perhaps served as a welcome reminder that all feeling had not been lost in the slow process of brutalization that was a consequence of war, and when people turned to prisoners' tales they did so not just to watch southern barbarity but also to confirm their own sensitivity.[44]

Evidence suggests that there is a close connection between the stories told by fugitive slaves and by survivors of southern prisons. But what do the connections between these stories signify? Smoking guns are rare in cultural history, and it is difficult to prove an argument based solely on evidence of the imagination. Yet the stories of heroic suffering told by prisoners perhaps played a small part in shaping policies of Reconstruction.

Perhaps those who might have best responded to the claims of the freed-people actually better remembered the stories that made the pain of white soldiers more pressing than the rights of former slaves.

As memories of war faded, success in pension claims depended on de-vices—official records and the testimony of witnesses—that marked a story as true. But did the assertions of "truth," which soldiers marshaled to describe what had happened to them, extend to their descriptions of the freedpeople who helped them? It is striking that narratives of "fact," stamped with official approval, contained comic portraits of a people who seem to stand outside history. As we will see, prisoners' stories recapitu-late Frederick Douglass's well-known chiasmus—"You have seen how a man was made a slave; you shall see how a slave was made a man"—but they give it a different outcome. Prisoners showed their readers how a white soldier might become a black slave and how an enslaved and black-ened soldier might become again a free white man. Left behind in the process that made heroes of those who struggled for liberty were men and women who had only recently gained their freedom.[45]

LIKE SLAVES IN THE HANDS OF SLAVEHOLDERS

Some northern soldiers felt that imprisonment had placed their manhood on trial, and they made joking comparisons between themselves and women as they draped themselves in blankets and washed their few clothes.[46] But most imprisoned soldiers compared their experience to that of slaves: after all, they were captives of a slaveholding enemy. We should remember that in some fashion all mid-century Americans were schooled in the vocabulary of slavery, and it is hardly surprising that the rhetoric of slavery and abolition runs through prisoners' narratives. But the opposition between chattel slavery and free citizenship that had proved so crucial in the formation of the northern white working class dis-appeared just when soldiers set out to describe themselves as captives in the South.[47]

The emancipation of the slaves altered the identity of the white working class as surely as it altered the legal status of former slaves. "If Northern white workers," as historian David Roediger puts it,

> developed new attitudes toward people of color only slowly and contradictorily, emancipation made for much more consistent and dramatic changes in how such workers conceived of *themselves*. No longer could whiteness be an unambiguous source of self-satisfaction. No longer could a counterpoint with slaves define whites as "free labor." No longer could the supposedly servile, lazy, natural and sensual African-American serve as so clear a counterpoint to white labor and as so convenient a repository for values that white workers longed for and despised.[48]

Stories from southern prisons were one of the places where "new attitudes toward people of color" were developed. Emancipation made it possible for prisoners-turned-writers to imagine themselves as slaves, for they now lived in world where, in fact, there were no slaves. An imagined identification with slaves that a generation of northern workers had shunned suddenly became freely available as a metaphor. In identifying with slaves, white prisoners who published their stories helped to reconstruct hard lines of race that nursed racism through the risky period of Reconstruction.

Most of the former prisoners who wrote experiences for publication explained ill-treatment by southern captors as part and parcel of slaveholders' attitudes toward slaves: southerners treated their prisoners as slaveholders treated their slaves. Some soldiers had found army life reminiscent of slavery, but prison life was worse. Unlike Union officers, southern guards were accustomed to the disciplinary practices of a slave system, and even if they themselves had never held slaves, they seemed to know full well the cruelest practices of those who did. As the report of the Sanitary Commission concluded, long habits of despotic power had led southerners to "do as they please, not only to their slaves, but to all mankind who differ from them." S. S. Boggs remembered his eighteen-month imprisonment in the hands of keepers "whose notoriety for cruelty as slave-drivers gained their appointment as prison-keepers, where they could satisfy their barbarous appetites on helpless captives who possessed no property value."[49]

It was but a small step from such general observation to individual cases. Casting themselves as slaves, prisoners found a rich collection of cultural references for the absence of freedom they experienced. We also find them using many of the techniques storytelling fugitives had used to move northern audiences. Like fugitives from slavery, they announced that they refrained from detailing the worst of their experiences, lest apparent exaggeration cause audiences to question their stories' content.

Some recalled abolitionist publications and tried to dispel doubts about their stories by reminding readers of the skepticism that had greeted published accounts of slavery. "When the anti-slavery reformers of thirty years ago set forth the cruelties of the slave system," John McElroy wrote in 1879, "they were met with a storm of indignant denial, vilification and rebuke. When Theodore D. Weld issued his 'Testimony of a Thousand Witnesses,' to the cruelty of slavery, he introduced it with a few words pregnant with sound philosophy, which can be applied to the work now introduced, and may help the reader better to accept and appreciate its statements." McElroy warned readers that the cruelties described in his book were no more than they "should legitimately expect from men who, all their lives, have used whip and thumb screw, shot-gun and blood-hound, to keep human beings subservient to their will."[50]

Indeed, prisoners found it easy to rewrite their experiences in terms that drew upon published accounts of the mistreatment of former slaves. They turned sometimes to the Bible, Homer, Shakespeare, Bunyon, and Defoe. But just as often, they turned to experiences of American slaves. Imprisoned enlisted men complained that captors had bound them with chains forged for slaves, frightened them with instruments of torture fabricated to discipline slaves, and pursued them with dogs or with civilian patrols organized to supervise slaves on masterless plantations. One man complained to the Sanitary Commission that he had found himself at Libby Prison crammed into quarters where prisoners sat on their

FIGURE 15   "Capture of the Fugitives" (from A. O. Abbott, *Prison Life in the South*). Courtesy of the American Antiquarian Society.

haunches like individuals destined for slavery and weathering the "middle passage."[51]

Prisoners seemed particularly bothered by dogs, and nearly all of them described the beasts the guards used to track fugitives. Mr. Abbott incorporated a passage from a paper that warned "escaping Yankee Doodles. *We have hundreds of dogs trained to catch negroes, which are thirsting for blood, and are ready to be put upon trails of escaping Yankees, and we will use them for the benefit of all who attempt escape; and the best thing the Doodles can do is to remain under the protecting care of Colonel Wayne.*"[52]

The discussion of dogs also offered an occasion for several prisoners to recount conversations with guards about the meaning of the war. Many paraphrased conversations in which Confederate guards complained that when the Union authorities had begun to enlist black soldiers, they had turned the war from an honorable contest into a degraded spectacle, reducing white soldiers to "the level of the 'nigger.'" As Robert Kellogg remembered the exchange: "After he had gone on in this manner for some time, one of the prisoners interrupted him with the query, 'Captain, which is worse? We use the *negro* as a soldier. You employ blood-hounds to do a soldier's duty,' referring, of course, to the mode of pursuing the prisoners who made attempts to escape." The first act of degradation, in other words, had been the use of dogs on men, but the assumption that the use of slaves and the use of dogs were similar acts seems to have been shared by white prisoners and their captors.[53]

Prisoners spoke metaphorically of being slaves, then turned that metaphor to their own ends. Although some felt flattered when captors said that they were worth at least as much as a good slave, most white prisoners—who realized that they were "worth" far less, in the sense that they could not be sold as slaves—managed to represent themselves as worse off than either slaves or the black soldiers who suffered among them. Some prisoners rediscovered the racist argument that African Americans were immune to pain, in contrast to white people, who supposedly felt pain deeply.[54] Drawing on such arguments, a group of Andersonville prisoners sent a memorial to Lincoln in August 1864 in which they objected to the suspension of formal prisoner exchange; they insisted that they suffered far more than the soldiers from the colored regiments who had the good fortune either to have been killed or returned to hard labor. As they put it to the president, "The whites are confined in such prisons as Libby and Andersonville, starved and treated with a barbarism unknown to civilized nations. The blacks, on the contrary, are seldom imprisoned. They are distributed among the citizens, or employed on government works. Under these circumstances they receive enough to eat, and are worked no harder than they have been accustomed to be."[55]

White soldiers, unaccustomed to starvation, filth, and loss of liberty, complained that they suffered more than slaves. Slavery, they said, was preferable to confinement; even death was better than imprisonment. After listening to the soldiers' litany of wrongs, the congressional committee concluded that the black soldiers who had been massacred at Fort Pillow were better off than the white soldiers who had been captured alive. "While the murder of these Union soldiers was more merciful than the starvation of the white troops, it was no less startling and striking in its de-

FIGURE 16   "Hanging by the Thumbs" (from Robert Kellogg, *Life and Death in Rebel Prisons*). Courtesy of the American Antiquarian Society.

velopment of the savage cruelty which seems to have usurped in the breasts of the confederate officials the kindlier sentiments of humanity, which among civilized people tend to assuage and mitigate the sufferings incident to war."[56] It is not surprising that soldiers weary of battle and spent by suffering had come to envy the dead: Virgil gave just such sentiments to Aeneas who had survived war with the Greeks only to face the wrath of Juno. White soldiers and congressional investigators, however, made the American version a chapter in the history of race. Perhaps surviving soldiers envied the dead their peace, but they also claimed for themselves the moral superiority of those who suffered most.

It was easy for prisoners to understand that guards might treat them as they had treated slaves, but stories suggest more complex connections among soldiers, slaves, and slavery; an identity that could no longer be constructed on the basis of servitude was, in prisoners' stories, reconstituted on the basis of race. White men who had lost their freedom not only had been enslaved; they had been blackened. The imagined line between slavery and freedom that had separated white workers in the North from slave laborers in the South disappeared in prison camps. In the filth and excrement of the prison yard, white men lost their distinctive racial identity. Without external markers of skin or status, racial identity was up for grabs. White prisoners sometimes found a race ascribed to them against their will, and sometimes they took advantage of the play of racial identity and put on black faces that helped them survive captivity or elude pursuers.

Former prisoners remembered meeting white soldiers so filthy they appeared black. When Warren Lee Goss arrived at Andersonville in May 1864, he was greeted by men whose "faces were so begrimed with pitch-pine smoke and dirt, that for a while we could not discern whether they were negroes or white men." Eugene Forbes wondered about his own racial identity: "I am somewhat in doubt as to whether I am a mulatto or a quadroon—I certainly don't look like a white man." And, although after confinement at Andersonville, Lessel Long still considered himself a German, he admitted that "from my appearance and dress [I] might equally as well have claimed nativity near the sources of the river Nile."[57]

Others made explicit the connections between black face and the minstrel stage. According to Mr. McElroy, since pitch pine "burned with a very sooty flame, the effect upon the appearance of the hoverers was startling. Face, neck and hands became covered as thick as heavy brown paper, and absolutely irremovable by water alone. The hair became of midnight blackness, and gummed up into elf-locks of fantastic shape and effect. Any one of us could have gone on the negro minstrel stage, without changing a hair, and put to blush the most elaborate make-up of the grotesque burnt-cork artists."[58]

Some prisoners found advantages in voluntarily blacking up. Roach remembered prisoners at Macon and Columbia who had "blacked their faces and passed out as negro workmen." Others had blackened their faces in order to be assigned the work details that entitled African American prisoners to larger rations. Others donned black masks in their run to freedom. After Alvan Bacon escaped from prison at Macon, Georgia, he and his companions traveled by night, pretending "whenever we pass a skiff, or a person going fishing, . . . in negro dialect, that we were 'goin' down to the next plantation to see our gal.'"[59]

If, as scholars have contended, minstrelsy was the most widespread form of popular entertainment in the antebellum North, it is hardly surprising that the men of the Union army drew upon a large repertoire of minstrel images to describe their own behavior (blacking up) and to describe (often with sympathy) the activities of the freedpeople they met.[60] Yet if we think of these stories as one of the places where postemancipation racial relations were imagined, then we recognize that something more than monetary compensation for suffering rode on soldiers' descriptions. In soldiers' narratives, the prison camp became a crucible for remaking race. White soldiers descended into blackness but reemerged as free white men. Nowhere in these accounts is this racial exchange more striking than in descriptions of men living in excrement.

Beneath white faces blackened by soot, prisoners discovered white bodies blackened by excrement. In the prison yards, the two strands—the comic and the erotic (or, if one prefers, the cerebral and the corporeal)—that literary critics have found in the idea of the "other" came unraveled. The grotesque black bodies that white performers put upon the minstrel stage offered the happy attractions of a careless, preindustrial life, but the grotesque body was also always potentially scatological. As though a discourse often repressed in peace was deployed in war, prisoners who described their camps and observers who described prisoners in camps were forced to recognize that prisoners, especially the men in Andersonville who suffered from severe diarrhea, were men living in their own excrement. In prisoners' descriptions of life along the banks of Andersonville's rancid stream, the ambivalent "other" of the stage became the unambivalent other of the prison, and the racial identities that had been softened in confinement were recast hard and new for the postwar world.[61]

The degradation of capture, confinement, exposure, and starvation was most extreme by the banks of the putrid stream that ran through the Georgia compound. The committees that worked through soldiers' accounts first noted the lesser slights—prisoners stripped of clothes, blankets, money, and even the family photographs that connected them to those they had left behind. "Pictures of wife and children, father or mother, brother or sister, of no value to the stranger, but inexpressedly dear to him who was to linger for months in hopeless confinement, were wantonly torn from their possession and made the subject of ribald jest and ridicule."[62]

Such small privations irked the officers held at Libby prison in Richmond, but they paled beside accounts of lice-covered enlisted men, fed rations barely sufficient to sustain life, who were exposed to the elements and left to wallow in their own filth. The congressional committee concluded that such mistreatment was part of a deliberate, diabolical plan either to kill Union soldiers or to render them unfit for future service. "The facts disclose a cool and malicious disregard of the condition and comfort of prisoners taken in battle, and an evident intention on the part of the confederate authorities to lose no time in the attempt to break them down in body and in spirit and render them unfit for future service to their country." Authorities forced the wounded to make long marches, leaving unburied by the roadside the bodies of those who died along the way. Even prisoners transported by train fared little better. They were crammed into box cars "immediately after cattle had been taken out of them, and the excrement of the beast was the bed of the men."[63]

The committee deployed poetic phrasing to sensational effect, shocking a northern middle class recently schooled in sanitation and cleanliness. Even the normally circumspect diarist George Templeton Strong noted an encounter with an Andersonville prisoner who described "his brethren there on their hands and knees around the latrines of that infernal pen, grubbing among the faeces for undigested beans and grains of corn wherewith to mitigate the pains of slow starvation."[64]

Stephen Greenblatt has argued that some nineteenth-century writers used a horror of excrement to mark their refinement. For the members of the Sanitary Commission, who had assumed as their particular mission the task of preventing in army camps precisely the kind of sanitary disaster they witnessed at Andersonville, the utter neglect of cleanliness in the prisons marked their southern enemies' unredeemable savagery. Conscientious (and well publicized) efforts on the part of northern reformers to combat the diarrhea, dysentery, maggots, and gangrene so common to army field hospitals made their presence at Andersonville all the more striking. The evidence from Andersonville also suggested that not only did the enemy neglect captive soldiers, but also that some captive soldiers forgot the sanitary habits the army had tried to inculcate in new recruits. Desperate, degraded, and too ill to care, the men forgot to dig trench latrines and bury their feces and therefore suffered the consequences.[65]

Many common soldiers noticed the filth around them, and some wrote of the lessons in cleanliness they had learned all too well in prison. A Mr. G. M. Van Buren who wrote to the congressional committee from Columbia County, New York, chronicled the systematic degradations he had witnessed in southern prisons. He remembered that at Andersonville he had seen men so "covered with dirt so as to be almost black, and the involuntary evacuations had encrusted their legs from the thighs down with foul excrement, so that the stench was almost intolerable at one hundred yards distant, where I stood." And among the things that Alonzo Cooper learned in Andersonville was that "[t]here is nothing so invigorating to the system as a daily bath in pure, cold water, and on the other hand there is nothing more debilitating, or conducive to disease and death, than crowded and filthy quarters, without the necessary sanitary conveniences to permit the enjoyment of this invigorating luxury."[66]

All this might be dismissed as mere literal description were it not for the fact that a whole set of racial associations of blackness and filth accompanied the descriptions of men living in their excrement. One prisoner captured with many during the battle of Chickamauga in September

1863 insisted that he did not "feel like a white man" until he had a "good scrub."[67] Writing near the close of the century, B. F. Booth recalled an inhabitant of Georgia who complained of the smell of excrement that emanated from Andersonville. "'I didn't know you all smelt so;'" he quoted him as saying, "why, you Yanks smells worse than niggers!'"[68] The journalist John McElroy quoted at length from testimony delivered at the trial of Andersonville commandant Henry Wirz: a Confederate surgeon who had visited the camp testified that "the volume of water was not sufficient to wash away the feces, and they accumulated in such quantities in the lower portion of the stream as to form a mass of liquid excrement." The Confederate surgeon went on to portray Union soldiers who had come to resent a government that broke off agreements on prisoner exchange and left them to rot in filth, all in what he said was a vain attempt to "make the negro equal to the white man." In his description, they had instead made white men equal to negroes, leaving them "begrimed from head to foot with their own excrements, and so black from smoke and filth that they resembled negros rather than white men."[69]

The stories told by former prisoners contain the raw materials of postwar racism. Although northern soldiers condemned the cruelty of their southern captors, praised the bravery of their comrades, and lauded the generosity of the freedpeople, they also visited the sewers of a cultural unconscious and found there the makings of a white racism better suited for postwar racial formation.

"I NEVER BEGUN TO BE SO BAD OFF AS THEY WAS"

White soldiers, so deprived of racial characteristics based on freedom and cleanliness, used episodes of escape to recover whiteness. If they borrowed from slave narratives the language and imagery to describe their sufferings at the hands of Confederate captors, so they borrowed from freedpeople the knowledge and techniques needed to escape from southern prisons. But escapees paid limited tribute to the freedpeople who helped them. Historians who have extracted from prison tales evidence of the aid freedpeople offered Union soldiers have sometimes failed to contextualize such material. Descriptions that might be read as tribute could also serve as insult.

When Union soldiers escaped from Confederate prisons, they asked the former slaves they met for food, shelter, and direction. They learned from them how to elude tracking dogs, how to survive in swamps, and how to lie to inquisitive strangers. Like fugitives from slavery, prisoners hid by day and traveled by night, navigating by the North Star and seeking shelter in households linked by what they specifically remembered as an "underground railroad." Many acknowledged their black friends, thanking the former slaves who led them to freedom. They would not, many admitted, have survived without them.[70]

To elude pursuers prisoners needed the help of former slaves. Freedpeople provided food and shelter, but they also knew the whereabouts of Union forces. Knowledge elevated them in the eyes of fleeing prisoners, who learned that those they had regarded as "unreliable and stupid" possessed, in fact, "much valuable information."[71] Prisoners who had lost their way were particularly impressed by the geographic knowledge of former slaves. As Abbott remarked, "The negroes appear to be perfectly familiar with every stump and tree in their neighborhood. No matter how dense the forest, or how close the thicket through which we were obliged to travel, we always found our negro guides able to pilot us through without losing their way."[72] William B. McCreery remembered a guide who was "intelligent, thoroughly acquainted with every foot of country, and knew the location of every picket post."[73] What appeared as impenetrable forest and swamp to white fugitives was familiar ground to slave hosts.

More important to starving soldiers, the former slaves seemed to possess an abundant supply of food. The freedpeople appeared in the woods, like magical providers, bearing the nourishment that escaping prisoners so badly needed. Narrators who had lived with want wrote veritable hymns to the apparent wealth of the families who had stayed on plantations to tend the crops of their former masters. As Mr. Hadley remembered "Sometimes twenty negroes, male and female, would come to

FIGURE 17   "Fed by Darkies" (from J. Madison Drake, *Fast and Loose in Dixie*). Collection of the New-York Historical Society.

us from one plantation, each one bringing something to give and lay at our feet—in the aggregate, corn-bread and potatoes enough to feed us a week."[74] The food they carried seemed the product of neither suffering nor labor, and on the rare occasion when soldiers had money to pay for the provisions provided them, cash was declined. The passage of prisoners through the communities of freedpeople more closely resembled a sequence from a fairy tale than scenes from the true stories that the soldiers had pledged to tell. Former slaves, their labor, their suffering, and their distinct identities were all lost in vague abstractions. In effect, the prisoners, who tried so hard to document with precision all that had happened to them while they were in southern hands, gave play to their imaginations as they recounted their escapes and the people they met on their way north.

Prisoners were thankful for the help given them, but a peculiar narrative logic undermines the gratitude in their descriptions of escape. What had been fact becomes fiction; what had been tragedy becomes comedy;

what had been grim and precise reality becomes airy fantasy. And even in writing tributes to those who helped them, escaping prisoners seemed to relegate the former slaves to realms of fancy. John Ransom, for example, promised that when made wealthy by the sales of his printed diary he would "visit this country and make every negro who has helped us millionaires." To his white helpers, he offered gratitude less extravagant but more useful, and once he and his companions reached Union lines, he made certain that the Union officers made restitution for the food and livestock the soldiers had taken from white southerners.[75]

However shattering their experiences of confinement, white soldiers readily deployed the elements of the comic and the exotic that frequently shaped white writers' descriptions of black people. So conditioned were the soldiers that they resorted easily to such stereotypes. Long passages of dialogue, written in black dialect, interrupt unvarnished narratives of fact. And soldiers whose names, ranks, and regimental affiliations were sure signs of the historical weight of the stories told are suddenly joined by people addressed only by the generic first names of slavery or the honorific "Uncle" and "Aunty" of old age. The freedpeople roll their eyes, show their teeth, and respond in comic dialect to soldiers' questions about the nature of the war.[76]

A passage from Warren Lee Goss—one of the writers whom the congressional committee deemed particularly reliable—is typical. He described how he learned to trust the former slaves. He hailed an old man he found working in the woods. "'Uncle, I suppose you know what kind of fellows we are.' 'Well, I reckon,' he replied, rolling up the whites of his eyes. 'We are hungry, and want something to eat sadly.' 'Well,' said uncle, 'you does look mighty kind o'lean. Step into de bushes while I peers round to see if we've got some hoe-cake,' and off he trotted." When the man returned with food, Goss turned his interrogation to the subject of the war. "'Well uncle,' I said, 'I suppose you know that Uncle Abe is coming down this way to set you all free when he gets the rebs licked.' "Yes, yes,' said the venerable negro, 'I's believe the day of jubilee is comin'; but pears to me, it's a long time; looks like it wouldn't come in my time.'"[77]

Three things are striking about Goss's description of this exchange. First, he substitutes dialogue for precise description, suggesting to readers that when white writers enter black communities, the weighty "narrative of fact" gives way to inconsequential invention. Second, although Goss lists the name of every Union soldier buried at Andersonville, his black helpers remain unnamed. And third, when Goss encounters freedpeople, he imposes on them the passivity he is in the process of escaping. When they speak, it is only in response to Goss's questions. They never initiate dialogue and never volunteer information. Indeed, information is extracted from them by aggressive soldiers determined to seek freedom. The soldiers' superior humanity is underscored by descriptions of the movements of black helpers. When they move, they do so like domestic animals, "trotting off" in search of food for fleeing prisoners. Although the freedpeople were not precisely slaves, soldiers' stories cast them as natural servants. License, anonymity, and passivity all set the contributions of former slaves outside the history the soldiers were so busy making.[78]

Moreover, former prisoners gradually turned to minstrel stereotypes to depict freedpeople, painting as ignorant and unknowing the very people whose willingness to share food and geographical knowledge made possible the soldiers' passage home. In the midst of the high seriousness of war and suffering, prisoners staged encounters with slaves as minstrel comedy. Writing in 1868, John Hadley, an Indiana soldier, saw fit to describe a slave he approached as "frightened out of his wits, if he ever had any." Cooper described a man who "jumped two feet straight up, when I thus abruptly saluted him. As soon as he could speak, he said, 'Golly, massa, how you skeered me!'" Or consider the following exchange from the prison narrative of Willard Glazier: "We asked our kind informant if he could guide us to our lines. He replied, 'I'ze neber ben down dar, massa, sense Massa Sherman's company went to Savannah; but I reckon you'uns can git massa Jones, a free cullerd man, to take you ober. He's a mighty bright pusson, and understands de swamps jest like a book.'"[79]

As the passage from Glazier suggests, the images are more complicated than simple racist stereotypes. Here is knowledge, but depicted in dialect. Uncharacteristically, Glazier allows his informant to know what Jones knows; in most instances, prisoners described freedpeople as entirely unconscious of the knowledge they possessed. Most significant, as soldiers worked their way to the northern lines through country alive with people in motion, they described freedpeople who seemed to be sitting still. The congressional committee concluded from the prisoners' testimony that although the freedpeople had been "our true and faithful auxiliaries," they had more often been "the calm and waiting spectators of the great struggle, in which the interests of their race were so deeply involved." Prisoners heading north must have encountered hundreds or even thousands of freedpeople making their way to new lives. Nevertheless, they constantly depicted former slaves as a passive people waiting for the Union soldiers to deliver them from bondage. Former prisoners cast themselves as those who struggled and suffered for freedom. Such representations of freedpeople underlined the fact that, even though prisoners had once been treated as slaves, the condition of servitude had in no way deprived them of their deep commitment to freedom. Nor had dirt and degradation deprived them of whiteness. As soldiers incorporated their suffering into their quest for freedom, they racialized their willingness to make personal sacrifice for the sake of freedom and used their tales of heroism to recover their racial identity as white men.[80]

In the years following the war, as the contributions of former slaves disappeared from the public mind, narratives kept the pain of former prisoners in full view. Prisoners' complaints leaked from their stories into the postwar world and entered the cultural contest over rewards for suffering and heroic sacrifice. Shortly after the war, the journalist J. T. Trowbridge visited the sites of the Confederate prisons, and he, too, employed the language of comparative suffering. Outside the prison at Macon, he found a man who remembered, "'I used to hear 'em yell for water . . . I was bad off as a slave, but I never begun to be so bad off as they was.

Some of 'em had no shoes for winter, and almost no clothes.'" In effect, Trowbridge had a freedman cede the contest over suffering to the barefoot soldiers.[81]

In September 1864, when he was sixteen years old, Charles Cummings enlisted in the Michigan Infantry Volunteers and spent a few months in the army watching over a herd of cattle. After the war he returned home and went to work on the railroad as a brakeman. One rainy day in October 1873, he slipped from the roof of a moving train and fell beneath its wheels. Both his feet were crushed. Every brakeman lived with the possibility of such an accident, and Cummings's awful fate was not unusual. What he did about it, however, was surprising. When he recovered from his double amputation, he supported himself by peddling lead pencils and hawking a pamphlet decorated with his portrait surrounded by patriotic symbols and emblazoned with the title "The Great War Relic."[82]

Even though the war had nothing to do with Cummings's maiming, it was clearly to his advantage to be taken for a wounded veteran, and thus on the cover of his pamphlet he appeared as "The Great War Relic" itself. There were other tales available for dismembered men, and had Cummings been a drinking man, he might well have cast his accident as a cautionary temperance tale and set out on a similar circuit, peddling his story as he traveled the country. Like reformed drunks, Cummings selected from a repertoire of tales and used the war to add significance to his work-related injury. Rather than telling readers outright that work had disabled him (and might well do the same for any of them) Cummings encouraged readers to buy his book as a gesture of support for every man who had been killed or wounded in the war.[83]

Like many of the propertyless writers of the nineteenth century, Cummings understood how to turn his suffering into a salable commodity. To do so, he produced a little book and borrowed the image of the wounded

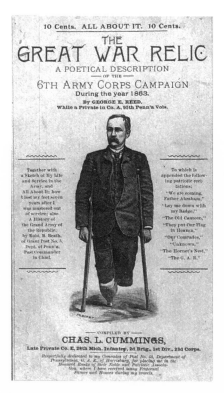

FIGURE 18   *The Great War Relic.* Collection of the author.

veteran, very much as veterans borrowed from the suffering slave. He saw that his body marked him as different and deliberately set out to profit from the curiosity his difference aroused. Instead of standing as a silent figure of pity, he seized the opportunity to represent himself. "I once heard of a railroad company that employed a blind man at a salary of $100 per month to answer questions at one of its stations," he wrote, "and he had to give it up. Well, if a man can't endure the selfish-never-let-up-quizzer at $100 per month, how is a man going to answer all the questions they will fire at him like shot from a gatling gun, when he gets only abuse in return for it." Cummings told his troubles to his "esteemed comrade," George Reed, who explained to him "there was one of two things a good

American will do when he is busted: he will either write a book or take up a collection."[84] Cummings did both—he wrote a book and *thereby* took up a collection. Those curious to know the history of his crippling would have to pay a dime to get his story.[85]

It would probably be difficult to find widespread agreement with Reed's description of the strategies available for "good Americans." Former soldiers who found themselves "busted" and felt that military service entitled them to compensation were more likely to craft stories into pension claims for the government than to publish them as books and peddle them to the public. But Cummings was certainly not the only man who capitalized on the soldier's privilege to tell his story. Taking advantage of a boom in war reminiscences in the 1880s, Cummings produced five editions of his pamphlet between 1886 and 1887 and asserted in the last of them that sympathetic readers had already purchased some thirty-five thousand copies. In its various versions, the pamphlet contained an account of Cummings's accident, a long poem by his friend George Reed about the Sixth Army Corps, a tribute to the Grand Army of the Republic, several patriotic recitations, and advertisements for a cutlery house, patent medicines, various Harrisburg businesses, and Crandall's Patent Crutch (with an endorsement by Mr. Cummings). In effect, the printed pamphlet carried the goods the dismembered peddler could not transport.[86] Like the maimed bricklayer disguised as a wounded sailor who appeared among the London beggars, Cummings sensed that some stories were better to tell than others. There was more drama in seafaring and war than in hard work. It was probably easier also for audiences to accept a tale of a man disfigured in the service of the state than to face the possibility that their own jobs in factories, brickyards, and rail yards could produce similarly devastating injuries.[87]

Although Cummings was certainly the hero of his story, one version of his pamphlet includes the tale of another man who had lost his feet, and here we can see how the racial confusion of the prison camps persisted long after the war. John January, a Union soldier whose photograph was redrawn for reproduction and reprinted in several publications on Confederate prisons, had gained fame on the lecture circuit by describing how he had cut off his own gangrenous feet while an inmate in the prison at Florence, South Carolina. But Reed had a different story, which Cummings reported in his pamphlet: Reed insisted that after he had been captured by Rebel forces, he had been paroled to work as a nurse in the prison hospital, and in the course of his duties, had himself been the one to snip January's tendons and remove his feet. According to Reed, January had been so covered with grime that Reed had been unable to distinguish the color of his skin. When questioned about his racial identity, January had replied, "I am a white man."

The final edition of Cummings's pamphlet printed January's response to Reed's version of events. The footless soldier assured them that he had never meant to deceive those who came to hear him lecture, but that somehow the story of self-amputation had gotten started, and once it had "lodged in the public mind," it had proved, unlike his feet, difficult to remove. In 1869, January had written to the congressional committee investigating abuses in southern prisons, testifying simply that his "feet turned black and dropped off, one of my nurses cutting the cords with an old knife." He continued, "I went from home full of hope, with an ardent desire to do something for my country, flushed with health and strength; I came home worn down with sickness and suffering, and a cripple for life, with nothing to comfort me only the thought that I have tried to do my duty, and that my sufferings were for a good cause."[88]

Perhaps the accusations directed against January served to distract readers from Cummings's own deceit, but the mixture of war, dismemberment, race, and commerce in even so trivial a document as "The Great War Relic" suggests the role such narratives played in reimagining the nation in the years following the war. Many stories surface in Cummings's pamphlet—a story of the personal consequences in the postwar railroad boom, a story of disabled veterans growing old as the war receded into the past, and a story of commercial life in central Pennsylvania. Moreover, in

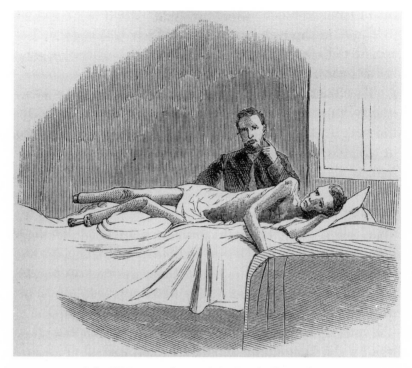

FIGURE 19   John W. January, Corporal Co. B, 4th Illinois (from A. O. Abbott, *Prison Life in the South*).

their account of January's story lurks a racism that characterizes many of the Union soldiers' narratives of imprisonment.

Just as Cummings borrowed from a genre designed for the stories of heroic veterans, so prisoners borrowed from a genre that had once served to represent the suffering of slaves. We can see both the pain and the fraud in Cummings's story: he did, indeed, lose his legs, yet with a friend's help he crafted a version of his story designed to reap profit. In doing so, he practiced just the sort of deceit that had troubled Henry Mayhew and his colleagues when they encountered the armless bricklayer posing as a sailor or the wandering folks pretending to have once been slaves.

Is there also dishonesty at work in the prisoners' narratives? Perhaps. And perhaps there is consequence in the fact that the narratives borrow rhetorical strategies from the tales of former slaves—people who might have used those strategies not to call forth pity, but to present their tales as exchanges between equals. Discovering race at work in prisoners' stories, we are reminded that racism has not been passed down without a good deal of imaginative work. Prisoners' stories were among the places where such work went on—episodes, if you will, in the history of racism. Even if prisoners intended merely to offer accounts of things they had seen, heard, felt, and tasted, the version of pain and suffering they recounted had unforeseen consequences for the freedpeople who sought acknowledgment for their contributions in the war.

In many cases, white soldiers took lessons both in suffering and in talking about suffering from men and women who had been slaves. Here were people practiced in the arts needed for survival in confinement and adept at turning the literary tools of sentimental culture to their own ends. But in the years following the war, white pupils surpassed their instructors in the school of suffering and reserved for themselves the larger portion of the heroism offered as a reward for waging war. In their own distinctive way, the stories they told documented the efforts by freedpeople on behalf of the Union cause. But they also made it possible to overlook those efforts by setting them down in stories that privileged the travails, privations, sufferings, and steadfast resolve of white prisoners.

Epilogue

Lovers, Farm Wives, and Tramps

Every man and woman has lived at least one big story which has the ring of truth for which authors of fictions strive with might and main.

True Story Magazine (January 1923)

There ain't a jack man of us that ain't got a history to him as good as any that ever was printed.

Claude Mckay,
Banjo: A Story without a Plot (1929)

TRUE STORIES

In January 1919 Bernarr Macfadden, "physical culturalist," self-promoter, and publisher, printed the first issue of a pulp magazine he called *True Story*. In it, he promised readers he would reprint their own stories of love and romance. *True Story* was an astounding success, read in the mid 1920s by more Americans—male and female—than any other magazine. As one contemporary remarked, "The rage for unadorned truth as to personal experiences finds its expression in the 'true story' and 'confession' group, where veracious narratives of titillating human experiences thrill literally millions of readers."[1]

Although the pledge to print readers' stories was probably little more than a convenient fiction, Macfadden reaped great profit from stories that seemed to come unvarnished from ordinary lives and thus captured emotional truths for his readers. He made a personal fortune out of materials that he insisted had come from the people themselves. He promised would-be writers both the validation of publication and, with publication, forgiveness for transgression. Macfadden operated in a world of mass culture where most people had little to do with actually producing the cultural artifacts (the movies, music, and magazines) they consumed, but he encouraged his readers to believe that their experiences appeared in his magazines. Moreover, he told them that they were the ones best qualified to turn their experiences into stories. He flattered readers with the idea that events in their lives were worth writing about and with the thought that ordinary people were those best able to do the writing. His promises were pleasing lies, of course, but he sustained his fictional world of true stories by borrowing the devices that had served to support the "truth" of poor people's personal narratives. The early-twentieth-century market for true stories bore little resemblance to its nineteenth-century counterpart, but the subtle play of power at the margins of culture reappeared in Macfadden's mass circulation magazines.[2]

Macfadden was the original ninety-pound weakling—a man who used the arts of "physical culture" to transform himself from a weak-chested wimp into the very embodiment of masculine strength.[3] Throughout the 1920s and 1930s, he appeared all over the American cultural landscape, a sort of low double of William Randolph Hearst. Like Hearst, he published magazines, produced movies and radio shows, and entertained political ambitions. But Macfadden also started a utopian community, opened sanitoria, ran cheap health-food restaurants, promoted beauty pageants, proclaimed the virtues of fresh air and exercise, and touted his personal techniques for making men more virile and women more fertile.

Macfadden offers us a way to reconsider questions raised in discussions of stories produced by beggars, slaves, convicts, and prisoners. Who gets to appear in print? Who assures the authenticity of printed documents? Does truth reside in a document or in the manner of reading a document? Who must forego art and stick to unembellished experience?

Macfadden is not the culmination of the story of plain unvarnished truths, but his career as a publisher of "true stories" suggests links between our present-day passion for revealing stories and the projects of nineteenth-century sufferers. Beggars, convicts, slaves, and soldiers approached readers with stories that connected incidents in individual lives to the larger moral and political dramas unfolding in the world around them. The shared narrative for Macfadden readers was most often a story of sexuality. In his hands, material that had once been private became shared public narrative; material that had once moved as gossip over the back fence or around the kitchen table was made to carry advertisements. In his magazines, an eccentric and muscled character with a taste for carrots presented himself as a cultural authority.

THE TRUE STORY OF BERNARR MACFADDEN

The first "true story" Macfadden published was his own. Bernarr Macfadden was born Bernard McFadden on a rundown farm in southeastern Missouri in 1868, the son of an alcoholic father and a consumptive mother. Orphaned as a boy, he spent his childhood bound out to various relatives. He survived his bouts with tuberculosis, changed his name from the soft-sounding Bernard to "Bernarr," a name he supposedly pronounced with a sustained manly roar, and turned his triumph over physical trials into living testimony for his methods of self-improvement. For Macfadden, self-improvement began as a purely physical proposition, but physical improvement got him off the farm and into the city.[4] He changed his body and, through his body, altered his social position: he became a performer, an athletic director, an author, and an expert. Male bodies like his own were his first concern, but women's stories would make his fortune.[5]

Macfadden lived for a time in St. Louis, supporting himself as an exhibition wrestler and exercise instructor. He called himself a professor of "kinistherapy." In 1893, he caught a glimpse of bigger things when he went to the World's Columbian Exposition in Chicago to demonstrate a system of pulleys he called the "Macfadden Health Exerciser." In Chicago, he saw on display classical nude male statues and the weight lifter Eugen Sandow's imitations of them. Macfadden would go on posing for the rest of his life, touting the wonders of his own body well into his seventies.[6]

To live off his body, Macfadden needed to find outlets into commercial culture. Opportunities appeared scarce in the Midwest, so Macfadden moved to New York to set himself up as an exercise specialist. He promoted a breakfast cereal, which he called "Strenthro," and opened a chain of one-cent vegetarian restaurants. He lent his name to several sanitoriums, promising doctors half the fees paid by any patients they referred. He started a utopian community, called Physical Culture City, in New Jersey, and ran a boarding school and a physical culture hotel. But it was in print that he came into his own.[7]

All his "accomplishments" might have passed unnoticed had he not publicized himself. In the 1920s he hired Edward L. Bernays, one of the pioneers of public relations, but by then Mcfadden had already spent a quarter of a century keeping himself in the public eye.[8] When his first literary project, a novel, was rejected by publishers as "hopelessly crude and devoid of all interest," Macfadden published it himself.[9] His preparation for a literary career was scant. He knew nothing of English grammar, and he read no books. As his estranged wife put it, "Aside from his own works, he really read nothing."[10] By the mid 1920s, Macfadden presided over an eccentric, but highly profitable, publishing empire, producing texts and products that bore his image and signature. All his publications appeared in a tightly closed system, each promoting all the others, all promoting the man, and all based on his self-proclaimed expertise in things physical. In all venues, he called for exercise, sexual knowledge, and dietary reform, and he encouraged audiences to imitate him and forward to him experiences he could reprint.[11] Macfadden dominated a peculiar cultural empire where power was so diffuse it became invisible. "The people" presided. But who were the people? Macfadden signed every product. But who was Macfadden but a series of inventions?

In 1899 Macfadden published the first issue of *Physical Culture*, a magazine dedicated to health, exercise, and the cultivation of various body parts. Under the slogan "Weakness Is a Crime. Don't Be a Criminal," Macfadden lavished advice on readers.[12] The magazine was filled with halftone illustrations, most of which depicted Macfadden himself, but from time to time he also reprinted images of classical nude male statues (or his own imitations of them) and copies of W. A. Bouguereau fleshy female nudes. In its pages he carried on a steady campaign against the medical establishment, proposing his own regimes of exercise, fresh air, fasting, and healthy eating as alternatives to professional medicine.[13]

Unlike *Physical Culture*, which at its height attracted no more than 150,000 subscribers, *True Story* was an instant and astounding success. By the middle of the 1920s, the magazine reached two million readers, and it remained among the most widely read American magazines through the 1930s. Its popularity suggests that Macfadden had found a style that meant something to his readers and had indeed tapped into their concerns about love and sex.[14]

When Macfadden launched *True Story* in 1919, he directed contributors to write up the materials of their daily lives—not great adventures and spiritual fantasies, but the complicated sexual encounters lived by "most people." Even the earliest issues of *True Story* were filled with pleas for readers to send their stories. "Remember," Macfadden wrote in a promotion for one *True Story* contest, "the story is the thing that counts—not literary skill." "Tell it naturally, simply, in your own words and the judges will consider it entirely upon its qualities as a story. If it contains the human quality we seek, it will receive preference over tales of less merit no matter how cleverly, beautifully, or skillfully written they may be."[15]

There is controversy over the genesis of *True Story*, although all parties agree that Macfadden's version of the confession magazine grew out of letters sent to *Physical Culture*. For years, Macfadden had been printing readers' letters in sections under titles like "Comment, Counsel, and Criticism by Our Readers" and "The Virtues of Our Methods Proven." Most correspondents worried about health, exercise, and visible muscles, and few discussed sex and romance. But surely renewed health was not the last adventure of their lives, and Macfadden sensed a sometimes latent content in letters from those who boasted of their newly straight backs, broad chests, and renewed physical vigor. In *Physical Culture*, Macfadden had promised "rewards" to those he published: for any letter published, a subscription to his magazine; for the best suggestion "as to just how to make the magazine provide readers with the greatest possible pleasure and profit," a subscription and any one of his books.[16]

Years later, his estranged and angry wife claimed that the idea for *True Story* had been hers and not his. She said she had first tried the idea out on her maid, who had replied "Everybody will want to read *that* one. All the working girls go through the same love troubles. This will be about themselves and *written* by themselves. Oh my!" If the maid did indeed make such a speech, she was the first of many working-class women whose tributes to *True Story* appeared as testimony to the publication in the magazine's own pages.[17]

Evidence suggests, however, that Macfadden, his wife, and his readers were already amply schooled in the possibilities of first-person confessions. One set of working-class life stories appeared at the turn of the century in a series running in *The Independent*, a paper that Henry Ward Beecher had once edited as a religious and antislavery journal. In the 1890s, its editor Hamilton Holt turned it into a general interest journal with a national circulation. Holt found a good deal of "human interest" in life stories of workers and immigrants; among the stories he published were the lives of an Irish cook, a Greek peddler, a French dressmaker, an Italian bootblack, and a "negro peon."[18] Though it may be true that Holt brought immigrant voices into the polyglot community of early-twentieth-century United States, his publication of first-person narratives sometimes revealed the compromises necessary to present to the public the stories of the poor and unschooled. As we have seen throughout this study, the power gained in publishing true stories of experience is tenuous at best.

In February 1905, Holt printed the story of "One Farmer's Wife," an Illinois woman who harbored inappropriate literary aspirations. The "farmer's wife" confessed that she was an impractical woman with an oft-thwarted passion for reading. Her father had taken away the love stories she read as a girl; her husband accused her of wasting time reading novels and stories. Still, she managed to squeeze reading (and an active correspondence) into a life of labor. "When knitting stockings for the family," she wrote, "I always have a book or paper in reading distance; or if I have a moment to rest or to wait on something, I pick up something and read during the time. I even take a paper with me to the fields." She managed, as well, to produce a story she sent off to a contest, and with her minister's encouragement, she subscribed to a correspondence school that promised to teach "short story writing by mail." To her relief, the school proved "trustworthy."[19]

Read one way, her strivings were incredible efforts at self-culture, yet Hamilton Holt prefaced her life story with a warning against the false hope that she had indeed become a writer.

> We are glad to be able to add to our series of representative "personal confessions" the following narrative of an Illinois farmer's wife. It was not originally submitted to us in its present form, but was a brief account of farm life from a woman's point of view, and was sent in to us at the suggestion of the correspondence school mentioned in the text. The article was unavailable as it stood, but it seemed to have "possibilities," so we returned the manuscript to her with the suggestion that she write a truthful narrative of her life and "tell everything." In response to the request we received the following article, which we publish without change. We hope that the money received for it and the joy of seeing it in print will not induce the author to neglect entirely her domestic duties to attempt a literary career.[20]

Macfadden, too, was slow to grant of cultural authority. In *True Story*, Macfadden directed would-be contributors to draw from their own lives

and from those of their neighbors, relatives, friends, and "local characters." "[E]very man and woman," one *True Story* solicitation read, "has
lived at least one big story which has the ring of truth for which authors of
fictions strive with might and main." To write a story, solicitations urged,
was a simple thing. One need only describe what had happened. Life frequently unfolded in patterns "as stirring and dramatic as the most far-
reaching imagination and the most gifted narrator could depict." No imagination, gifts, or expertise were necessary for a Macfadden writer.[21]

In January 1923, "The Magazine That Is Written by Its Readers" displayed a panel of eminent figures—including F. Scott Fitzgerald, Hendrik
Van Loon, Fannie Hurst, and D. W. Griffith—who knew the value of a
"true story" because they had learned to "dress the product of the imagination to the semblance of the simple truth." In this, Macfadden's "amateur illiterates" had an advantage on the professionals, because they had
no need to curtail imagination. Professionals now agreed to judge "the
great $5000 story contest." Every issue was larded with similar solicita-
tions urging readers to turn life's "happenings" into cash. "Never before
did men and women who are not professional writers have such a glorious
opportunity to turn their life experiences into handsome sums of
money."[22]

On the pages of *True Story*, Macfadden also hawked shares of stock in
his corporation, printed coupons to send to theater owners requesting
"True Story Films," posed questions about personal relationships for
readers to answer, and promised readers as much as "$15 for the best let-
ter criticizing" the contents of each issue of the magazine. "In your letter
tell us the story you think is the best. If there is any story that you don't
particularly care for, tell us about that one too. You will be having a real
part in deciding what stories shall appear in future issues of *True Story*."
He also promised that the best stories would reappear in movie theaters as
"True Story Films," a pledge he reinforced by illustrating each story with
posed photographs designed to recall with gesture, lighting, and makeup
movie stills rather than documentary truths.[23]

Readers like Mrs. Macfadden's maid were cheap sources of material for Macfadden, and he made sure they would remain cheap by offering contributors "prizes" rather than a fair price for their writing. His reader-contributors would retain the status of amateurs, entirely anonymous figures earning their money in lucky windfalls and never by skill, art, or expertise. Anonymity may have made "true stories" seem the collective outpouring of a class, rather than the unique complaints of individuals, but it elevated Macfadden as the single most identifiable figure on the pages of his publications.[24]

Once Macfadden and his editors had found the proper formula, *True Story* quickly turned a profit, attracting millions of readers, male and female, with a mix of sex and romance and boasting advertising revenues in excess of three million dollars. The magazine became the flagship of a small publishing empire, and in the mid 1920s, Macfadden claimed that 16,500,000 people regularly read his writings and stories. Such boasts surely inspired the Fawcett Publishing Company in 1922 to launch a competing magazine: the better-remembered and more aptly titled *True Confessions*. But it was Macfadden who presided over an empire of "true stories," with the four most profitable of his eleven magazines claiming to be produced by readers.[25]

Any account of the success of *True Story* risks being taken in by the magazine's own publicity, and one should remember that Macfadden and his staff might have inflated numbers to tempt advertisers. Nevertheless, an ample readership is evidence of the magazine's cultural importance. Macfadden's own polls found the average reader to be the twenty-five-year-old wife of a "skilled laborer," but in a study of *The Reading Interests of Young Workers*, conducted at the University of Chicago in the mid 1930s, *True Story* appeared on the lists of the ten magazines most read by both men and women. In 1924 and again in 1932, female readers named it the most popular magazine. Among men, *True Story* ranked first in 1924, but by 1932 it had dropped to sixth on the list, yielding the top spot to *Popular Mechanics*, a magazine well-suited to Depression householders who could no longer afford to hire help and were compelled to do maintenance and repair themselves.[26]

By the 1940s, Macfadden's appeals to advertisers touted an ability to reach working-class women, claiming an audience composed of waitresses, file clerks, and the wives of men with "work shirt backgrounds." Early issues from the 1920s employed a more muted language of class, telling stories of teachers, librarians, lawyers, ministers, clerks, and reporters, but always offering intimate advice to the lovelorn, the heartbroken, the abandoned, and the betrayed. The first issues addressed men as well as women, publishing tales of romance and adventure told by male narrators (like the explorer Martin Johnson's "If a Cannibal King Wanted Your Wife for His Harem") and advertisements for courses to promote careers in electricity, radio, and sales.[27] By the early 1930s, however, female stories dominated the table of contents, and ads for beauty products, romance novels, and Macfadden's own publications replaced descriptions of courses for men.

The issue from February 1926 is typical of the magazine at the height of its popularity. That month, as it did throughout the mid 1920s, the magazine sold on newsstands for twenty-five cents. (During the Depression, the price of an issue dropped to fifteen cents.) The magazine encouraged purchasers to consider that quarter a sound investment, promising on the cover that "true stories" of their own might be worth fifty thousand dollars in prize money (that the fifty thousand was to be spread among as many writers was hidden in the fine print). The notion that the magazine was a collaborative project in which readers played essential roles appeared on nearly every page.

The February issue opened with several full-page advertisements. "Private Secretaries to Famous Men" praised Royal Typewriters; Prof. Eugene Feuchtinger offered "The Secret of Caruso's Amazing Vocal Power"; others promised to help readers become "auto experts," "electrical experts," and "finger print experts"; and still others held the keys to growing hair, developing the bustline, reducing the waistline, and clearing up the complexion.

In the body of the magazine, readers had advice of their own to offer. In "True Story's Own Domestic Relations Court," the editors posed a problem for readers and then published as "prize letters" the best solutions to the previous month's domestic dispute. For jokes submitted by readers, they promised to pay "two cents a word, and not less than two dollars for any real laugh we print." Following such regular columns, a typical issue ran more than a dozen "true stories," each continued at the back of the issue, where columns of text ran beside columns of advertisements and promotions for Macfadden's other publications.

Although stories offered a variety of narrators and a variety of romantic and professional problems, each and every story was told in the first person. Narrators whispered their secrets, moving readers into a first circle of intimacy and offering them both instruction in coping with the problems of modern life and forgiveness for their errors. The February 1926 issue is no exception to this rule; the opening paragraph of "When a Woman Loves" sets the scene in typical fashion. "The telephone clicked," the narrator writes. "I sat dazed; tears of wounded pride and anger filled my eyes. I dried them quickly for fear someone might see them. I rushed to my room, but just as I reached the door a slight girlish figure almost ran into me." From this slight young woman and from all the other characters in the story, the narrator hid the truth she now promised to reveal to readers. Likewise, "His Misjudged Wife" begins with the tantalizing claim that "this story of mine, I could not tell even to my mother, if she were living." And the narrator of "Why I Shall Never Marry" declares, "For years I have kept silent about my life."[28] Most stories revolved around sex and romance: in the early years, the stories focused on the consequences of unwanted pregnancy; in the late 1920s, as the magazine came specifically to target young married women, its tales stressed the consequences of choosing whether and whom to marry.[29]

Macfadden found "thinking clergymen" willing to "acclaim TRUE STORY." Rev. C. P. Chewning of Olar, South Carolina, commended the "plan of having a Ministerial Board pass on your stories before being published." "I think," Olar continued, "that if more mothers would provide this magazine for their girls to read, we ministers would hear less of the sad stories of fallen girls. May God bless you in your work of helping the young by warning them of the dangers in life that are controlled by that satanic power in the world today." According to Rev. J. W. Richardson of Kerby Knob, Kentucky, *True Story* was a surrogate mother for his daughter. "My daughter, fourteen years of age," he wrote to Macfadden, "reads all of them she can get, and I do not object, for I hope she will learn some of the lessons from the experiences of others which she reads in TRUE STORY, knowledge of which she has been deprived of by the loss of her mother several years ago."[30]

Most stories with moral lessons were probably written by Macfadden employees. That fact, as well as the success of confession magazines in general, annoyed rival editor Oswald Garrison Villard. "Veracious personal experiences," he protested for genteel readers in *The Atlantic*, "are written by small groups of industrious workers who turn out from 30,000 to 50,000 words a month and are paid from two to six cents or more a word. Hence most of the sad wives and disillusioned flappers whose touching narratives appear every month are in reality mature gentlemen residing in Harlem or Greenwich Village." The trade publication *Writer's Market* ran columns to teach readers "How to Hit *True Story*" and published articles that admitted "I Sell Confessions" or exposed "The Truth about *True Story*." And some reporters admitted that they cultivated a side-market for news stories and submitted to confession magazines the experiences of women "whose stories they had covered in the course of their daily work."[31]

Nevertheless, like many who published the writings of poor and unschooled authors, Macfadden designed affidavits to attest that these stories were true.[32] He also cautioned against plagiarism, warning potential contributors that they could be found "guilty of a Federal offense in using the mails to defraud" if they submitted, as their own, stories that had appeared in other magazines.

The publishers of TRUE STORY are anxious—as are all reputable publishers—to stamp out this form of literary theft and piracy, and are advising all magazines from which such stories have been copied of such plagiarism, and are offering to co-operate with the publishers thereof to punish the guilty persons.

Notice is hereby given to all who have submitted stories that the same must be *original* and *true*.[33]

But what did it mean for a story to be original and true? What purpose did Macfadden's affidavits serve? Here, too, he revived a pattern long associated with the publication of personal narratives, but one which, as we have seen, changed a great deal over the course of the nineteenth century. Moses Smith and Michael Smith had local political and religious allies to vouch for their stories. Robert Adams had his "gentlemen." Convicts, even illiterate convicts, had ministers and editors to support their stories. Slaves had abolitionists, and prisoners of war had the Sanitary Commission and congressional committees. The stories Macfadden presented as true came blessed instead by the marketplace. His stories were not literal renditions of experience produced by those who had suffered or sinned. But writers and readers liked to pretend they were. To be "true," a story had only to seem so to its readers. He captured not the particular truths of an individual life, but general truths he ascribed to all modern lives.

In a series of newspaper advertisements published throughout the year 1929, Macfadden presented his vision of the American people united in a land where desire could be satisfied by the purchase of goods. Personal narratives, he said, mapped desire, and they did so particularly well for advertisers who wished to reach potential consumers. "A whole new layer of society is taking its first cultural steps," a Macfadden advertisement proclaimed, "in what might be termed its primitive or folk literature. The first step, as all students of literature know, is a personal narrative recited by one to whom the incident has happened, and listened to or read by those to whom the same incident has happened, or may still happen."

Macfadden made it his mission to publish and preserve this primitive literature, this "great mass of personal experiences" of a group "making its first cultural effort along the lines of physical acquisitions." He made no effort to hide his commercial intent. Macfadden told would-be advertisers that "characters" in the stories he published (and by extension readers of his publications, insofar as they were one and the same) were "now exchanging gifts instead of miseries." His storytellers, in other words, had stopped talking so much and become consumers, a development sure to appeal to potential advertisers, but one that suggests a diminishing supply of stories for his pages.[34]

Read another way, Macfadden and his publicists were aligning the stories they published with what they saw as the great modern saga of getting and spending. And here they did something writers and publishers of personal narratives had done before: they made a series of eccentric personal accounts into chapters of a much larger story. For the cooper, the minister, and the sailor, this had been the story of the nation; for convicts, it had been the story of sin and evil; for slaves and soldiers, it had been the story of freedom. Even if Macfadden thought that the stories he published were scenes in a history of consumption, it did not mean his readers read them only that way. Evidence suggests that some found in them a different kind of "truth," one suited to a people willing to credit a world of emotions and willing to help those who appeared to be suffering. In other words, readers and not writers created the "truths" of *True Story*.[35]

And readers' responses bothered Villard and the genteel folk who read *The Atlantic*. Those who wrote specious stories, Villard contended, received "several thousand letters from fascinated readers." "They come from all over the country, and many are from kindhearted and benevolent persons who offer the reformed sister or abandoned wife a home and indefinite use of their best parlor-bedroom. If she will just telegraph they will meet her train, ask no questions, and receive her as a daughter." It was not the art of the stories that annoyed him, but rather that in seeming to forego art as a condition of publication, writers of "true stories" deceived readers.[36]

Villard's description of *True Story* served to distinguish his middle-class readers from Macfadden's naive working-class constituency, but his criticism recalls for us the disputes that swirled around poor peoples' stories nearly a century earlier. What difference did it make whether stories were literally true? Lydia Maria Child was willing to accept James Williams's story as touching the deepest truths of slavery, even if he had embellished his experiences. But what if Williams had asked her for money? When was a storyteller an artist? When a figure to be pitied? When a deceiver?

For Villard the deceit would lie with Macfadden, the man who presented stories as true. Macfadden assumed the role of mediator, taking advantage of a loophole, if you will, in the logic of plain, unvarnished tales. True stories—whether by beggars, convicts, slaves, prisoners, or "problem girls"—have never appeared without mediators. But the place of the mediator and the role of mediation changed. Frames and framing devices were intrinsic to the stories of beggars, convicts, and slaves—an essential part of each story itself. Congressional approval was external to prisoners' stories, yet crucial to substantiating the claims made in prisoners' narratives. Macfadden, too, stood outside the stories he published, but from the outside he could become an impresario of "truth." Macfadden was a fertile man, fathering at least eight children, but his progeny in the realm of culture (talk-show hosts, literary agents, and tabloid reporters) have outdone his biological offspring.

A BEGGING WRITER

I began this book by describing the careers of writing beggars who tried to get readers to give them money, food, or shelter for their tales of woe. With every successful exchange of a story, they managed to wrest a little cultural authority from readers, but it was a vexed and contingent authority, dependent on a pose of humility and a pledge to forego art. To be taken as true, every story had to be ratified by those with more evident social or cultural power. Although most cultural authorities acted in concert with the aims of the storytellers, in the process of ratification these artless tales could be hijacked for ends little intended by their writers.

Readers or audiences could find their own meanings in artless tales. When an artist went begging, things could get very confused. In 1907, Jack

London published several stories about his tramping days in the 1890s in Nevada and Utah. "Confession," the first story that appears in *The Road*, is presented as an explanation to a woman in Reno to whom the narrator "once lied continuously, consistently, and shamelessly." The story also details a sort of apprenticeship in the writer's trade. "To this training of my tramp days," London writes, "is due much of my success as a story-writer. In order to get the food whereby I lived, I was compelled to tell tales that rang true. At the back door, out of inexorable necessity, is developed the convincingness and sincerity laid down by all authorities on the art of the short-story. Also, I quite believe it was my tramping apprenticeship that made a realist out of me. Realism constitutes the only goods one can exchange at the kitchen door for grub."[37] When Whittier wrote of beggars in the 1840s, he cast himself as a would-be philanthropist, one who dispensed charity, not one who made stories. London, in contrast, cast his lot with the beggars. By his lights, every successful beggar was an artist. And perhaps, after a fashion, every artist is a beggar.

London said that he learned his lessons in realism while begging. But his experience reminds us that the unvarnished tales that supported writers and moved readers also left their mark on literature. In the middle of the nineteenth century, Melville saw the risks of making a beggar the center of a story; in the early twentieth century, London saw the benefits. London also learned that those who gave money to storytelling beggars still preferred to think that the beggars told the truth. London's narrator is broke, hungry, and wants to get to San Francisco. He invents for the Reno woman a tale of woe—an orphan's story—a "lurk" straight from the collections of the likes of Henry Mayhew. The poor boy needs to get to the home of a married sister in Salt Lake City. In response to his story, the kind woman gives him food and warm socks, an exchange that surely would have pleased the sailor Robert Adams. But she insists on helping him further by arranging with a relative in the railway mail service for the begging boy to ride the mail car to Salt Lake City. "To her," as London put it, "my story was 'true.'" And for her, to take his story as "true" was to act on it.

Every beggar who used a story to ask for relief, every old soldier who used a story in lieu of a pension, every convict who asked support for his innocence or pennies for his orphans, every former slave who told a tale of escape to advance the cause of emancipation, and every maimed and suffering prisoner who asked for support similarly demanded action from audiences and readers. London's begging narrator was relieved to learn that the relative in the mail service was not passing through Reno, and well supplied with socks and food, he made his way over the mountains to California. Perhaps in old age, the Reno woman (like John Greenleaf Whittier) entertained fond memories of the begging boys who sometimes told stories in her kitchen. Perhaps she fed them still, joining the venerable crowd of listeners and readers willing to find truth in tales told by the most marginal members of society. Perhaps she resented their impositions. Perhaps she relished their inventions. Perhaps she knew that tellers of plain unvarnished tales sometimes used their stories not only to alter their own lives but to change the world.

NOTES

PREFACE

1. Bruce Weber, "Lawyer in Shooting Case Offers Girl's Story for Bail," *New York Times*, 9 June 1992, sec. B, p. 4.

2. The tactic has become commonplace; eyewitness stories tailored to the market are now the expected by-products of every scandal. Those who followed the trial of O. J. Simpson could have followed as well the literary production of each of the trial's many participants, not one of whom could claim, by profession, skill, accomplishment, or training, to be a writer. And Bill Clinton's sex life has produced a miniboom in marketable stories. Early on, according to the *New York Times*, William Ginsburg, Monica Lewinsky's first lawyer, predicted "that Ms. Lewinsky will have no choice but to write a book or sell her story in order to pay off her legal bills." Jill Abramson, "Dream Team, Nightmare Tab," *New York Times*, 7 June 1998, sec. 4, p. 3. And so she has. Doreen Carvajal, "A Star in Scandal, and Now the Selling of Her Story Begins," *New York Times*, 28 February 1999, p. 1, 18.

INTRODUCTION

1. Herman Melville, *Israel Potter: His Fifty Years of Exile* (1855; reprint, with a foreword by Alfred Kazin, New York: Warner Books, 1974), 210–11.

2. *Life and Remarkable Adventures of Israel R. Potter (a native of Cranston, Rhode-Island,): who was a soldier in the American Revolution, and took a distinguished part in the Battle of Bunker Hill (in which he received three wounds,) after which he was taken prisoner by the British, conveyed to England, where for 30 years he obtained a livelihood for himself and his family, by crying "Old chairs to mend," through the streets of London* (Providence: Printed by Henry Trumbull, 1824). Melville purchased Henry Trumbull's pamphlet life of Israel Potter in London in 1849 but did not "serve up the Revolutionary narrative of the beggar" until 1855. Melville lifted passages and incidents from Trumbull's pamphlet but altered the story with the portraits of Benjamin Franklin, John Paul Jones, and Ethan Allen that give the novel its tension between the fate of the common soldier and the myths of the Revolution's heroes. He also eliminated much of Potter's description of begging in London and replaced it with a discussion of the literary problem posed by the beggar. Scott Casper has suggested that Melville's novel is a thinly veiled attack on Jared Sparks's hagiographic biographies of American patriots. Casper, *Constructing American Lives: Biography and Culture in Nineteenth-Century America* (Chapel Hill: University of North Carolina Press, 1999), 155–57.

3. My thinking about these "plebeian" narratives has been influenced by Natalie Zemon Davis, *Fiction in the Archives: Pardon Tales and Their Tellers in Sixteenth-Century France* (Stanford: Stanford University Press, 1987); Richard Rabinowitz, *The Spiritual Self in Everyday Life: The Transformation of Personal Religious Experience in Nineteenth-Century New England* (Boston: Northeastern University Press, 1989); and material in several recent studies: Daniel Walker Howe, *Making the American Self: Jonathan Edward to Abraham Lincoln* (Cambridge: Harvard University Press, 1997), 3–17; Joyce Appleby, "New Cultural Heroes in the Early National Period," in *The Culture of the Market: Historical Essays*, ed. Thomas L. Haskell and Richard F. Teichgraeber III (Cambridge: Cambridge University Press, 1993), 163–88; Joyce Appleby, ed., *Recollections of the Early Republic: Selected Autobiographies* (Boston: Northeastern University Press, 1997); Mechal Sobel, "The Revolution in Selves: Black and White Inner Aliens," in *Through a Glass Darkly: Reflections on Personal Identity in Early*

America, ed. Ronald Hoffman, Mechal Sobel, and Fredrika J. Teute (Chapel Hill: University of North Carolina Press, 1997), 163–205; R. Jackson Wilson, *Figures of Speech: American Writers and the Literary Marketplace, from Benjamin Franklin to Emily Dickinson* (New York: Alfred A. Knopf, 1989); and Charles Taylor, *Sources of the Self: The Making of Modern Identity* (Cambridge: Harvard University Press, 1989).

4. The studies of print culture in eighteenth- and nineteenth-century America that I have found most helpful include Cathy N. Davidson, *Revolution and the Word: The Rise of the Novel in America* (New York: Oxford University Press, 1986); William J. Gilmore, *Reading Becomes a Necessity of Life: Material and Cultural Life in Rural New England, 1780–1835* (Knoxville: University of Tennessee Press, 1989); David D. Hall, *Cultures of Print: Essays in the History of the Book* (Amherst: University of Massachusetts Press, 1996); William Charvat, *The Profession of Authorship in America, 1800–1870*, ed. Matthew J. Bruccoli (Columbus: University of Ohio Press, 1968); Christopher Grasso, "Print, Poetry, and Politics: John Trumbull and the Transformation of Public Discourse in Revolutionary America," *Early American Literature* 30 (1995): 5–31; Ronald J. Zboray, *A Fictive People: Antebellum Economic Development and the American Reading Public* (New York: Oxford University Press, 1993); Michael Gilmore, *American Romanticism and the Marketplace* (Chicago: University of Chicago Press, 1985); Kenneth Lockridge, *Literacy in Colonial New England: An Inquiry into the Social Context of Literacy of the Early Modern West* (New York: W. W. Norton, 1974); and E. Jennifer Monaghan, "Literacy Instruction and Gender in Colonial New England," in *Reading in America: Literary and Social History*, ed. Cathy N. Davidson (Baltimore: Johns Hopkins University Press, 1989), 53–80. On the importance of intellectual milieu and social context in understanding narrative, see Thomas Laqueur, "Bodies, Details, and the Humanitarian Narrative," in *The New Cultural History*, ed. Lynn Hunt (Berkeley: University of California Press, 1989), 200.

5. Benedict Anderson, *Imagined Communities: Reflections on the Origin and Spread of Nationalism* (London: Verso, 1983); Michael Warner, *Letters of the Republic: Publication and the Public Sphere in Eighteenth-Century America* (Cambridge: Harvard University Press, 1990), 34–72. See also David Waldstreicher, *In the Midst of Perpetual Fetes: The Making of American Nationalism, 1776–1820* (Chapel Hill: University of North Carolina Press, 1997).

6. Richard L. Bushman, *The Refinement of America: Persons, Houses, Cities* (New York: Vintage Books, 1993), 280–87, 473. Perhaps by looking at this

countertradition of letters, we can sometimes, as Bushman wished, hear "ordinary people talk back to their superiors" (405).

7. Consider, for example, the eccentric "K. White" (a woman, but one taken often for a man in drag). Her gender trouble begins when a woman flirts with her, insisting that White is a man dressed as a woman. White also suffers through bankruptcy, captivity among American Indians, and countless romantic betrayals. *A Narrative of the Life, Occurrence, Vicissitudes and Present Situation of K. White* (Schenectady: Printed for the Authoress, 1809). See also *The Female Shipwright, or, Life and Extraordinary Adventures of Mary Lacy* (New York: Printed for Georg Sinclair, 1807); Cordelia Stark, *The Female Wanderer: Containing an account of her nativity, parentage, &c.* (United States: Printed for the Publishers, 1826); Lucy Brewer, *Affecting Narrative of Louisa Baker* (New York: Luther Wales, 1815); *The Surprising Adventures of Almira Paul* (Boston: N. Coverly, Jun., 1816). See also Jane Kamensky, "Talk Like a Man: Speech, Power, and Masculinity in Early New England," *Gender and History* 8 (April 1996): 22–47.

8. James W. Parker, *Narrative of the Perilous Adventures, Miraculous Escapes and Sufferings of Rev. James W. Parker, during a frontier residence in Texas of fifteen years; with an impartial geographical description of the climate, soil, timber, water &c., &c., &c. of Texas; written by himself* (Lexington, Ky.: Printed at the Morning Courier Office, 1844), 4.

9. Informative literature on captivity narratives includes Richard Slotkin, *Regeneration through Violence: The Mythology of the American Frontier, 1600–1860* (Middletown, Conn.: Wesleyan University Press, 1973); June Namias, *White Captives: Gender and Ethnicity on the American Frontier* (Chapel Hill: University of North Carolina Press, 1993); and Christopher Castiglia, *Bound and Determined: Captivity, Culture-Crossing, and White Womanhood from Mary Rowlandson to Patty Hearst* (Chicago: University of Chicago Press, 1996). Richard White suggests that captivity narratives turned wars waged against native peoples by Euro-Americans into "defensive" maneuvers. Richard White, "Frederick Jackson Turner and Buffalo Bill," in *The Frontier in American Culture: Essays by Richard White and Patricia Nelson Limerick*, ed. James R. Grossman (Berkeley: University of California Press, 1994). On African American autobiography and captivity, see John Saillant, "'Remarkably Emancipated from Bondage, Slavery and Death': An African American's Retelling of the Puritan Captivity Narrative, 1820," *Early American Literature* 29 (1994): 122–40; John Sekora, "Red, White, and Black: Indian Captivities, Colonial Printers, and the Early African-American Narrative,"

in *A Mixed Race: Ethnicity in Early America*, ed. Frank Shuffleton (New York: Oxford University Press, 1993), 92–104.

10. On the seeds of sensationalism in early-nineteenth-century narratives, see Karen Halttunen, "Early American Murder Narratives: The Birth of Horror," in *The Power of Culture: Critical Essays in American History*, ed. Richard Wightman Fox and T. J. Jackson Lears (Chicago: University of Chicago Press, 1993); Halttunen, *Murder Most Foul: The Killer and the American Gothic Imagination* (Cambridge: Harvard University Press, 1998); and Daniel A. Cohen, *Pillars of Salt, Monuments of Grace: New England Crime Literature and the Origins of American Popular Culture, 1674–1860* (New York: Oxford University Press, 1993). On such narratives' effect as literary inspiration, see David Reynolds, *Beneath the American Renaissance: The Subversive Imagination in the Age of Emerson and Melville* (Cambridge: Harvard University Press, 1988). One could argue that even the narratives of reformed drunks added to the canon of our national literature, providing William James with material to use in his exploration of the claims of experience, *The Varieties of Religious Experience* (New York: Longmans, Green, 1902).

11. On the cultural legacies of slave narratives, see Henry Louis Gates Jr., *Figures in Black: Words, Signs, and the "Racial" Self* (New York: Oxford University Press, 1987), 3–42; see also Henry Louis Gates Jr., "Introduction: Writing 'Race' and the Difference It Makes," in *"Race," Writing, and Difference*, ed. Henry Louis Gates Jr. (Chicago: University of Chicago Press, 1986), 7–15; and William L. Andrews, *To Tell a Free Story: The First Century of Afro-American Autobiography, 1760–1865* (Urbana: University of Illinois Press, 1988), 123–38.

Hard as it was for fugitive men to tell their stories, it was even more difficult for women. As Harriet Jacobs makes clear in her narrative, she cannot cross-dress, cannot appropriate masculine forms of storytelling, and cannot tell her tale within the conventions available to her, and so she develops her story by making her case around, through, and against both domestic injunctions to practice sexual purity and the abolitionist urge to publicize the sexual degradation of slave women. The ability to read, which so clearly led Douglass to freedom, only makes Jacobs more available to the sexual overtures written to her by her master, and the ability to write, which serves Douglass as an engine of manhood, causes pain to Jacobs. Harriet Jacobs, *Incidents in the Life of a Slave Girl*, ed. Jean Fagan Yellin (Cambridge: Harvard University Press, 1987). A reading of the conflicting rhetorics in Jacobs's story is beautifully developed by Franny Nudelman, "Harriet

Jacobs and the Sentimental Politics of Female Suffering," *American Literary History* 59 (1992): 939–64. I borrow the argument about writing from Jacqueline Goldsby, "'I disguised my hand': Writing Versions of the Truth in Harriet Jacobs, *Incidents in the Life of a Slave Girl* and John Jacobs, *A True Tale of Slavery*," in *Harriet Jacobs and Incidents in the Life of a Slave Girl: New Critical Essays*, ed. Deborah M. Garfield and Rafia Zafar (Cambridge: Cambridge University Press, 1996), 11–43. See also Karen Sánchez-Eppler, "Bodily Bonds: The Intersecting Rhetorics of Feminism and Abolition," in *The New American Studies: Essays from Representations*, ed. Philip Fisher (Berkeley: University of California Press, 1991), 228–59.

12. In claiming this artless honesty, the narrators denied that they played a role in making the stories they told. If they followed a philosopher, it would be David Carr, who argues that narrative structures, rather than being imposed after the fact on a chaos of events, inhere in events themselves. See Carr, *Time, Narrative, and History* (Bloomington: Indiana University Press, 1986). In contrast, Hayden White argues that the world does not "present itself to perception in the form of well-made stories, with central subject, proper beginning, middles and ends." H. White, "The Value of Narrativity in the Representation of Reality," in *On Narrative*, ed. W. J. T. Mitchell (Chicago: University of Chicago Press, 1981), 23. Students of personal narratives have sometimes found it more useful to follow White because he seems to allow the powerless a greater part in shaping their narrative worlds. See Davis, *Fiction in the Archives*, 3; and Halttunen, "Early American Murder Narratives," 67. But if we pay attention to the exchange of stories, Carr too leads us into the social world where stories circulated.

13. Raymond Williams, *The Long Revolution* (New York: Columbia University Press, 1961), 26, 38.

14. Joan Scott challenged naive assumptions that articulations of the experience of and by marginalized group would prove liberatory. "Standpoint epistemology" does not change the shape of knowledge. Nor does it challenge the way history has been written. Scott, "The Evidence of Experience," *Critical Inquiry* 17 (summer 1991): 779–80, 777. Laura Lee Downs offered a feminist critique, reiterating the need to write "histories of difference." Downs, "If 'Woman' Is Just an Empty Category, Then Why Am I Afraid to Walk Alone at Night? Identity Politics Meets the Postmodern Subject," *Comparative Studies in Society and History* 35 (April 1993): 414–51. See also Sandra Harding, "Subjectivity, Experience, and Knowledge: An Epistemology from/for Rainbow Coalition Politics," in *Who Can*

Speak? Authority and Critical Identity, ed. Judith Root and Robyn Wiegman (Urbana: University of Illinois Press, 1995), 120–36.

CHAPTER ONE

1. *History of the Adventures and Sufferings of Moses Smith during five years of his life; from the beginning of the year 1806, when he was betrayed into the Miranda Expedition, until June 1811, when he was nonsuited in an action at law which lasted three years and a half* (Brooklyn: Thomas Kirk, for the author, 1812). A second edition of Smith's book was printed in Albany by Packard and Van Benthuysen in 1814.

2. Michael Smith, *A Narrative of the Sufferings in Upper Canada, with his family in the Late War and Journey to Virginia and Kentucky* (Lexington, Ky.: Printed for the Author by Worsley and Smith, 1816).

3. *The narrative of Robert Adams, an American sailor who was wrecked on the Western coast of Africa, in the year 1810; was detained three years in slavery by the Arabs of the great desert, and resided several months in the City of Tombuctoo* (Boston: Wells and Lilly, 1817), ix–xi. A London edition was published by John Murray in 1816, a Paris edition by Michaud in 1817, a Stockholm edition by A. Gadelius in 1817, and an Amsterdam edition by J. C. Seepen Zoon in 1818. The American edition of Adams's story appeared in 1817 in a handsome two-hundred-page book published by Wells and Lilly in Boston with the help of Mathew Carey in Philadelphia. On April 30, 1817, Mathew Carey noted an expense of 275 dollars for the two hundred copies of Adams's *Narrative* that he ordered from Wells and Lilly. Accounts, vol. 31, 1818, Papers of Mathew Carey, American Antiquarian Society, Worcester, Massachusetts.

4. Mechal Sobel, "The Revolution in Selves: Black and White Inner Aliens," in *Through a Glass Darkly: Reflections on Personal Identity in Early America*, ed. Ronald Hoffman, Mechal Sobel, and Fredrika J. Teute (Chapel Hill: University of North Carolina Press, 1998), 163–205; and Joyce Appleby, "New Cultural Heroes in the Early National Period," in *The Culture of the Market: Historical Essays*, ed. Thomas I. Haskell and Richard F. Teichgraeber III (Cambridge: Cambridge University Press, 1993), 163–88.

5. Richard L. Bushman, *The Refinement of America: Persons, Houses, Cities* (New York: Vintage Books, 1993), 280–87. On the "golden age" of American

printing, see William Charvat, *Literary Publishing in America, 1790–1850* (Amherst: University of Massachusetts Press, 1959), 17–37; and David Hall, "The Uses of Literacy," in *Printing and Society in Early America*, ed. William Joyce, et al. (Worcester, Mass.: American Antiquarian Society, 1983).

6. On beggars' books, see John Cumming, "Mendicant Pieces," *The American Book Collector* (March 1966): 17–19. Other books that begin with a writer reduced to poverty include *A Narrative of the Life and Travels of John Robert Shaw, the well-digger, now resident in Lexington, Kentucky* (Lexington: Printed by Daniel Bradford, 1807); *The Life of Captain David Perry, a soldier in the French and Revolutionary Wars. Recollections of an Old Soldier. Containing many extraordinary occurrences relating to his own private history, and an account of some interesting events in the history of the times in which he lived, no-where else recorded* (Windsor, Vt.: The Republican and Yeoman, 1822); and *A Narrative of the Travels and Voyages of Davis Bill. Late a Mariner in the British Navy, and formerly of New-Fame, Vermont* (Brattleboro: William Fessenden, 1811). Those who appealed to readers to buy stories to help them recover from financial losses include James Riley, *Authentic Narrative of the Loss of the American Brig* Commerce (New York: For the Author, 1817); *Narrative of the Adventures and Sufferings of Samuel Patterson* (Palmer, Mass.: The Press in Palmer, 1817); Owen Chase, *Narrative of the Most Extraordinary and Distressing Shipwreck of the Whaleship* Essex *of Nantucket* (New York: W. B. Gilley, 1821); Elisha Dexter, *Narrative of the Loss of the Whaling Brig* William and Joseph, *of Martha's Vineyard* (Boston: Charles C. Mead, 1848); and Lloyd Burt, *An Account of the Loss of the Ship* Rose in Bloom (Massachusetts: n.p., 1829).

7. Raymond A. Mohl, *Poverty in New York, 1783–1825* (New York: Oxford University Press, 1971), 37–38, 164. See also Christine Stansell, *City of Women: Sex and Class in New York, 1789–1860* (Urbana: University of Illinois Press, 1987), 30–37.

8. On reading, printing, and publishing, see Charvat, *Literary Publishing*, 17–37; Rollo G. Silver, *The American Printer, 1787–1825* (Charlottesville: University Press of Virginia, 1967); Milton Hamilton, *The Country Printer: New York State, 1785–1830* (New York: Columbia University Press, 1936); Robert Darnton, "What Is the History of Books?" *Daedalus* (summer 1982): 65–83; and Ronald J. Zboray, *A Fictive People: Antebellum Economic Development and the American Reading Public* (New York: Oxford University Press, 1993), 17–36. Although scholars have questioned the rigid opposition between oral and literate cultures so important to much of his work, Walter J. Ong describes the episodic patterns

that characterized the narratives of an oral culture. Ong, *Orality and Literacy: The Technologizing of the Word* (London: Metheun, 1982), 147–51.

9. A list of those executed and those incarcerated appears in *The History of Don Francisco de Miranda's attempt to effect a Revolution in South America in a series of letters. By a Gentleman who was an Officer under that General, to his friends in the United States. To which are annexed, Sketches of the Life of Miranda, and Geographical Notices of Caracas* (1808; reprint, Boston: Oliver and Munroe, 1812), 242–43. See also *Mechanics of New York, read the heart-rending Truth! Sixty American Citizens enslaved—Ten beheaded and hung by the nefarious scheme of Miranda, the would-be King of America, the Duke of Braintree, a Burrite Col. And a Nova Scotia Tory, F***k, together with a tory-federal merchant, S. O—n* (New York: n.p, 1806). In his haste, the composer of the broadside surely reversed the sequence of punishment, because it is hard to imagine a man being beheaded before he is hanged.

10. *History of the Adventures* (1814), 124. Historians of the Early Republic have used the story of Miranda's first expedition to illustrate the troubled state of diplomatic relations with Spain during Jefferson's second administration. Miranda made friends in high places. Benjamin Rush arranged for the charming Miranda to dine with Jefferson and Madison, and Miranda then operated as though he had tacit approval from the president and his secretary of state. Although Jefferson avoided war with Spain, Federalists tried to use the episode to discredit Madison. See Dumas Malone, *Jefferson the President, Second Term, 1805- 1809* (Boston: Little, Brown and Company, 1974), 80; Henry Adams, *History of the United States of America during the Second Administration of Thomas Jefferson* (New York: Charles Scribner's Sons, 1890), 1:189–96; and Irving Brant, *James Madison: Secretary of State* (Indianapolis: Bobbs-Merrill, 1953), 326–35. For a fuller portrait of Miranda's extraordinary career, see William Spence Robertson, *The Life of Miranda* (Chapel Hill: University of North Carolina Press, 1929).

11. *History of the Adventures*, 121–23. John Sherman, *A General Account of Miranda's Expedition. Including the Trial and Execution of Ten of his Officers and an Account of the Imprisonment and Sufferings of the Remainder of his Officers and Men who were Taken Prisoners* (New York: McFarlane and Long, 1808), 19. Although Sherman admitted that the men recruited to join Miranda were deceived, he also thought it possible that some were enticed by a promise of easy wealth. For Smith's story to work the way he intended it, he needed to present himself as a man governed by the purest motives. The idea that Smith and others

enlisted in order to guard the mail is repeated in *Report of the Committee to whom was referred the Petition of Sundry Citizens of the United States confined at Carthagena in South America* (Washington, D.C.: A. and G. Way, Printers, 1809), 3. See also "An Account of the Sufferings of the Crew of two Schooners, part of the Squadron of General Miranda, which were taken by two Spanish Guarda Costas, in June 1806. Written by one of the Sufferers who made his escape," *Select Reviews and Spirit of the Foreign Magazines* 2 (1809): 44–55.

12. Robertson, *Life of Miranda*.

13. *History of the Adventures*, 99. Walter Flavius McCaleb documents the earlier interest in Miranda's ventures. McCaleb, *The Aaron Burr Conspiracy* (New York: Dodd, Mead, and Co., 1903), 114–15.

14. *History of the Adventures*, 104–5, 107. Smith's confidence that he would find in a tavern a welcome reception, good fellowship, and people interested in politics was not entirely unfounded. See David W. Conroy, *In Public Houses: Drink and the Revolution of Authority in Colonial Massachusetts* (Chapel Hill: Institute of Early American History and Culture, 1995), 10–11, 313–14; and Rhys Isaac, *The Transformation of Virginia: 1740–1790* (Chapel Hill: Institute of Early American History and Culture, 1982), 94–98. A few years before Smith appeared, the notorious Stephen Burroughs begged his way through the Maryland countryside. Burroughs, however, addressed himself to the wealthy and respectable, who accepted him as one of their own fallen on hard times. *Memoirs of the Notorious Stephen Burroughs* (1798; 1804; reprint, ed. Philip F. Gura, Boston: Northeastern University Press, 1989), 326–37.

15. *History of the Adventures*, 99.

16. *Narrative of Henry Bird, who was carried away by Indians after the murder of his whole family in 1811* (Bridgeport: n.p., 1811), 7.

17. *A Son of the Forest: The Experience of William Apess, a Native of the Forest,* in *On Our Own Ground: The Complete Writing of William Apess, a Pequot,* ed. Barry O'Connell (Amherst: University of Massachusetts Press, 1992), 24. Karim M. Tiro, "Denominated 'SAVAGE': Methodism, Writing, and Identity in the Works of William Apess, a Pequot," *American Quarterly* 48 (December 1996): 653.

18. Smith apologized for the poor quality of his travelogue. "It is of importance to my story, that the reader should understand the nature of the territory, which is now the scene of action. It cannot be expected that my description should be entirely accurate, as I was more intent upon concealing myself from view, than on making observations." *History of the Adventures*, 83–84.

19. *History of the Adventures*, 32–33, 75, 78. On the conventions that characterize Gothic fiction, see Karen Halttunen, *Murder Most Foul: The Killer and the American Gothic Imagination* (Cambridge: Harvard University Press, 1998), 3–6.

20. *History of the Adventures*, 20. Certainly "experience" described in accents of a humble narrator was useful to a novelist like Daniel Defoe. He was a mere "editor" of *Moll Flanders* (1722). On novels, see Ian Watt, *The Rise of the Novel* (1957; reprint, Berkeley: University of California Press, 1967); Lennard Davis, *Factual Fictions: The Origins of the English Novel* (New York: Columbia University Press, 1983), 123–37; and Cathy Davidson, *Revolution and the Word: The Rise of the Novel in America* (New York: Oxford University Press, 1986), 15–37; 70–79.

21. *History of the Adventures*, 104–8.

22. A jury had already acquitted the two most prominent of Miranda's supporters—the "tory-federal merchant" Samuel Ogden and Colonel William Stephens Smith, who was the son-in-law of John Adams, the surveyor of the New York port, and an old traveling companion of Miranda. Although Smith and Ogden had acquired arms for Miranda and helped him recruit, by ruse, his little band of mercenaries, they had broken no law. From the evidence presented, the jury could not conclude that Colonel Smith and Mr. Ogden had intended to provoke war with Spain. *The Trials of William S. Smith and Samuel G. Ogden, for Misdemeanors, had in the Circuit Court of the United States for the New-York District, in July 1806* (New York: Printed by and for I. Riley and Co., 1807); *Mechanics of New York, read the heart-rending Truth!*

23. "It was too evident from this sentence, that our judges did not credit our story, true as it was, that any man could dare to do, in a country where there are laws and civilization, an act so audacious as that which Mr. Fink did, when he entrapped fifteen of us into this desperate adventure, under pretence of an authority to enlist us for a guard to the Washington mail." *History of the Adventures*, 44.

24. *History of the Adventures*, 119.

25. According to William Charvat, subscription publishing, which was common in eighteenth-century Britain, had begun by the early years of the nineteenth century to fall out of favor. Personal ventures like Smith's, however, were still common in the United States in the 1810s and 1820s. William Charvat, *The Profession of Authorship in America, 1800–1870*, ed. Matthew J. Bruccoli (1968; reprint, New York: Columbia University Press, 1992), 21. For examples of such ventures, see *The Life and Adventures of Robert Bailey from his Infancy up to*

December, 1821 (Richmond, Va.: For the Author, 1822); *Narrative of the Adventures and Sufferings of Samuel Patterson*, and *Narrative of the Travels and Voyages of Davis Bill*. On the form of subscription publishing common later in the nineteenth century, see Michael Hackenberg, "The Subscription Publishing Network in Nineteenth-Century America," in *Getting Books Out: Papers of the Chicago Conference on the Book in Nineteenth-Century America*, ed. Michael Hackenberg (Washington, D.C.: Library of Congress, Center for the Book, 1987), 45–75.

26. On Smith's subscribers, see *Elliot's Improved New-York Double Directory* (New York: William Elliot, 1812). The political nature of Smith's argument is suggested not only by his association with Thomas Kirk, the Democratic-Republican printer of the *Long Island Star*, but also by his repeated assertions of a Federalist conspiracy. See Hamilton, *Country Printer*, 52. On the contests for the political loyalties of New York artisans and renewed intensity of party rivalries during the War of 1812, see Howard Rock, *Artisans of the New Republic: The Tradesmen of New York City in the Age of Jefferson* (New York: New York University Press, 1979), 77–100. An advertisement printed in Boston in *The Literary Mirror* (10 September 1808) suggests why Smith sensed there might be interest in his story. In the paper, the publishers, Oliver and Munroe, recommended their *History of Don Francisco de Miranda's attempt to effect a Revolution in South America in a series of letters* because the "unstudied simplicity of the narration carries conviction of its truth. . . . It has so much of incident that it will engage the curious reader; so much of disaster as to fix on sensibility and carries proof of such depraved hypocrisy in the leader as to interest every lover of truth" (120).

27. *History of the Adventures*, 89–90, 104.

28. Under the Articles of Confederation, paupers and vagabonds were explicitly excluded from privileges and immunities of citizenship, "but the federal Constitution did not repeat the phrase." Linda K. Kerber, "The Meanings of Citizenship," *Journal of American History* 84 (December 1997): 843.

Although the phrasing is surely foreign to the plain style Smith espoused, perhaps one could follow the literary scholar Lauren Berlant and credit Smith with working out his own "structure of personal/national representation." Berlant, *The Anatomy of National Fantasy: Hawthorne, Utopia, and Everyday Life* (Chicago: University of Chicago Press, 1991), 3.

29. *History of the Adventures*, 115. Perhaps Smith manages here to elevate himself above those who found injustice in small and private failure. See Toby Ditz, "Shipwrecked; or Masculinity Imperiled: Mercantile Representations of

Failure and the Gendered Self in Eighteenth-Century Philadelphia," *Journal of American History* 81 (June 1994): 51–80.

30. For a discussion of the ways in which political conflict over the War of 1812 shaped publication, see Daniel A. Cohen, "'The Female Marine' in the Era of Good Feeling: Cross Dressing and the 'Genius' of Nathaniel Coverly, Jr.," *Proceedings of the American Antiquarian Society* 103 (October 1994): 359–93.

31. *Human Sorrow and Divine Comfort; or a short narrative of the suffering, travel and present feelings and situation of M. Smith, preacher of the gospel, author of the view of Upper Canada and British Possessions. Intended to illustrate the goodness of God* (Richmond: Samuel Pleasants, 1814), 9. *A Geographical View of the Province of Upper Canada, and Promiscuous Remarks Upon the Government in Two Parts, With an Appendix: Containing a complete description of Niagara Falls. And remarks relative to the situation of the inhabitants respecting the war* (Hartford: Printed for the Author by Hale and Hosmer, 1813), 4.

32. *Geographical View* (Hartford), 5–6; *Narrative of the Sufferings,* 5–13. George Sheppard, *Plunder, Profit, and Parole: A Social History of the War of 1812 in Upper Canada* (Montreal: McGill-Queen's University Press, 1994), 79–91, 98; and Alan Taylor, "John Graves Simcoe's Colonists: A Canadian Perspective on the Legacies of the American Revolution" (paper presented at the Columbia University Early American Seminar, May 12, 1998). In fact, civilians such as Smith spied for both sides during the war. See Donald R. Hickey, *The War of 1812: A Forgotten Conflict* (Urbana: University of Illinois, 1990), 38–39.

33. On the Loyalist emigration from the United States to Canada, see Alfred Leroy Burt and John Bartlett Brebner, *The Mingling of the Canadian and the American Peoples* (New Haven: Yale University Press, 1945), 87.

34. *Geographical View* (Hartford), 4–5.

35. *A Geographical View of the British Possessions in North America: comprehending Nova Scotia, New Brunswick, New Britain, Lower and Upper Canada, with all the country to the Frozen Sea on the North and the Pacific Ocean on the West: with an appendix containing a concise history of the war in Canada to the date of this volume* (Baltimore: Printed for the Author by P. Mauro, 1814), v.

36. *Narrative of the Sufferings,* 67.

37. *A Complete History of the Late American War with Great Britain and her allies: from the commencement of hostilities in 1812 till the conclusion of peace with the Algerines in 1815: with geographical notes relative to the seat of war and scene of battle, and biographical sketches of the principal actors* (Lexington: Printed for

the Author by F. Bradford Jun., 1816), 269–70. To put a fine face on Smith's travels, we might label him an itinerant entrepreneur in the religious line. See Stephen A. Marini, "Evangelical Itinerancy in Rural New England: New Gloucester, Maine, 1754–1807," in *Itinerancy in New England and New York*, ed. Peter Benes and Jane Montague Benes (Boston: Boston University Press, 1984), 63. O. K. Armstrong and Marjorie Armstrong, *The Baptists in America* (Garden City, New York: Doubleday, 1979), 103–17.

38. *Human Sorrow and Divine Comfort*, 30. Jack Larkin, "The Merriams of Brookfield: Printing in the Economy and Culture of Rural Massachusetts in the Early Nineteenth Century," *Proceedings of the American Antiquarian Society* 96 (1986): 39–73; and Philip F. Gura, "Early Nineteenth-Century Printing in Rural Massachusetts: John Howe of Greenwich and Enfield, ca. 1803–1845," *Proceedings of the American Antiquarian Society* 101 (1991): 25–62.

39. *Complete History of the Late American War*, iv.

40. *Narrative of the Sufferings*, 32. In 1813, Smith produced editions in New York (printed by Pelsoe and Gould), Philadelphia (printed by J. Bioren for Thomas and Robert Desilver), and Trenton (printed by W. and D. Robinson for More and Lake). Although each edition of Smith's book contained the same basic geography with which he had begun, as he worked his way south, he changed its title, adding a "concise history" of the war's progress "to the present date." When he reached Richmond in 1814, he changed the title of the book to *A Continuation of the History of the War*, and after the Treaty of Ghent was signed in February 1815, he changed it once more to *A Complete History of the Late American War*.

41. On peddlers, see Lewis Perry, *Boats against the Current: American Culture between Revolution and Modernity, 1820–1860* (New York: Oxford University Press, 1993), 174–89; Zboray, *Fictive People*, 38–42; and William J. Gilmore, "Peddlers and the Dissemination of Printed Material in Northern New England, 1780–1840," in Benes and Benes, *Itinerancy in New England and New York*, 76–87.

42. David Jaffee, "The Village Enlightenment in New England, 1760–1820," *William and Mary Quarterly* 47 (July 1990): 327–46. Smith, *Narrative of the Sufferings* (1817), 99–100; 116–18.

43. Hickey, *War of 1812*, 227–31. A conscientious search for customers predisposed to accept his patriotic account perhaps explains why Smith never produced an edition of his book in Massachusetts, a state most important to the New England book trade, but one whose Federalist majority was hardly enthusiastic

about war with England. On Massachusetts printers and the New England book trade, see Larkin, "Merriams of Brookfield."

44. *Narrative of the Sufferings*, 282. On preachers' wages, see Armstrong and Armstrong, *Baptists in America*, 116.

45. *Narrative of the Sufferings*, 275–80; Charvat, *Profession of Authorship*, 18; Zboray, *Fictive People*, 42.

46. *Narrative of the Sufferings* (1817), 124–25.

47. Ibid., 120, 104, 282.

48. *Geographical View* (Baltimore), ix.

49. *Human Sorrow and Divine Comfort*, 35–36.

50. *Narrative of the Sufferings* (1817), 104–5, 135–37, 123–24. *Beauties of Divine Poetry, or, Appropriate Hymns and Spiritual Songs* (Lexington: Printed for the Author by Worsley and Smith, 1817). The first version of Smith's personal narrative (*Human Sorrow and Divine Comfort* [Richmond: Samuel Pleasants, 1814]) appeared as an appendix to his book on the war. In Lexington, he published two subsequent editions as *A Narrative of the Sufferings in Upper Canada, with his family* . . . : one was printed by F. Bradford, Jun. in 1816; the other was printed by Worsley and Smith in 1817. On evangelical publishing, see Nathan Hatch, *The Democratization of American Christianity* (New Haven: Yale University Press, 1989), 141–44; David Paul Nord, "Evangelical Origins of Mass Media in America, 1815–1835," *Journalism Monographs* 88 (1984); and R. Laurence Moore, *Selling God: American Religion in the Marketplace of Culture* (New York: Oxford University Press, 1994), 13–27.

51. *Narrative of the Sufferings* (1817), 120.

52. Ibid., 76.

53. On changing patterns of relief for the poor, see Mohl, *Poverty in New York*, 15–38, 67–83, 161–64; and Elizabeth Blackmar, *Manhattan for Rent, 1785–1850* (Ithaca: Cornell University Press, 1989), 170–71. See also Michael Katz, *In the Shadow of the Poorhouse: A Social History of Welfare in America* (New York: Basic Books, 1986), 3–66; Gary B. Nash, *The Urban Crucible: Social Change, Political Consciousness, and the Origins of the American Revolution* (Cambridge: Harvard University Press, 1979), 253–63; and David J. Rothman, *The Discovery of the Asylum: Social Order and Disorder in the New Republic* (Boston: Little, Brown and Company, 1971), 155–68. It was not until after the Civil War that beggars appeared conspicuous enough in the United States to be deemed endemic. For an astute reading of the application of measures against begging in the 1870s, see Amy Dru

Stanley, "Beggars Can't Be Choosers," in *From Bondage to Contract: Wage Labor, Marriage, and the Market in the Age of Slave Emancipation* (Cambridge: Cambridge University Press, 1998), 98–137.

54. *Narrative of the Sufferings* (1817), 118–19.

55. For examples of extensive appendices in African travel narratives, see Mungo Park, *Travels in the Interior Districts of Africa performed under the Direction and Patronage of the African Association in the years 1795, 1796, and 1797* (London: W. Bulmer and Co., 1799); and René Caillié, *Travels through Central Africa* (London: Henry Colburn and Richard Bentley, 1830).

56. *Narrative of Robert Adams,* [1].

57. Laurence Sterne's novel concludes "L—d! said my mother, what is all this story about?—A COCK and a BULL, said Yorick—And one of the best of its kind, I ever heard." Sterne, *The Life and Opinions of Tristam Shandy, Gentleman* (1759–1767; reprint, ed. Melvyn New and Joan New, with an introductory essay by Christopher Ricks, London: Penguin Books, 1967), 543. The phrase "cock and bull story" is an old one, dating back at least to the second half of the seventeenth century. Adams's tale was indeed a "long, rambling idle story." Or it could have been, more precisely, a deliberate sham, an "idle, concocted, incredible story; a canard." *The Oxford English Dictionary* (New York: Oxford University Press, 1971), 2: 569. On the African Association, see Mary Louise Pratt, *Imperial Eyes: Travel Writing and Transculturation* (London: Routledge, 1993), 69–70.

58. The first edition of fifteen hundred copies of Mungo Park's book sold out almost immediately, and versions of his travels have remained in print for most of the two hundred years since its initial appearance. Christopher Lloyd, *The Search for the Niger* (London: Collins, 1973), 46.

59. On European exploration of Africa, see Robert Rotberg, *Africa and Its Explorers: Motives, Methods, and Impact* (Cambridge: Harvard University Press, 1970). On Timbuktu, see Christopher Hibbert, *Africa Explored: Europeans in the Dark Continent, 1769–1889* (London: Allen Lane, 1982), 154–77.

60. *Narrative of Robert Adams,* x, xv.

61. Ibid., xxi.

62. "The Narrative of Robert Adams," *North American Review* 5 (July 1817): 205–6.

63. *Narrative of Robert Adams,* 38.

64. Paul Baepler, "The Barbary Captivity Narrative in Early America," *Early American Literature* 30 (1995): 95–120. Adams's book could not com-

pete with James Riley's story of his Barbary captivity. Riley, *An Authentic Narrative of the Loss of the American Brig* Commerce. According to Baepler, nearly one million copies of Riley's book appeared in different editions between 1817 and 1851 (115).

65. *Narrative of Robert Adams,* 165. On the origins of slavery, see James W. C. Pennington, *A Text Book of the Origin and History, &c. &c. of the Colored People* (Hartford: L. Skinner, 1841), 39–42.

66. *The Narrative of Robert Adams,* 40, 43, 146, 155n.

67. Ibid., 146–47.

68. Ibid., 143, xiv.

69. Ibid., 107, n. 28.

70. Ibid., 108. "During the crisis of the autumn and winter of 1816," Peter Linebaugh wrote, "the municipal authorities took active steps to control the independent mobilization of the urban proletariat." Those responsible for maintaining order in the city of London paid particular attention to African American sailors, because authorities saw "the danger of a nautical proletariat joining London's idle apprentice in insurrectionary alliance." Linebaugh, "A Little Jubilee? The Literacy of Robert Wedderburn in 1817," in *Protest and Survival: Essays for E. P. Thompson,* ed. John Rule and Robert Malcolmson (New York: The New Press, 1993), 207. See also Stanley Palmer, *Police and Protest in England and Ireland, 1780–1850* (Cambridge: Cambridge University Press, 1988), 169. Artlessness, according to Jay Fliegelman, was mandated for all poor storytellers. Fliegelman, *Declaring Independence: Jefferson, Natural Language, and the Culture of Performance* (Stanford: Stanford University Press, 1993), 59.

71. Although he studied an earlier generation, Steven Shapin's work on gentlemen scientists sheds light on the role that social position could play even in a book such as Adams's. Shapin, *A Social History of Truth: Civility and Science in Seventeenth-Century England* (Chicago: University of Chicago Press, 1995), 65–125. *Narrative of Robert Adams,* xi, xiii.

72. John W. Blassingame, *The Slave Community: Plantation Life in the Antebellum South* (1972; reprint, New York: Oxford University Press, 1979), 49–63.

73. *Narrative of Robert Adams,* xxi, 68, xviii, 56, 116, n.37.

74. "The Narrative of Robert Adams," 211–12, 221.

75. Ibid., 205–6, 209. "Interiour of Africa," *North American Review and Miscellaneous Journal* 5 (May 1817): 12. "The Narrative of Robert Adams," *The Atheneum or, Spirit of the English Magazines* 1 (April–September 1817): 60.

In his *Travels of Richard Lander into the Interior of Africa, for the discovery of the course of the Niger* (London: W. Wright, 1836), Robert Huish accepts Adams's story, despite its inconsistencies (132–63). He thought Adams was probably the "first Christian who ever reached the far-famed city of Timbuctoo" (161).

76. "The Narrative of Robert Adams," *The North American Review* 5, no. 2 (July 1817): 220, 222, 223–24. On the American Colonization Society, see Paul Goodman, *Of One Blood: Abolitionism and the Origins of Racial Equality* (Berkeley: University of California Press, 1998), 11–25.

77. "René Caillié, *Journal d'un Voyage à Tomboctou et à Jenne dans l'Afrique Central, pendant les années, 1824, 1825, 1826, 1827, 1828,*" *North American Review* 36 (January 1833): 48–49.

78. *Life and Remarkable Adventures of Israel R. Potter (a native of Cranston, Rhode-Island,): who was a soldier in the American Revolution, and took a distinguished part in the Battle of Bunker Hill (in which he received three wounds,) after which he was taken prisoner by the British, conveyed to England, where for 30 years he obtained a livelihood for himself and his family, by crying "Old chairs to mend," through the streets of London* (Providence: Printed by Henry Trumbull, 1824), 88, 95–96. Henry Trumbull of Providence held the copyright to this version of Potter's story. J. Howard, also of Providence, printed another edition for Potter later that same year. The second edition sold for thirty-one cents. In *A History of Vagrants and Vagrancy and Beggars and Begging*, C. J. Ribton Turner described men and women who survived, like Potter, by scavenging the waste of the streets (London: Chapman and Hall, 1887). Charles Dickens put scavengers at the center of *Our Mutual Friend* (1864–1865).

79. *Life and Remarkable Adventures of Israel R. Potter*, 62–63.

80. *Life and Remarkable Adventures of Israel R. Potter*, 100.

81. *Life and Remarkable Adventures of Israel R. Potter*, 105. On pensions, see John P. Resch, "Politics and Public Culture: The Revolutionary War Pensions Act of 1818," *Journal of the Early Republic* 8 (1988): 139–58.

82. David Perry, another veteran of the Revolution, also peddled a book when denied a pension. His printer-publisher at the *Republican & Yeoman* in Windsor, Vermont, promised to allocate his own share of the earnings from the sale of Perry's book to underwrite publication of the narratives of other impoverished veterans. *The Life of Captain David Perry.*

83. At the start of the fifty-seventh chapter of *Moby Dick*, Ishmael pauses to acknowledge the artistry of a crippled "kedger" who has survived for some ten

years by begging beside a painting "representing the tragic scene in which he lost his leg." Whether his story was true did not matter, for Ishmael offered him "justification," judging his whales "as good whales as were ever published in Wapping, at any rate; and his stump as unquestionable as any you will find in the western clearings." Herman Melville, *Moby-Dick or, The Whale* (1851; reprint, ed. Charles Fiedelson, Indianapolis: Bobbs-Merrill, 1971), 357–58.

84. Petitions of Alexander Dobbins, Bridget McLaughlin, Mary Dorsey, Mrs. Porter, and Ann Banta, "Markets—Petitions, Stalls and Licenses," City Clerk's Documents, Box 57, 1810, New York City, Municipal Archives. See also John Yates, "Report of the Secretary of State in 1824 on the Relief and Settlement of the Poor," in *The Almshouse Experience*, ed. David Rothman (New York: Arno Press, 1971), 941–1009; and *Report to the Managers of the Society for the Prevention of Pauperism in New-York; by Their Committee on Idleness and Sources of Employment* (New York: Published by Order of the Board, 1819). On shop rents and contests over space at the bottom of the economy, see Blackmar, *Manhattan for Rent*, 171-72.

85. John Greenleaf Whittier, "The Yankee Gypsies," in *Margaret Smith's Journal, Tales and Sketches* (Boston: Houghton, Mifflin, 1892), 328–29. On Whittier, disguise, masquerade, and the wholesale pursuit of gain, see Perry, *Boats against the Current*, 154–59.

86. Lennard Davis and Robert Darnton have both investigated connections between the intellectual and criminal subcultures of Grub Street. Davis, *Factual Fictions*, 125–31; and Robert Darnton, "A Police Inspector Sorts His Files: The Anatomy of the Republic of Letters," in *The Great Cat Massacre and Other Episodes in French Cultural History* (New York: Basic Books, 1984), 145–89. For the evolution of professional authorship in the United States, see Charvat, *Profession of Authorship*, 5–48. Of course Melville, and not Whittier, saw the irony in the kinship between writing beggars and begging writers.

87. Henry Mayhew, *London Labour and the London Poor* (1851–1852; reprint, New York: Dover Publications, 1968), 403, 425, 427–28. See also Wendy Lesser, "On Philanthropy," in *The Amateur: An Independent Life of Letters* (New York: Pantheon, 1999), 137–56. The writer Joseph Mitchell learned that "decayed literary gentlemen" continued to practice their begging arts well into the twentieth century. See Mitchell, "Professor Sea Gull" and "Joe Gould's Secret," in *Up in the Old Hotel* (New York: Vintage Books, 1993), 52–70 and 623–716. The story of Mr. Gould first appeared in *The New Yorker* in 1964.

88. Lloyd B. Burt, a former ship's steward, began to sell his book about a ship-wreck after he lost three fingers in a factory accident. Burt, *An Account of the Loss of the Ship* Rose in Bloom, 11–12. The association of sailors with stories has a long and venerable history. Publishers in the 1840s actively solicited sea stories. Charles Ellms concludes his *Robinson Crusoe's Own Book; or the Voice of Adventure, from the Civilized Man Cut Off from his Fellows, by Force of Accident, or Inclination and from the Wanderer in Strange Seas and Lands* (1842; reprint, Boston: Joshua V. Pierce, 1846) with a "Card," inviting "mariners of every grade" to send him ac-counts of "adventures sufficiently remarkable for publication, . . . such as ship-wrecks, and extraordinary escapes from these and other disasters; [and] inter-course with uncivilized people, whether of a peaceful or warlike character."

On the importance of being Uncle Tom, see Robin Winks, "The Making of a Fugitive Slave Narrative: Josiah Henson and Uncle Tom—A Case Study," in *The Slaves' Narrative*, ed. Charles T. Davis and Henry Louis Gates Jr. (New York: Oxford University Press, 1986), 112–46. Victorian diarist Arthur Munby took a special interest in white working-class women who masqueraded as black. See Anne McClintock, *Imperial Leather: Race, Gender, and Sexuality in the Colonial Contest* (New York: Routledge, 1995), 108.

89. George Fitzhugh, *Cannibals All! or, Slaves without Masters* (1856; reprint, ed. C. Vann Woodward, Cambridge: Harvard University Press, 1960), 137–45. Fitzhugh's chapter is little more than an extended quotation from an ar-ticle published in July 1852 in the *Edinburgh Review*. The article itself, "Mendac-ity: Its Causes and Statistics," was little more than a pamphlet previously pub-lished in Birmingham. Turner traced the "lurk" from the Welsh *llerc*, which he defined as a "fit of loitering." Turner, *A History of Vagrants and Vagrancy*, 311.

90. Fitzhugh, *Cannibals All!*, 250.

CHAPTER TWO

1. Michael Smith, *A Geographical View of the Province of Upper Canada and Promiscuous Remarks on the Government* (Hartford: Printed for the Author by Hale and Hosmer, 1813), [5]. On writers' ties to the criminal subculture in eighteenth-century England, see Lennard Davis, *Factual Fictions: The Origins of the English Novel* (New York: Columbia University Press, 1983), 124.

2. Jeremy Bentham, *Rationale of Judicial Evidence: Specially Applied to English Practice* (London: Hunt and Clarke, 1827), quoted in John Henry Wigmore, *A Treatise on the System of Evidence in Trials at Common Law, including Statutes and Judicial Decisions of all Jurisdictions of the United States* (Boston: Little, Brown, 1904–1905), 520.

3. Davis, *Factual Fictions*, 126.

4. Michel Foucault, *Discipline and Punish: The Birth of the Prison*, trans. Alan Sheridan (New York: Vintage Books, 1979), 32–69. Here perhaps is a beginning for our current disputes over so-called Son-of-Sam laws"—attempts by the states to control the profits from sales of criminals' stories. For an account of New York State's defense of its law before the Supreme Court, see Linda Greenhouse, "High Court Upsets Seizing of Profits on Convicts' Books," *New York Times*, 11 December 1991, sec. A, p. 1.

5. On popular print culture, see David S. Reynolds, *Beneath the American Renaissance: The Subversive Imagination in the Age of Emerson and Melville* (Cambridge: Harvard University Press, 1988). On culture and the market, see Michael Gilmore, *American Romanticism and the Marketplace* (Chicago: University of Chicago Press, 1985) and Walter Benn Michaels, "Romance and Real Estate" in *The Gold Standard and the Logic of Naturalism: American Literature at the Turn of the Century* (Berkeley: University of California Press, 1987), 87–112.

6. Karen Halttunen, "Early American Murder Narratives: The Birth of Horror," in *The Power of Culture: Critical Essays in American History*, ed. Richard Wightman Fox and T. J. Jackson Lears (Chicago: University of Chicago Press, 1993), 73. See also Karen Halttunen, *Murder Most Foul: The Killer and the American Gothic Imagination* (Cambridge: Harvard University Press, 1998).

7. In addition to Halttunen, the historians whose work shaped the discussion that follows include Daniel A. Cohen, *Pillars of Salt, Monuments of Grace: New England Crime Literature and the Origins of American Popular Culture, 1674–1860* (New York: Oxford, 1993); Lawrence W. Towner, "True Confessions and Dying Warnings in Colonial New England," in *Sibley's Heir: A Volume in Memory of Clifford Kenyon Shipton* (Boston: Colonial Society of Massachusetts, 1982), 523–39; Ronald Bosco, "Lectures at the Pillory: The Early American Execution Sermon," *American Quarterly* 30 (1978): 156–76; Patricia Cline Cohen, "Unregulated Youth: Masculinity and Murder in the 1830s' City," *Radical History Review* 52 (1992): 33–52; Patricia Cline Cohen, *The Murder of Helen Jewett: The*

Life and Death of a Prostitute in Nineteenth-Century New York (New York: Alfred
A. Knopf, 1998); Daniel Williams, "'Behold a Tragic Scene Strangely Changed
into a Theater of Mercy': The Structure and Significance of Criminal Conversion
Narratives in Early New England," *American Quarterly* 38 (1986): 827–47; David
Ray Papke, *Framing the Criminal: Crime, Cultural Work, and the Loss of Critical Perspective, 1830–1900* (Hamden, Conn.: Archon Books, 1987); Mike Hepworth and Bryan S. Turner, *Confessions: Studies in Deviance and Religion* (London: Routledge and Kegan Paul, 1982); and Thomas M. McDade, *The Annals of
Murder: A Bibliography of Books and Pamphlets on American Murders from Colonial Times to 1990* (Norman: University of Oklahoma Press, 1961).

8. Halttunen, "Early American Murder Narratives," 78. On the triumph of law
and decline of ministerial authority, see Cohen, *Pillars of Salt*, 28–30; Donald
Scott, *From Office to Profession: The New England Ministry, 1750–1850* (Philadelphia: University of Pennsylvania Press, 1978), 46–49; and Ann Douglas, *The Femi-
nization of American Culture* (New York: Avon Books, 1977), 143–240. On sensationalism and crime literature, see Reynolds, *Beneath the American Renaissance*,
178; and Richard D. Altick, *Deadly Encounters: Two Victorian Sensations* (Philadelphia: University of Pennsylvania Press, 1986). On traffic in crime literature, see
Thomas McDade, "Christian Brown—Wanted for Murder," *New-York Historical
Quarterly* 52 (April 1968): 119–38; and Daniel A. Cohen, "'The Female Marine' in
the Era of Good Feeling: Cross Dressing and the 'Genius' of Nathaniel Coverly Jr.,"
Proceedings of the American Antiquarian Society 103 (October 1994): 359–93.

9. Halttunen, "Early American Murder Narratives," 96, 83, and Halttunen,
Murder Most Foul, 55–59. In *Pillars of Salt*, Cohen adds a detailed chronology to
the history of criminal narratives. Cohen follows murderers from roles as "insid-
ers" to "outsiders" and "alongsiders" and traces the narrative logic of criminal literature from theological condemnation to legal romanticism and literary senti-
mentalism and sensationalism. He is less forthcoming in his explanations for such
changes than is Halttunen, who argues clearly that changes in the ways murder
has been represented can be traced to the spread of Enlightenment assumptions
about human nature and liberal explanations for sin and evil. In her work, Halttunen has contributed to a history of consciousness; Cohen has contributed to a
history of publishing on crime.

10. Louis P. Masur, *Rites of Execution: Capital Punishment and the Transformation of American Culture, 1776–1865* (New York: Oxford University Press,
1989), 95–115. On the United States, see David J. Rothman, *The Discovery of the*

Asylum (Boston: Little, Brown, 1971). Wendy Lesser has written an excellent essay on the theatrical aspects of execution, *Pictures at an Execution: An Inquiry into the Subject of Murder* (Cambridge: Harvard University Press, 1993).

11. Masur writes: "What had been thought too corrupting to witness publicly, even with the attendant safeguards of ministers' sermons and formulized moral messages, could now be experienced privately through a printed medium that reported the execution without emphasizing its didactic purpose." Masur, *Rites of Execution*, 115. According to Richard Brodhead, restraint in punishment became one of tokens of the superiority of the new middle class. See Brodhead, "Sparing the Rod: Discipline and Fiction in Antebellum America," in *Cultures of Letters: Scenes of Reading and Writing in Nineteenth-Century America* (Chicago: University of Chicago Press, 1993), 13–47. On Victorians and public punishment, see Martin J. Weiner, "Market Culture, Passion, and Victorian Punishment," in *The Culture of the Market: Historical Essays*, ed. Thomas L. Haskell and Richard F. Teichgraeber III (Cambridge: Cambridge University Press, 1993), 136–60, esp. 152–54. For discussions of the humanitarian sensibilities that help explain new attitudes toward punishment, see Karen Halttunen, "Humanitarianism and the Pornography of Pain in Anglo-American Culture," *American Historical Review* 100 (April 1995): 303–34; G. J. Barker-Benfield, *The Culture of Sensibility: Sex and Society in Eighteenth-Century Britain* (Chicago: University of Chicago Press, 1992); Norbert Elias, *The Civilizing Process: The History of Manners*, trans. Edmund Jephcott (New York: Blackwell, 1978); Richard Bushman, *The Refinement of America: Persons, Houses, Cities* (New York: Vintage, 1993); and John F. Kasson, *Rudeness and Civility: Manners in Nineteenth-Century Urban America* (New York: Hill and Wang, 1990).

12. *Narrative of the Murder of James Murray and the Circumstances of its Detection with the Trial of John Johnson* (New York: S. King, 1824), iv. The Rev. William Winnis, for example, reported that the first edition of two thousand copies of a confession of a wife-murderer was "exhausted by public demand within a few hours of leaving the press." Winnis, *Life, Trial, Execution and Dying Confession of John Erpenstein: convicted of poisoning his wife . . . written by himself, and translated from the German* (Newark: Printed at the Daily Advertiser Office, 1852), v. William Goodwin, Winnis's colleague in the commerce of confession, also set his sights on a big market, offering his pamphlet on a particularly nasty New Haven man, who drugged, raped, and murdered his little cousin, to wholesalers at "$1 per dozen or $8 per hundred." How well his pamphlet sold, we

do not know. Goodwin, *Death Cell Scenes, or, Notes, sketches and memorandums of the last sixteen days and last night of Henry Leander Foote: together with an account of his execution for the murder of Emily H. Cooper* (New Haven: J. H. Benham, Printer, 1850), 15. Publishers Fay and Burt of Rutland, Vermont, sold copies of *Trial of Stephen and Jesse Boorn for the murder of Russell Colvin: before an adjourned term of the Supreme Court of Vermont* (Rutland: Fay and Burt, 1819) by "the dozen, hundred or thousand" (title page).

13. *A Statement of the Trial of Charles R. S. Boyington: who was indicted for the murder of Nathaniel Frost / written by himself; to which is added a number of fugitive pieces, in verse, also written and composed by him* (Mobile: Printed at the Office of Mercantile Advertiser, 1835), 4, 31.

14. *An Account of the Life and Crimes of Lucian Hall, the Murderer of Mrs. Bacon, of Westfield, Conn.* (New Haven: Printed for the Publisher, 1844), 3. A similar sentiment appears in *The Bowery Tragedy!: the Trial of Joseph Jewell, for the Murder of Luciese Louis Leuba, of the City Watch* (New York: R. H. Elton, 1836), 2.

15. *The Dying Confession of John Lechler, who was convicted for the murder of his wife, Mary Lechler . . . made in the presence of Samuel Carpenter, mayor of the city of Lancaster, and others* (Lancaster: S. C. Stambaugh, 1822), 2. Or as the murderer Richard Johnson wrote, "I have reason to expect the publication and dissemination of numerous trifling, obscene, and untrue statements of my former life, in the form of a Confession, Dying Speeches, &c. To guard against this, and prevent injustice to my memory when dead, is one of the principal reasons that has prevailed upon me to make this publication. It is the only one I shall make, under any circumstances whatever." Johnson, *A Brief Summary of Some of the Principal Incidents, Relative the Life of Ursula Newman: and the Intercourse Subsisting between her and Richard Johnson* (New York: Elam Bliss, 1829), iv.

16. Lechler's sorry history sparked such curiosity and controversy that his execution prompted Pennsylvania lawmakers to contemplate staging their hangings away from the public. See Masur, *Rites of Execution*, 96–97. Some of the condemned endorsed a publication on the steps of the gallows. Peter Matthias "there requested, that the audience should be informed, that the confession he had made (which was in the hands of Mr. Allen) was a true one, and he wanted no alterations made." Rev. Richard Allen held the copyright to the printed confession. *Confession of Peter Matthias, alias Mathews, who was executed on Monday, the 14th of March 1808 for the Murder of Mrs. Sarah Cross; with an Address to the Public, and People of Colour* (Philadelphia: For the Benefit of Bethel Church, 1808), 23.

17. *The Life and Confession of George Swearingen: who was Executed at Cumberland, Allegany County, Md. On the 2d day of October, 1829 for the murder of his wife / written at his solicitation by the Rev. N. R. Little* (Hagers-town, Md.: William D. Bell, 1829), 78. *Life and Confession of Amos Miner, who was tried and convicted before the Hon. Supreme Court of Rhode-Island, at their March term, 1833 of the murder of John Smith, Esq. town-sergeant of Foster, while in performance of his duty in said town, on the 20th day of June, 1832: and by said court sentenced to be hanged July 5, 1833: taken from his own mouth and published by his request* (Providence: n.p., 1833), 3.

18. *Life and Confession of John Tuhi (a youth of 17 years) who was executed at Utica, on Friday July 25, 1817 for the murder of his brother Joseph Tuhi* (New York: John Low, ca. 1817), 11.

19. *An Authentic Statement of the Case and Conduct of Rose Butler: who was tried, convicted, and executed for the Crime of Arson / reviewed and approved by the Rev. John Stanford, M.A., Chaplain to the Public Institutions* (New York: Printed and Sold by Broderick and Ritter, 1819), 13. Pamphlets containing crowd estimates include *The Trial, Sentence, and Confession of Antoine Le Blanc, who was executed at Morristown, N.J. on Friday the 6th Sept. 1833 for the Murder of Mr. Sayre and family* (Morriston, N.Y.: n.p., 1833), title page; *The Authentic Confession of Jesse Strang, executed at Albany, August 24, 1827, for the murder of John Whipple: as made to the Rev. Mr. Lacey, rector of St. Peter's Church, Albany* (New York: E. M. Murden and A. Ming Jr., 1827), 17; *Life and Dying Confession of John Van Alstine, who was tried and found guilty . . . and was executed on the 19th day of March, 1819, for the murder of William Huddleston* (Newburgh: Printed for Benjamin F. Lewis), 12; and *An Account of the Murder of Thomas Williams: the apprehension and correction of Peter Stout, who committed the murder* (Trenton: Printed by Sherman and Mershon, 1803), where "4 or 5,000" people "on foot, on horseback, in carriages and in trees" witnessed the execution (12).

20. Daniel Defoe, *An Essay Upon Literature or an Inquiry into the Antiquity and Original Letters* (London: Thomas Bowles, 1726), quoted in Davis, *Factual Fictions*, 127.

21. *Trial and Confession of John Schild* (Reading, Pa.: n.p., 1813), 10, 11, 31. See also *The Confession of Adam Horn, alias Andrew Hellman, embodying particulars of his life: convicted on the 27th of November, 1843, in Baltimore County Court, of the murder of his wife* (Baltimore: Printed by James Young, 1843), 21–22; *The Trial of David Mayberry, for the murder of Andrew Alger* (Janesville, Wis.:

Baker, Burnett and Hall, 1855); and *Trial and Sentence of John Johnson, for the murder of James Murray, Connected with his Life and Confession* (New York: Joseph Desnoues, 1824), 22. A sympathetic publisher protected one author as follows: "As many exaggerated rumors have prevailed in various sections of the country, since his conviction, relative to his participation in other crimes—and in the commission of other murders—it may not, perhaps, be amiss to remark, in this place, that, when questioned, he pertinaciously denied that he had ever taken the life of a fellow being, except in the horrid instance now disclosed." *Report of the Trial and Conviction of John Earls, for the Murder of his Wife, Catharine Earls, late of Muncy Creek Township, Lycoming County, Pennsylvania* (Williamsport: Wm. F. Packer and A. Cummings Jr., 1836), 188.

22. *Life of Michael Powers, now under Sentence of Death for the Murder of Timothy Kennedy* (Boston: Russell and Gardner, 1820), 5. The "gentleman of the Bar," who produced a brief narrative of the trial of Levi Weeks, confronted "A thousand rumors of a vague and incongruous nature . . . circulated by the tongue of public report." *A Brief Narrative of the Trial for the Bloody and Mysterious Murder of the Unfortunate Young Woman in the Famous Manhattan Well* (New York: David Longworth, 1800), 4.

23. *Life and Confession of Amasa E. Walmsley: who was tried and convicted . . . of the murder of John Burke and Hannah Frank, in Burrillville, R.I.* (Providence: n.p., 1832), 15.

24. Several who published confessions of men who had murdered their wives designated profits for orphan children. See, for example, *Report of the Trial and Conviction of John Earls*, and *Life, Trial, Execution and Dying Confession of John Erpenstein.* The condemned also considered their widows. See, for example, *A Brief Account of the Trial of Winslow Russell for the murder of Michael Bockus: to which is added, the voluntary confession of the said Winslow Russell, and an interesting narrative of his life* (Troy: n.p., 1811), 11; and *Trial and Confession of Robt. McConaghy, the inhuman butcher of six of his own relatives* (Huntington: Published under the direction of a committee for the benefit of the wife and family of the wretched criminal, 1840).

25. *The Life and Confession of John W. Cowan, who murdered his wife and two children in the 10th of October, 1835 in the city of Cincinnati / written by himself, and arranged for the press, and published by James Allen* (Cincinnati: Printed for the Publisher by Kendall and Henry), iii.

26. Recent work on literacy and on the history of the book and printing makes the case that there is no great chasm—either historical or metaphysical—separating oral cultures from cultures of print. Literacy, it is argued, cannot be reduced to a mere technique of decoding; reading is an interpretive art, a cultural practice, embedded in the "structural, political and ideological features of the society in question." Brian V. Street, *Literacy in Theory and Practice* (Cambridge: Cambridge University Press, 1984), 95–125. The "autonomous model" of literacy that Street rejects is most closely associated with the work of Jack Goody. See Jack Goody, ed., *Literacy in Traditional Societies* (Cambridge: Cambridge University Press, 1968). See also Walter J. Ong, *Orality and Literacy: The Technologizing of the Word* (London: Methuen, 1982). On the ideological significance of describing a man as literate, see Peter Linebaugh, "A Little Jubilee? The Literacy of Robert Wedderburn in 1817," in *Protest and Survival: Essays for E. P. Thompson*, ed. John Rule and Robert Malcolmson (New York: New Press, 1993), 174–220.

27. *Report of the Trial and Conviction of John Earls*, 188; *The Last Words of Ebenezer Mason: who was executed at Dedham, October 7, 1802, for the murder of William Pitt Allen, his brother-in-law, on the 18th of May 1802: taken from his own mouth a few hours previous to his execution* (Dedham: Printed and Sold at the Minerva Office, 1802), iv. Confessions signed with marks include *Life and Confession of Amasa E. Walmsley*; *Confession of John Joyce, alias Davis* (Philadelphia: For the Benefit of Bethel Church, 1808); and *A Short Account of the Life of Cyrus Emlay, a black man, who was convicted of robbery, arson and murder* (Burlington: S. C. Ustick, 1810).

28. *The Life and Confession of Charles O'Donnel, who was executed at Morgantown, June 19, 1797* (Lancaster, Pa.: W. and R. Dickson, 1798), 4. *The Trial and Life and Confession of John F. Van Patten, who was indicted, tried, and convicted of the murder of Mrs. Maria Schermerhorn, on the 4th of October last, and sentenced to be executed on the 25th of February, 1825* (New York: Christian Brown, 1825), 7–8. See also *Trial of Robert McConaghy, together with his confession and execution: who murdered his six relatives* (Philadelphia: n.p., 1840), 20.

29. *The Life and Confession of John W. Cowan*, iii, 22.

30. Michel Foucault and his students excavated a particularly compelling case of a murderer made writer. Michel Foucault, ed., *I, Pierre Rivière, having slaughtered my mother, my sister, and my brother: A case of parricide in the 19th century*, trans. Frank Jellinek (1973; reprint, Lincoln: University of Nebraska Press, 1982),

204–5. In many cases, literacy was a key descriptive feature of convicts. For example, the compiler of *The Trial of Augostino Rabello for the murder of Ferris Beardsley: at New Preston, Con. [sic] April 27, 1835* (Litchfield: Printed for Birdsay Gibbs, 1835) concludes his pamphlet, "He is rather short, and writes a good hand" (48).

31. On occasion, illiterates were called upon to verify printed tales. In 1872, Fanny Kelly published "a plain unvarnished narrative" of her five months of captivity among the Ogalalla Sioux, hoping thereby to encourage the government to reimburse her for property lost during her capture. With a plan to settle "among the golden hills of Idaho," she and her companions had headed across the Kansas plains in the summer of 1864, where they encountered a band of Sioux, who stripped them of their provisions, killed several of the party's members, and held Mrs. Kelly for ransom. She was released at Fort Sully in December 1864.

Kelly's was a "late" captivity narrative, published at a time when most such accounts appeared as sensational fiction, and to have her story be read as true, Kelly needed the corroboration of the illiterate Sioux who had held her captive. Illiteracy, in this context, seemed to ensure veracity. She concluded her story dramatically with a "CERTIFICATE OF INDIAN CHIEFS." The document, which appeared over the marks of sixteen "chiefs and warriors," confessed to the destruction of Kelly's property and expressed the wish that she be compensated "out of any moneys now due our nation." The marks of the chiefs and warriors were themselves witnessed by several interpreters, one of whom had his own mark witnessed by an army officer. Kelly, *Narrative of My Captivity among the Sioux Indians* (Hartford: Mutual Publishing Company, 1872), 270–73.

32. *Life and Confession of John Washburn: (partner of Lovett, Jones &c,) the Great Robber and Murderer: who was executed for the murder of Wm. Beaver, Cincinnati, Ohio, on the 6th of January, 1837, and who was also concerned in the murder of thirty different individuals / dictated by himself and written by a fellow prisoner* (Philadelphia: n.p., 1837), title page, 8, 10, 15. According to literary scholar Mark Seltzer, serial killing became a "career option" at the turn of the twentieth century. Seltzer, *Serial Killers: Death and Life in America's Wound Culture* (New York: Routledge, 1998), [1].

33. *Life and Confession of John Washburn*, 23.

34. Cohen, *Pillars of Salt*, 22.

35. Confession of Peter Matthias, 15–21. *The Life and Confession of Miner Babcock: who was executed at Norwich, Connecticut, June 6th, 1816, for the murder of London, a blackman / taken by the County Gaoler, at his request* (New London:

Printed by Samuel Green for the Proprietor of the Copy-Right, 1816), 4–8. James Hamilton also described his life before the War of 1812 by listing jobs and wages. *The Life and Dying Confessions of James Hamilton: executed for the murder of Major Benjamin Birdsall, Nov. 6, 1818: at Albany* (New York: Printed and sold at the printing-office, over the bookstore, corner of Wall and Broad streets, 1818), 5–6. Lewis Wilber ordered his life by listing his earnings as a laborer and boat-hand on the Erie Canal. *Dying Confession of Lewis Wilber, who was executed October 3, 1839 . . . for the murder of Robert Barber; including a sketch of his life and character* (Morrisville, [N.Y.]: Printed at the Office of the *Madison Observer*, 1839).

36. The editor of the confession of Jereboam O. Beauchamp also admitted to expurgation. "I do certify that the foregoing Narative [*sic*], is a true copy taken from, and printed from the original manuscript, written by J. O. Beauchamp, as presented to me by Mr. G. S. Hammond; some trifling and unimportant alterations excepted—some hard expressions against individuals were softened or expunged." *The Confession of Jereboam Beauchamp / (written by himself) who was executed at Frankfort, Ky. for the murder of Solomon P. Sharp* (Frankfort, Ky.: H. T. Goodsell, 1854), 97. The confession of Hannah Kinney appeared "almost verbatim" from the "pen of the author." *A Review of the Principal Events of the Last Ten Years in the Life of Mrs. Hannah Kinney: together with some comments upon the late trial / written by herself* (Boston: J. N. Bradley and Co., 1841), title page. See also *The Trial of Charles Stevens, for the Murder of Charles Henry C. Stevens: before the Supreme Court at York, April term, 1823* (Kennebunk: Printed by James K. Remich, 1823), [3]; and *A Narrative of the Life and Conversion of Alexander White: who was executed at Cambridge, November 18, 1784, for the murder of a captain White, at sea* (Boston: Powers and Willis, 1784), 5–6.

37. "The compiler" put out several versions of Miner's tale. *Trial, Life and Confession of Amos Miner, who was executed in Friday, Dec. 27, 1833, for the murder of John Smith, Esq., late town-sergeant of Foster: with his speech under the gallows: also, the trial and sentence of Charles Brown for highway robbery* (Providence: Published by Request, 1834), 7. Miner's confession was also reprinted in the early anthology *Confessions, Trials and Biographical Sketches of the Most Cold Blooded Murderers who have been executed in this Country* (Hartford: S. Andrus and Son, 1844 [1837]), 168–87.

38. On the growth of national markets for information, see Richard D. Brown, *Knowledge Is Power: The Diffusion of Information in Early America, 1700–1865* (New York: Oxford University Press, 1989), 3–15, 268–96.

39. *Narrative of the Murder of James Murray*, iii–iv. In editing Harriet Jacob's manuscript, Lydia Maria Child confessed that she collected the most gruesome scenes into a chapter she called "Neighboring Planters," "[i]n order that those who shrink from 'supping upon horrors' might omit them." The quotation from Child appears in Jean Fagan Yellin's introduction to Harriet Jacobs, *Incidents in the Life of a Slave Girl* (Cambridge: Harvard University Press, 1987), xxii.

40. Daniel Cohen explores contentions about truth in *Pillars of Salt*, 249–50. *The Address of Abraham Johnstone, a Black Man,: who was hanged at Woodbury, in the county of Glocester, and state of New Jersey* (Philadelphia: n.p., 1797), 5. *Life of Samuel Green: executed at Boston, April 25, 1822, for the murder of Billy Williams, a fellow convict with Green in state prison / written by himself* (Boston: David Felt, 1822), 47. See also *Life and Confession of Amos Miner*, 3; and "Narrative of the life of Thomas Qua who was executed at Salem, (N.Y.) August 12th, 1808, for the murder of his wife Margaret Qua," in *The trial of Rufus Hill, for the murder of Mary Sisson, May 30th, 1808* (New York: n.p., 1808).

41. On connections between bodily displays and assertions of truth, see Elaine Scarry, *The Body in Pain: The Making and Unmaking of the World* (New York: Oxford University Press, 1985), 125. See also Foucault, *Discipline and Punish*, 37–39, 66.

42. References to mouth, tongue, and lips have long appeared in the printed versions of stories told by illiterates. See Natalie Zemon Davis, *Fiction in the Archives: Pardon Tales and Their Tellers in Sixteenth-Century France* (Stanford: Stanford University Press, 1987), 17. Such references also appear in Elijah Waterman, *A Sermon Preached at Windham, November 29th, 1803, being the day of execution of Caleb Adams, for the murder of Oliver Woodworth* (Windham: Printed by John Byrne, 1803), 23; *A Short Narrative of the Life and Execution of Cornelius Jones: who suffered death November 15th, 1817, at Bethan[y], Wayne County, for the murder of his step-father Mr. Isaac Roswell* ([Wilkes-Barre, 1817?]), 6; *The Last Words of Ebenezer Mason*; *Life and Confession of Amos Miner*; and *The Trial and a Sketch of the Life of Oliver Watkins, now under sentence of death in Brooklin jail, for the murder of his wife, March 22, 1829; the facts of his history obtained in part from his own mouth and partly from the testimony of others* (Providence: H. H. Brown, Printer, 1830).

43. *Confession of Winslow Curtis alias Sylvester Colson: convicted of the murder on the high seas, of Edward Selfridge, captain of the schooner* Fairy *of Boston* (Boston: Dutton and Wentworth, 1827), back cover. Murderer David How concludes, "I must know close my narrative, and sign it with a trembling hand,

which is soon to become cold in death." A merchant and a minister witnessed his signing. *Life and Confession of David D. How, who was executed at Angelica, Alleghany County, N. Y. On Friday, March 18, 1824, for the murder of Othello Church* (New York [State]: n.p., 1824), 12.

44. *A Full and Particular Narrative of the Life, Character and Conduct of John Banks, a native of Nieuport, in Austrian Flanders, who was executed on the 11th day of July, 1086 [sic], for the willful murder of his wife Margaret Banks; to which is prefixed, a correct copy of his trial and condemnation, with an appendix, containing his confession, voluntarily made by himself, in the presence of the editor, attended by one of the keepers, who, (if required,) will testify to its truth* (New York: Printed for the Proprietor, 1807).

45. *The Address of Abraham Johnstone*, [2]; *Trial, Sentence, and Confession of Jesse Strang for the Murder of John Whipple* (New York: C. Brown, 1827), 23.

46. The other illustrations depict the author and his drunken friends and a burning building. *A Voice from the Leverett Street Prison, or The Life, Trial, and Confession of Simeon L. Crockett, who was executed for arson, March 16, 1836* (Boston: Society for the Promotion of Temperance, 1836), 19.

47. *The Lives and Confessions of James M'Gowan & James Jameson, who were executed at Harrisburgh, for the murder and robbery of Mr. Jacob Eshelman on the night of the 28th August, 1806* (Harrisburgh: Printed by John Wyeth, 1807), 5.

48. *The Life and Confession of George Swearingen*, 10. See also *An Account of the Apprehension, Trial, Conviction and Condemnation of Manuel Philip Garcia and Jose Demas Garcia Castellano . . . for a most horrid murder . . . on Peter Lagoardette* (Norfolk: C. Hall, 1821); and Davis, *Factual Fictions*, 114.

49. *S. P. Hull's report of the Trial and Conviction of Antoine Le Blanc for the murder of the Sayre family: at Morristown, N.J. on the night of the 11th of May, 1833: with the confession, as given to Mr. A. Boisaubin, the interpreter* (New York: Lewis Nichols, Printer, 1833), title page, 20. Editor Hull referred to *Mutiny and Murder: Confession of Charles Gibbs, a native of Rhode Island, who with Thomas Wansley was doomed to be hung in New York on the 22d of April last, for the murder of the captain and mate of the brig Vineyard, on her passage from New Orleans to Philadelphia, in November 1830* (Providence: Israel Smith, 1831); *Confessions of Two Malefactors, Teller and Reynolds: who were executed at Hartford, Connecticut, on the sixth of September, 1833, for the murder of Ezra Hoskins at the Connecticut State Prison: containing an account of their numerous robberies,*

burglaries, &c. (Hartford: Hanmer and Comstock, Printers, 1833); and *The Life and Confession of George Swearingen.*

50. Stenographers, too, used confessions to advertise their skills. A Mr. M. T. C. Gould recorded *The Trial of Joseph Mason, for the killing of William Farrel* (Onondaga, N.Y.: L. H. Redfield, 1820); *Trial of Medad M'Kay, for the murder of his wife* (Albany: Websters and Skinners, 1821); *Trials of Twenty Four Journeymen Tailors* (Philadelphia: n.p., 1827); and *Trial of John F. Bradee, in the United States District Court for Western Pennsylvania* (Pittsburgh: R. G. Berford, 1841).

51. For discussions of the role of religious publication and Protestant ministers in the spread of popular print culture, see R. Laurence Moore, *Selling God: American Religion in the Market Place of Culture* (New York: Oxford University Press, 1994); and David Paul Nord, "The Evangelical Origins of Mass Media in America, 1815–1835," *Journalism Monographs* 88 (May 1984).

52. Donald Scott found that although the spread of print culture might have brought Americans into a "common field of discourse," all that was integrative—the press, national political parties, and Evangelical Christianity—was also divisive. Intolerance of Catholics grew, he suggests, as people were recruited into evangelical sects. Scott, "Print and the Public Lecture System, 1840–1860," in *Printing and Society in Early America*, ed. William Joyce, et al. (Worcester, Mass.: American Antiquarian Society, 1983), 278–99.

53. *A Transcript of the Writings of Joseph J. Sager, while confined in the jail at Augusta, Me.: who was tried for the murder of his wife before the Supreme Court, Oct. Term, 1834: condemned and executed January 2, 1835* (Augusta: n.p., 1835), 14; *The Life of Cornelius Wilhelms one of the Braganza pirates, now under sentence of death: containing every important event in his life, and the full account of the diabolical murder of Capt. Turley / written from conversations with the prisoner* (New York: R. E. Elton, 1839), 15.

54. *Trial and Execution of Thomas Barrett: who first committed a rape on the person of Mrs. Houghton of Lunenburg . . . and then foully murdered her* (Boston: Skinner and Blanchard, 1845), 24. Other Irishmen who refused to confess to publishers included the wife-beater Donnelly (*A Sketch of the Trial of Edward Donally [sic] at Carlisle . . . for the murder of his wife* [Carlisle: From the Press of A. Loudon, 1808], 40) and the cousin-murderer Powers, whose confidant wrote, "It may be asked, why does not Powers come out with a full disclosure of the murder of Kennedy? What possible advantage could be derived from such a

confession? It is always bad policy, to urge men to confess what is plainly proved." *Life of Michael Powers*, 14. A publisher assumed that Samuel Perry refused to confess because he had "retained his early papal notions to the last." See *The Trial of Samuel Perry who murdered his wife on June 1, 1826: with a sketch of his life and death / by a neighbor* (Utica: Printed by William Williams, 1826), 14. On the difficulty of choosing to remain silent in the face of compulsion to confess, see Hepworth and Turner, *Confessions*, 12–14, 141.

55. *Life, Trial, Execution and Dying Confession of John Erpenstein*, 14.

56. "John Stanford Diary," New-York Historical Society, 12. Most of the diary was reprinted in Charles G. Sommers, *Memoir of the Rev. John Stanford, D.D. Late Chaplain to the Humane and Criminal Institutions in the City of New York* (New York: n.p., 1835). See also "Marriages Performed in New York City, 1794–1830 by Rev. John Stanford," *New-York Historical Society Quarterly Bulletin* 21 (June–October 1937): 23–30. For Stanford's many roles in New York philanthropic organizations, see Carroll Smith Rosenberg, *Religion and the Rise of the American City: The New York City Mission Movement, 1812–1870* (Ithaca: Cornell University Press, 1971), 53, 66, 77–79.

57. "John Stanford Diary," 28. For Stanford's connection with publishers, see McDade, "Christian Brown—Wanted for Murder," 119–38.

58. *Last Dying Words and Confession of James Reynolds, for the Murder of Captain Wm. West: together with his letters and correspondence, to his wife and other relations as written by himself* (New York: C. Brown, 1825), 11. The murder pamphlets Stanford had a hand in producing include *Trial, Conviction, Sentence and Only True Copy of the Confession of Catharine Cashiere, made to the Rev. John Stanford A.M. Chaplain to the Public Institutions, of the City of New York* (New York: Christian Brown, 1829); *The Commutation of the Punishment of William Miller, who was to be executed Jan. 26, 1827: with the notes of the Rev. John Stanford, who attended him during his confinement in the City Prison* (New York: Christian Brown, 1828); *An Authentic Statement of the Case and Conduct of Rose Butler*; *The Confessions of Isaac Fraser & George Vanderpool, under sentence of death for arson: with some account of Thomas Burke, for the murder of his wife* (New York: Elias Gould, 1816); and *A True Account of the Confessions and Contra Confessions of John Johnson: who was executed on Friday, the 2d of April, for the murder of James Murray: taken during his confinement, by the Rev. John Stanford* (New York: C. Brown and R. Tyrell, 1824).

59. New York *Spectator*, 23 November 1823, p. 1; 24 November 1823, p. 1.

60. *Trial and Sentence of John Johnson, for the Murder of James Murray*, 32–34. As murders go, Murray's death was not really sensational, but it took place in a lodging house, where travelers should expect to be safe. Reporters hoped that Johnson's death would serve as an example to "sailor landlords." Writing for his *National Advocate*, Thomas Snowden condemned Johnson for killing a man who had "every natural and moral claim to his protection." Snowden, "Execution of Johnson," *National Advocate*, 3 April 1824, p. 1.

61. *A True Account of the Confessions, and Contra Confessions*, 15. In addition to the Stanford and Brown publication on Johnson, his story appeared in *Complete Account of the Horrid Murder of James Murray!* (New York: n.p., 1823); *The Life and Confession of John Johnson, the murderer of James Murray: together with some particulars of his family, not generally known* (New York: Brown and Tyrell, 1824); *Narrative of the Murder of James Murray, and the circumstances of its detection with the trial of John Johnson* (New York: S. King, 1824); *Trial and Sentence of John Johnson, for the Murder of James Murray* (New York: Joseph Desnoues, 1824); and *The Trial of John Johnson for the murder of James Murray: before the court of Oyer & Terminer at New York* (Trenton: Francis S. Wiggins, 1824).

62. *Trial and Sentence of John Johnson, for the Murder of James Murray*, 31.

63. Ibid., title page.

64. *A True Account of the Confessions, and Contra Confessions*, 23–24; "Execution of Johnson," *New York Spectator*, 6 April 1824, p. 1.

65. *Authentic Narrative of the Murder of Mrs. Rademacher: with splendid illustrations, drawn and engraved especially for this work* (Philadelphia: G. B. Zeiber, 1848), 6–7. Here I draw on Karen Halttunen's argument that sensational pamphlets encouraged in readers a "horror-response . . . that would replicate the horror response of those who first came upon the scene of the crime." Halttunen, "Early American Murder Narratives," 89, and Halttunen, *Murder Most Foul*, 80–81.

CHAPTER THREE

1. Minutes of the Executive Committee of the American Anti-Slavery Society, 4 January 1838, p. 21, Papers of the American Anti-Slavery Society, Boston Public Library, Boston, Massachusetts.

2. "Correspondence between the Hon. F. H. Elmore and James G. Birney," *The Anti-Slavery Examiner* (New York: American Anti-Slavery Society, 1838), 19–20. On publication as part of abolitionist strategy, see Janet Wilson, "The Early Anti-Slavery Propaganda," *More Books: The Bulletin of the Boston Public Library* 19 (November 1944): 343–60; 19 (December 1944): 393–405; and 20 (February 1945): 51–67.

3. *Narrative of James Williams, an American Slave; who was for several years a driver on a cotton plantation in Alabama* (New York: American Anti-Slavery Society, 1838), 100, iv. On Williams and his story, see Marion Wilson Starling, *The Slave Narrative: Its Place in American History* (Washington, D.C.: Howard University Press, 1988), 228–33; and William L. Andrews, *To Tell a Free Story: The First Century of Afro-American Autobiography, 1760–1865* (Urbana: University of Illinois Press, 1988), 87–90. Patrick Reason worked as an engraver in New York in the 1830s and 1840s. With the support of antislavery groups, he published portraits of DeWitt Clinton, Granville Sharp, Peter Wheeler, and Henry Bibb. On his career, see James A. Porter, *Modern Negro Art* (New York: Arno Press, 1969), 35–38.

4. *Narrative of James Williams*, ix, x–xvi, xvii. As Kenneth S. Greenberg argues, slaveholders and abolitionists read scars differently. To slaveholders, scars were a sign of a slave's bad character; to abolitionists, they were a sign of a master's bad character. "The dispute," he continues, "involved not simply a difference of interpretation over the sign of the scar but also a different conception of the nature of reading signs. The abolitionists read for meaning beneath and beyond the surface. They found it important to imagine the scene behind the scar, and they recreated it endless times in word and woodcut. But men of honor did not linger over the scene that gave rise to the scar; it was irrelevant." Greenberg, *Honor and Slavery: Lies, Duels, Masks, Dressing as Women, Gifts, Strangers, Humanitarianism, Death, Slave Rebellions, The Proslavery Argument, Baseball, Hunting, Gambling in the Old South* (Princeton: Princeton University Press, 1997), 15.

5. *Narrative of James Williams*, xix–xx, xvii–xviii. *The Liberator*, 27 July 1838, p. 120. Advertisements for the narrative, which Isaac Knapp, the publisher of *The Liberator*, was selling for eighteen and three-quarters cents, appeared in the antislavery press throughout the spring and summer of 1838.

6. Some scholars (most notably Elizabeth Clark) have seen portraits of suffering as the occasion for fugitives from slavery to put their full humanity on display. See E. Clark, "'The Sacred Rights of the Weak': Pain, Sympathy, and the Culture of Individual Rights in Antebellum America," *Journal of American History* 82

(September 1995): 463–93. See also Philip Fisher, *Hard Facts: Setting and Form in the American Novel* (New York: Oxford University Press, 1985), 92–108. Clark argues that, however limiting appeals to suffering may have become, in the middle years of the nineteenth century, sentimental appeals provided a basis for claims to individual rights. In contrast, Saidiya V. Hartman argues that "rather than bespeaking the mutuality of social relations or the expressive and affective capacities of the subject, sentiment, enjoyment, affinity, will, and desire facilitated subjugation, domination, and terror precisely by preying upon the flesh, the heart, and the soul." Hartman, *Scenes of Subjection: Terror, Slavery, and Self-Making in Nineteenth-Century America* (New York: Oxford University Press, 1997), 5.

7. *Narrative of James Williams*, 89, 95–98.

8. Ibid., 101, 103.

9. According to the sociologist Michael Schudson, it was in the late 1830s that newspaper reporters worked out the rules of objectivity. Schudson writes, "Objectivity, in this sense, means that a person's statements about the world can be trusted if they are submitted to established rules deemed legitimate by a professional community. Facts here are not aspects of the world, but consensually validated statements about it." *Discovering the News: A Social History of American Newspapers* (New York: Basic Books, 1978), 7, 12–60.

10. Events, in this reading, thus receive significance from their end point. See David Carr's discussion of the work of Wilhelm Dilthey, in *Time, Narrative, and History* (Bloomington: Indiana University Press, 1986), 78.

11. Eric Foner, "The Meaning of Freedom in the Age of Emancipation," *Journal of American History* 81 (September 1994): 444. According to Daniel Walker Howe, the model self of early-nineteenth-century America was based on an ideal of "balanced character." Such equilibrium, first the prerogative of elite males, gradually extended to poor men, women, and people of color. Howe, *Making the American Self: Jonathan Edwards to Abraham Lincoln* (Cambridge: Harvard University Press, 1997), 8.

12. For the discussion that follows I am indebted to the work of William L. Andrews. I return here to issues he addresses in "The Performance of Slave Narrative in the 1840s," the central chapter of *To Tell a Free Story*. My intent is to weave the controversies over the reliability of former slaves and the nature of the stories they told into a pattern that differs from the literary and philosophical analysis offered by Andrews. I also rely on John Sekora, "Black Message/White Envelope: Genre, Authenticity, and Authority in the Antebellum Slave Narra-

tive," *Callaloo* 10 (summer 1987): 482–515; and Robert Stepto, "Narration, Authentication, and Authorial Control in Frederick Douglass' *Narrative* of 1845," in *African American Autobiography: A Collection of Critical Essays*, ed. William L. Andrews (Englewood Cliffs: Prentice Hall, 1993), 26–37.

13. *The Life of William Grimes, the runaway slave, written by himself* (New York: By the Author, 1825), iii.

14. *The Life of William Grimes the Runaway Slave, brought down to the present time / Written by Himself* (New Haven: Published by the Author, 1855), 58–59, 90.

15. Grimes described himself as a patriarch—the father of eighteen children who had scattered around the world. One son had gone off to seek gold in Australia, and Grimes's wife was in the gold fields in California. *Life of William Grimes* (1855), 84, 89. On the uses of celebrity for former slaves, see Nell Irvin Painter, "Representing Truth: Sojourner Truth's Knowing and Becoming Known," *Journal of American History* 81 (September 1994): 470–71.

16. *Life of William Grimes* (1825), 68. On Grimes, see Starling, *Slave Narrative*, 90–92; Andrews, *To Tell a Free Story*, 77–81; and Charles H. Nichols Jr., "The Case of William Grimes, the Runaway Slave," *William and Mary Quarterly* 8 (October 1951): 552–60.

17. *The Liberator*, 13 May 1838, p. 78; Andrews, *To Tell a Free Story*, 87. The passage from the *Herald of Freedom* appears in Starling, *Slave Narrative*, 115.

18. Abolitionists knew, when they sent publications to the South, that they risked strong responses from slaveholders. In 1835, a mob had stormed the post offices in South Carolina and burned abolitionist pamphlets. For a good discussion of the U.S. mail and the violence incited by antislavery propaganda, see Richard John, *Spreading the News: The American Postal System from Franklin to Morse* (Cambridge: Harvard University Press, 1995).

19. The circulation of accusation and counteraccusation was complicated. J. B. Rittenhouse published his charges in the Alabama *Beacon*, 10 May 1838. They were reprinted as a challenge to James Birney in the New York *Commercial Advertiser*, and then reprinted again in the Ohio abolitionist paper, *The Philanthropist*, 30 October 1838. The passages I use here are from *The Philanthropist*.

20. On Murrell, see Augustus Q. Walton [Virgil A. Stewart], *A History of the Detection, Conviction, Life and Designs of John A. Murel, the Great Western Land Pirate, together with his System of Villainy, and Plan of Exciting a Negro rebellion*

(Cincinnati: n.p., 1835); H. R. Howard, ed., *The History of Virgil A. Stewart, and his Adventure Capturing and Exposing the Great "Western Land Pirate" and His Gang in Connexion with the Evidence* (New York: n.p., 1836). See also Ann Fabian, *Card Sharps, Dream Books, and Bucket Shops: Gambling in Nineteenth-Century America* (Ithaca: Cornell University Press, 1990), 28–29; and Greenberg, *Honor and Slavery*, 143–44.

21. See Thomas R. R. Cobb, *An Inquiry into the Law of Negro Slavery in the United States of America* (Philadelphia: T. and J. W. Johnson and Co., 1858), 233. Some among the abolitionists clearly shared the slaveholders' assumptions about the honesty of slaves. In 1838, in a letter to the *Union Herald*, Gerrit Smith confessed, "Simple-hearted and truthful as these fugitives appeared to be, you must recollect that the slave, as a general thing, is a liar, as well as a drunkard and a thief." Smith quoted in Andrews, *To Tell a Free Story*, 3.

22. On decisions governing testimony by slaves, see Cobb, *An Inquiry into the Law of Negro Slavery*, 226–46; and Thomas D. Morris, *Slavery and Law, 1619–1860* (Chapel Hill: University of North Carolina Press, 1996), 229–45. The fugitive slave John Thompson described the punishments designed to keep slaves from lying under oath. A white man, trying to find stolen wheat, sought the testimony of slaves. "'Do you know the consequences of taking a false oath?'" he asked Thompson. "'I shall go to hell,' I answered. 'Yes, and that is not all,' he said, 'you will have your ears cropped.'" *The Life of John Thompson, a Fugitive Slave; containing His History of Twenty-Five Years in Bondage, and His Providential Escape; Written by Himself* (Worcester: n.p., 1856), 70. See also the section entitled "Exclusion from all Participation in the Administration of Justice," in *The Anti-Slavery Examiner on the Condition of the Free People of Color in the United States* (New York: American Anti-Slavery Society, 1839), 12. The question of whether to lie or to tell the truth was complicated for slaves by the fact that they could be punished for refusing to account for themselves when asked. A slave stopped and questioned by a white person had to say something.

23. Greenberg, *Honor and Slavery*, 12. The most useful discussion of the social authority of gentlemen and the construction of truth is found in Steven Shapin, *A Social History of Truth: Civility and Science in Seventeenth-Century England* (Chicago: University of Chicago Press, 1994), 65–125. On the importance of truth to gentlemen of honor, see Bertram Wyatt-Brown, *Southern Honor: Ethics and Behavior in the Old South* (New York: Oxford University Press, 1982); and Julian Pitt-Rivers, "Honor," in *International Encyclopedia of the Social Sci-*

ences, ed. David L. Sills (New York: Macmillan and The Free Press, 1968), 6: 503 – 11. On the lies of slaves as a form of resistance, see Eugene D. Genovese, *Roll, Jordon, Roll: The World the Slaves Made* (New York: Random House, 1976), 609 – 12; and Orlando Patterson, *Slavery and Social Death: A Comparative Study* (Cambridge: Harvard University Press, 1982), 96.

24. We can, perhaps, discern a trace of such concerns in Jean Fagan Yellin's edition of Harriet A. Jacobs, *Incidents in the Life of a Slave Girl* (Cambridge: Harvard University Press, 1987), xiii–xxxiv. Yellin writes her introduction to answer two questions: Did Jacobs write the story, and did the story happen as she wrote it? Yellin insists that the value of the narrative depends on an affirmative answer to both questions. For a fascinating discussion of Jacobs's possible use of artful lies, see Jacqueline Goldsby, "'I disguised my hand': Writing Versions of the Truth in Harriet Jacobs, *Incidents in the Life of a Slave Girl* and John Jacobs, *A True Tale of Slavery*," in *Harriet Jacobs and Incidents in the Life of a Slave Girl: New Critical Essays*, ed. Deborah M. Garfield and Rafia Zafar (Cambridge: Cambridge University Press, 1996), 11 – 43.

25. "Narrative of James Williams," *The Liberator*, 28 September 1838, p. 153.

26. Minutes of the Executive Committee of the American Anti-Slavery Society, 16 August 1838, p. 92; 18 October 1838, pp. 99, 101. The full report, signed by Birney and Tappan, was published in *The Emancipator* and reprinted in *The Liberator*, 2 November 1838.

27. James G. Birney, "James Williams," *The Philanthropist*, 6 November 1838.

28. Ibid.

29. The phrase comes from literary scholar Wai-chee Dimock, who reads a "nominating frenzy" at the opening of Melville's *Typee* as "the simplest and clearest sign of creativity." Dimock, *Empire for Liberty: Melville and the Poetics of Individualism* (Princeton: Princeton University Press, 1989), 49.

30. *Slavery in the United States: A Narrative of the Life and Adventures of Charles Ball, a Black Man* (Lewistown, Pa.: n.p., 1836), in *Recollections of the Early Republic: Selected Autobiographies*, ed. Joyce Appleby (Boston: Northeastern University Press, 1997), 109.

31. Levi Coffin, *Reminiscences of Levi Coffin, the Reputed President of the Underground Railroad* (London: Sampson, Low, Marston, Searles, and Rivington, 1879), 114.

32. Karen Sánchez-Eppler, *Touching Liberty: Abolition, Feminism, and the Politics of the Body* (Berkeley: University of California, 1993), 136.

33. "Lydia Maria Child and D. L. Child to Angelina and Theodore Weld, December 26, 1838," in *Letters of Theodore Dwight Weld, Angelina Grimké Weld and Sarah Grimké, 1822–1844*, ed. Gilbert H. Barnes and Dwight L. Dumond (New York: D. Appleton-Century Company, 1934), 2: 732; "Lydia Maria Child to Weld, December 29, 1838," in *Letters of Weld, Weld, and Grimké*, 2: 736.

34. E. Clark, "'The Sacred Rights of the Weak,'" 467, 477.

35. After the Williams debacle, abolitionists were more careful to check the authenticity of accounts they published, and according to John Blassingame, there "were no comparable exposés during the antebellum period." John W. Blassingame, "Critical Essay on Sources," in *The Slave Community: Plantation Life in the Antebellum South* (1972; reprint, New York: Oxford University Press, 1979), 372. For an account of a "colored imposter" operating in Worcester, Massachusetts, see *The National Anti-Slavery Standard*, 31 October 1850, p. 91. Frederick Douglass offered particular advice on detecting counterfeit fugitives: "So uniformly are good manners enforced among slaves, that I can easily detect a 'bogus' fugitive by his manners." Douglass, *My Bondage and My Freedom* (1855; reprint, Urbana: University of Illinois, 1987), 49. See also Harriet E. Wilson's description of one man who admitted that his "illiterate harangues were humbugs for hungry abolitionists." To satisfy abolitionist hunger was surely to ease his own. Wilson, *Our Nig; or, Sketches from the Life of a Free Black, in a Two-Story House, North. Showing that Slavery's Shadows Fall Even There* (1859; reprint, with an introduction and notes by Henry Louis Gates Jr., New York: Vintage Books, 1983), 128.

36. In his compilation of atrocities, *American Slavery as It Is: Testimony of a Thousand Witnesses* (New York: American Anti-Slavery Society, 1839), Theodore Weld likewise impaneled readers as a jury "to try a plain case and bring in an honest verdict." "The question at issue is not one of law, but of fact—'What is the actual condition of the slaves in the United States?'" (7).

37. On disputes within the antislavery movement, see Bertram Wyatt-Brown, *Lewis Tappan and the Evangelical War against Slavery* (Cleveland: Case Western Reserve University Press, 1969), 186–99; Lawrence J. Friedman, *Gregarious Saints: Self and Community in American Abolition, 1830–1870* (Cambridge: Cambridge University Press, 1982), 175–89; Ronald Walters, *The Antislavery Appeal: American Abolitionism after 1830* (1978; reprint, New York: W. W. Norton, 1984), 6–9; Robert H. Abzug, *Cosmos Crumbling: American Reform and the Religious Imagination* (New York: Oxford University Press, 1984), 161; and John L. Thomas, *The Liberator William Lloyd Garrison: A Biography* (Boston: Little, Brown, 1963), 250–270.

38. Dwight L. Dumond, ed., *Letters of James Gillespie Birney, 1831–1857* (Gloucester, Mass.: Peter Smith, 1966), 1: 408. "Correspondence between the Hon. F. H. Elmore and James G. Birney," 20.

39. Wyatt-Brown, *Lewis Tappan*, 227, 235. On the development of the Mercantile Agency, see 226–38.

40. William Taylor, *Cavalier and Yankee: The Old South and American National Character* (New York: Harper and Row, 1961); and Greenberg, *Honor and Slavery*, 11. Henry Watson described the sharp practices of slave markets. "Just before the doors are opened, it is usual for the keeper to grease the mouths of the slaves, so as to make it appear that they are well and hearty, and have just done eating fat meat; though they seldom, if ever, while in custody of the keeper taste a morsel of meat of any kind." *The Narrative of Henry Watson, a fugitive slave* (Boston: Bela March, 1848), 12. See also *Slave Life in Georgia: A Narrative of the Life, Sufferings, and Escape of John Brown, a Fugitive Slave, Now in England,* ed. L. A. Chamerovzow (London: W. M. Watts, 1855), 112–188; and Hartman, *Scenes of Subjection*, 39.

41. Henry Sumner Maine, *Ancient Law: Its Connection with the Early History of Society and Its Relation to Modern Ideas* (1861; reprint, Boston: Beacon Press, 1963), 295–96. Amy Dru Stanley has explored the contradictions in the application of contract. Stanley, *From Bondage to Contract: Wage Labor, Marriage, and the Market in the Age of Slave Emancipation* (Cambridge: Cambridge University Press, 1998). Or as Morton Horwitz has written,

> The contractarian ideology above all expressed a market conception of legal relations. Wages were the carefully calibrated instrument by which supposedly equal parties would bargain to arrive at the proper "mix" of risk and wages. In such a world the old ideal of legal relations shaped by a normative standard of substantive justice could scarcely coexist. Since the only measure of justice was the parties' own agreement, all preexisting legal duties were inevitably subordinated to the contract relation.

Horwitz, *The Transformation of American Law, 1780–1860* (Cambridge: Harvard University Press, 1977), 209.

42. Brook Thomas, *American Literary Realism and the Failed Promise of Contract* (Berkeley: University of California Press, 1997), 3. See also Walter Benn Michaels, "The Phenomenology of Contract," in *The Gold Standard and the Logic of Naturalism* (Berkeley: University of California Press, 1987), 115–36.

43. Hartman, *Scenes of Subjection*, 6.

44. The phrase "the quasi-freedom of inequality" is Eric Foner's. Foner, "The Meaning of Freedom," 452.

45. Dumond, *Letters of James Gillespie Birney*, 1: 502. "Authentic Narrative of James Williams, an American Slave" was listed among the titles for sale at the Ohio Anti-Slavery Depository in advertisements that ran in *The Philanthropist* throughout the spring of 1839.

46. The best account on the appeal of Barnum's schemes remains Neil Harris, *Humbug: The Art of P. T. Barnum* (Chicago: University of Chicago Press, 1973). See, in particular, Harris's description of Barnum's success exhibiting Joice Heth, the slave said to have been George Washington's nurse. Barnum "purchased" Heth in 1835 and, after a fashion, put on his own slave display. Harris, *Humbug*, 19–30. See also Bluford Adams, *E Pluribus Barnum* (Minneapolis: University of Minnesota Press, 1997), 1–10.

47. Collins to Garrison, *The Liberator*, 21 January 1842. Starling, *Slave Narrative*, 39. Of the more than fifty thousand men and women who fled slavery, the stories of only a few hundred appeared either in the pages of abolitionist newspapers or as separately published narratives. Books by former slaves sold exceptionally well. Starling, *Slave Narrative*, 235. On the sales of slaves' narratives, see Frances Smith Foster, *Witnessing Slavery: The Development of Ante-Bellum Slave Narratives* (1979; reprint, Madison: University of Wisconsin Press, 1984), 23; and Charles H. Nichols, "Who Read the Slave Narratives?" *Phylon* 20 (summer 1959): 149–62.

48. Among the most successful slave narrators were Frederick Douglass, William Wells Brown, Samuel R. Ward, Henry Bibb, Lewis and Milton Clarke, William and Ellen Craft, Henry "Box" Brown, Lunsford Lane, and James Pennington, but there were dozens of others. See Larry Gara, "The Professional Fugitive in the Abolition Movement," *Wisconsin Magazine of History* 48 (spring 1965): 196–204; and C. Peter Ripley, et al., ed., *The Black Abolitionist Papers* (Chapel Hill: University of North Carolina, 1991), 3: 28. See also Painter, "Representing Truth," 461–92. The fugitive Lunsford Lane described himself as a "colporteur" for the Baptists. William G. Hawkins, *Lunsford Lane; or, another Helper from North Carolina* (Boston: Crosby and Nichols, 1863), 177.

49. Douglass, *My Bondage and My Freedom*, 220. See also Gara, "Professional Fugitive in the Abolition Movement," 197. On decisions about when, where, and how to tell a story, see *Narrative of William Wells Brown, a Fugitive Slave, Written by Himself* (Boston: Anti-Slavery Office, 1847), reprinted in *Puttin' On Ole*

Massa: The Slave Narratives of Henry Bibb, William Wells Brown, and Solomon Northup, ed. Gilbert Osofsky (New York: Harper and Row, 1969), 216–19; Josiah Henson, *Father Henson's Story of His Own Life* (Boston: John P. Jewett and Company, 1858), 110–17, 122; and *The Narrative of Lunsford Lane formerly of Raleigh, N.C.* (1842; reprint, Boston: Published by Himself, 1845), 39.

50. *Narrative of Events in the Life of William Green, (formerly a slave) written by himself* (Springfield: L. M. Guernsey, Book, Job, and Card Printer, 1853), 20.

51. *Narrative of Henry Watson,* 39.

52. *The Liberator,* 25 July 1851, p. 118. Jane J. Pease and William H. Pease, *They Who Would Be Free: Blacks' Search for Freedom, 1830–1861* (New York: Atheneum, 1974), 66.

53. *Narrative of Henry Watson,* 40. Watson to Garrison in *The Liberator,* 24 May 1850, p. 83, quoted in Starling, *Slave Narrative,* 38; *Anti-Slavery Advocate* 11 (August 1853): 85.

54. *Narrative of Henry Watson,* 48.

55. *A Narrative of the Adventures and Escape of Moses Roper from American Slavery: with a preface by Rev. T. Price, D.D.* (London: Harvey and Darton, 1840), 26–27, 80.

56. *Narrative of the Adventures and Escape,* 28, 31, 86–87, 89–92. On Roper, see Starling, *Slave Narrative,* 106–12; and Andrews, *To Tell a Free Story,* 92–96. See also *Narrative of the Life of Moses Grandy; Late a Slave in the United States of America* (Boston: Oliver Johnson, 1845), iii.

57. "Review of *A Narrative of the Adventures and Escapes of Moses Roper from American Slavery, with a Preface by the Rev. T. Price, D.D. London,*" *The Liberator,* 30 March 1838. The review was reprinted from *The London Christian Advocate.*

58. *Narrative of the Life and Adventures of Henry Bibb, an American Slave, Written by Himself* (New York: Published for the Author, 1849), reprinted in *Puttin' on Ole Massa,* 53, 63.

59. *Narrative of the Sufferings of Lewis and Milton Clarke, Sons of a Soldier of the Revolution, during a captivity of more than twenty years among the slaveholders of Kentuck, one of the so called Christian States of North America* (Boston: Bela Marsh, 1846), 117–22.

60. *Narrative and Writing of Andrew Jackson of Kentucky; containing an account of his birth, and twenty-six years of his life while a slave; his escape; five years of freedom, together with anecdotes relating to slavery; journal of one year's*

travel, sketches, etc. Narrated by himself; written by a friend (Syracuse: Daily and Weekly Star Office, 1847), 82–84, 94, 105.

61. *A Narrative of the Life of Rev. Noah Davis, a colored man, written by himself, at the age of fifty-four* (Baltimore: John F. Weishampel Jr., 1859), 29–30, 68–70. On Davis, see Starling, *Slave Narrative*, 186.

62. Douglass, *My Bondage and My Freedom*, 220–21. William Craft broke the narrative of his and his wife's escape to complain about the poor English of the slaves he met on the coasts of Carolina and Georgia. He transcribed dialect speech. The scene perhaps served to celebrate his ability as a narrator, constructing something resembling a class alliance between the refined (and light-skinned) Crafts and their refined audiences. William Craft, *Running a Thousand Miles for Freedom; or, The Escape of William and Ellen Craft* (London: W. Tweedie, 1860), 53.

63. Hartman, *Scenes of Subjection*, 27.

64. Several recent studies argue for the importance of blackface minstrelsy in understanding the culture and politics of the antebellum North. On the complicated racial logic of blackface, see especially Eric Lott, *Love and Theft: Blackface Minstrelsy and the American Working Class* (New York; Oxford, 1993); and Michael Rogin, *Blackface, White Noise: Jewish Immigrants in the Hollywood Melting Pot* (Berkeley: University of California, 1996), 22–68. On minstrelsy's role in creating a white working class, see David Roediger, *The Wages of Whiteness: Race and the Making of the American Working Class* (London: Verso, 1991), 115–27. On minstrelsy's role in expressing the ideology of northern Democrats, see Alexander Saxton, *The Rise and Fall of the White Republic: Class Politics and Mass Culture in Nineteenth-Century America* (London: Verso, 1990), 165–82; and Paula Baker, *Affairs of Party: The Political Culture of Northern Democrats in the Mid-Nineteenth Century* (Ithaca: Cornell University Press, 1983), 213–258. Older studies include Robert C. Toll, *Blacking Up: The Minstrel Show in Nineteenth-Century America* (New York: Oxford, 1974); and David Grimsted, *Melodrama Unveiled: American Theater and Culture, 1800–1850* (Chicago: University of Chicago, 1968). The best recent study of the theater and music of minstrelsy is Dale Cockrell, *Demons of Disorder: Early Blackface Minstrels and Their World* (Cambridge: Cambridge University Press, 1997).

65. Ephraim Peabody, "Narrative of Fugitive Slaves," *Christian Examiner* 47 (July–September 1849): 61–93. Peabody reviewed the narratives of Henry Watson, Lewis and Milton Clarke, William Wells Brown, Frederick Douglass, and Josiah Henson. The review is reprinted in Charles T. Davis and Henry

Louis Gates Jr., eds., *The Slaves' Narrative* (New York: Oxford University Press, 1985), 9–28. In a speech delivered on August 8, 1849, the New England minister Theodore Parker expressed a similar conviction that fugitive narratives were America's contribution to literature. "We have one series of literary productions that could be written by none but Americans, and only here: I mean the Lives of Fugitive Slaves. But as these are not the work of men of superior culture, they hardly help to pay the scholar's debt. Yet all the original romance of America is in them, not in the white man's novels." Parker is quoted in Houston A. Baker Jr., introduction to *Narrative of the Life of Frederick Douglass, an American Slave*, by Frederick Douglass (1845; reprint, New York: Penguin Books, 1982), 12–13.

66. Edwin P. Christy, *Christy's Plantation Melodies No. 4*, quoted in Saxton, *Rise and Fall of the White Republic*, 166, and Rogin, *Blackface, White Noise*, 22.

67. On stage versions of *Uncle Tom's Cabin*, see Lott, *Love and Theft*, 215–28. On antislavery strains in minstrelsy, see Rogin, *Blackface, White Noise*, 41; and David Reynolds, *Walt Whitman's America: A Cultural Biography* (New York: Random House, 1995), 185–86. Saidiya Hartman dissents, arguing that every act of sympathetic identification induced by melodrama depended on staging subjection and degradation. See Hartman, *Scenes of Subjection*, 28–32. George W. Clark's several songsters suggest that abolitionists knew the power of minstrel tunes. See G. Clark, *The Liberty Minstrel* (New York: n.p., 1845). See also William L. Van Deburg, *Slavery and Race in American Popular Culture* (Madison: University of Wisconsin Press, 1984), 39–49.

68. Reynolds, *Walt Whitman's America*, 183–86. In 1844 Lydia Maria Child wrote disparagingly of the entertainments so popular with working-class New Yorkers. In her many published discussions of music, she never seems to have mentioned minstrel songs. "I speak playfully, yet the low, unsatisfactory, and demoralizing character of popular amusements is painful to me. Only by cultivation of the higher qualities of our nature, can sensual stimulus and fierce excitement be rendered unattractive." Child, "Letter XVIII, July 12, 1844," *Letters from New York* (New York: C. S. Francis and Co., 1846), 175.

69. As the title of Allen Sekora's essay "Black Message/White Envelope: Genre, Authenticity, and Authority in the Antebellum Slave Narrative" suggests, fugitive narratives can be read as a form of "whiteface."

70. On minstrelsy's theatrical circuits, see Saxton, *Rise and Fall of the White Republic*, 167–72; and Robert C. Allen, *Horrible Prettiness: Burlesque and American*

Culture (Chapel Hill: University of North Carolina Press, 1991), 163–78. On the antislavery lecture circuit, see Dorothy Sterling, *Ahead of Her Time: Abby Kelley and the Politics of Antislavery* (New York: W. W. Norton, 1991), 82–93, 150–71. Although Donald Scott says little about lectures and publications by fugitive slaves, his "Print and the Public Lecture System, 1840–1860" offers a helpful model for thinking about relations between public speaking and publication. Scott, *Printing and Society in Early America*, ed. William L. Joyce, et al. (Worcester: American Antiquarian Society, 1983), 278–99.

71. Black performers were not alone in taking advantage of a legacy left by blackface performance. Political scientist Michael Rogin recently found roots of twentieth-century burlesque, vaudeville, and early film in blackface minstrelsy. Blackface, he argues, provided immigrant Jewish filmmakers with stories that moved them into the mainstream of twentieth-century American culture. Rogin, *Blackface, White Noise*, 73–156. Arnold Rampersad, "Biography, Autobiography, and Afro-American Culture," *The Yale Review* 73 (October 1983): 1–16. E. Clark, "'The Sacred Rights of the Weak,'" 491.

72. Lott, *Love and Theft*, 115; Rogin, *Blackface, White Noise* 137; and Saxton, *Rise and Fall of the White Republic*, 168.

73. Douglass, *My Bondage and My Freedom*, 220.

74. See especially Stepto, "Narration, Authentication, and Authorial Control." See also Peter Walker, *Moral Choices: Memory, Desire, and Imagination in Nineteenth-Century American Abolition* (Baton Rouge: Louisiana State University Press, 1978), 211–45; Donald B. Gibson, "Reconciling Public and Private in Frederick Douglass' *Narrative*," *American Literature* 57 (December 1985): 549–69; Albert E. Stone, "Identity and Art in Frederick Douglass's *Narrative*," in *Critical Essays on Frederick Douglass*, ed. William L. Andrews (Boston: G. K. Hall, 1991), 62–78; and Lucinda H. MacKethan, "Metaphors of Mastery in the Slave Narrative," in *The Art of the Slave Narrative: Original Essays in Criticism and Theory*, ed. John Sekora and Darwin T. Turner (Macomb, Ill.: Western Illinois University Press, 1982), 55–80.

75. Douglass, *My Bondage and My Freedom*, 174–75. Douglass, *Narrative of the Life*, 127–128, 62.

76. *The Fugitive Blacksmith; or, Events in the History of James W. C. Pennington* (London: Charles Gilpin, 1849), 21, 22, 23–24.

77. The quotation is from C. B. Macpherson. The entire passage reads as follows:

The individual was seen neither as a moral whole, nor as part of a larger social whole, but as an owner of himself. The relation of ownership, having become for more and more men the critically important relation determining their actual freedom and actual prospect of realizing their full potentialities, was read back into the nature of the individual. The individual, it was thought, is free inasmuch as he is proprietor of his person and capacities. The human essence is freedom from dependence on the wills of others, and freedom is a function of possession.

Macpherson, *The Political Theory of Possessive Individualism: Hobbes to Locke* (New York: Oxford University Press, 1962), 3. As Henry Louis Gates Jr. suggested, literacy could serve slaves as a commodity "with which the African's right to be considered human could be traded." Gates Jr., *Figures in Black: Words, Signs, and the "Racial" Self* (New York: Oxford University Press, 1987), 11.

78. *Fugitive Blacksmith*, 18, 22, 30. On Cicero, see Shapin, *Social History of Truth*, 71–72. See also Sissela Bok, *Lying: Moral Choice in Public and Private Life* (New York: Random House, 1978).

79. Frederick Douglass, *Life and Times of Frederick Douglass* (1892; reprint, New York: Collier Books, 1962), 197–201.

80. Douglass, *My Bondage and My Freedom*, 196–97.

81. Douglass, *Narrative of the Life*, 78.

82. Douglass, *Life and Times*, 197.

CHAPTER FOUR

1. A. O. Abbott, *Prison Life in the South: at Richmond, Macon, Savannah, Charleston, Columbia, Charlotte, Raleigh, Goldsborough, and Andersonville, during the years 1864 and 1865* (New York: Harper and Brothers, 1865), [7]. Harper and Brothers signed a contract with Abbott in June 1865. The publishers agreed to pay him royalties of 10 percent of their list price for all copies above one thousand sold. In the same contract, Ole P. Dahl granted Harpers the right to use as illustration his sketches of "The Southern Prisons of U.S. Officers." Contract Books, Papers of Harper and Brothers (microfilm, Baker Library, Columbia University), Reel 1: 482.

2. In her study of Civil War stories published in popular magazines, the literary historian Kathleen Diffley suggests that stories that posed the "negro question"

helped to "prod the Union's potential futures out of its contested pasts by helping to set the stage for popular debate." Diffley, *Where My Heart Is Turning Ever:
Civil War Stories and Constitutional Reform, 1861–1876* (Athens, Ga.: University
of Georgia Press, 1992), xix.

3. William Best Hesseltine, *Civil War Prisons: A Study in War Psychology*
(Columbus: Ohio State University Press, 1930); William Marvel, *Andersonville:
The Last Depot* (Chapel Hill: University of North Carolina Press, 1994); and Ovid
Futch, "Prison Life at Andersonville, *Civil War History* 8 (June 1962): 121–35.

4. Leon F. Litwack, *Been in the Storm So Long: The Aftermath of Slavery*
(New York: Vintage Books, 1980), 50.

5. Randall C. Jimerson, *The Private Civil War: Popular Thought during the
Sectional Conflict* (Baton Rouge: Louisiana State University Press, 1988), 206–9.
Some slaveholders saw the filth and deprivation of soldiering in racial terms. One
Alabama officer expressed a longing to be home to his sister, concluding "then I
could sit down in a chair like a white man, and eat at a table like a white man and
feel for a little while like a white man once again!!" The passage appears in Reid
Mitchell, *Civil War Soldiers* (New York: Penguin Books, 1988), 60.

6. Inevitably, we think of present-day examples, which include movies such
as *Mississippi Burning*, where white FBI agents emerged as heroes of a Civil
Rights story.

7. The official memory of the war, Michael Kammen has written, helped "fa-
cilitate a reconciliation" between the North and the South but also "kept African-
Americans outside the mainstream of retrospective consciousness." Kammen,
*The Mystic Chords of Memory: The Transformation of Tradition in American Cul-
ture* (New York: Random House, 1991), 121. The "Sambo image," George
Fredrickson argues, was merely modified with the abolition of slavery. Fredrick-
son, *The Black Image in the White Mind: The Debate on Afro-American Character
and Destiny, 1817–1914* (1971; reprint, Middletown, Conn.: Wesleyan University
Press, 1987), 168–69. In contrast, Kirk Savage has looked at just how images of
African Americans were worked into the consciousness of a white nation. Savage,
*Standing Soldiers, Kneeling Slaves: Race, War, and Monument in Nineteenth-
Century America* (Princeton: Princeton University Press, 1997). In his study of
Frank Leslie's Illustrated Newspaper, the historian Josh Brown suggests that dur-
ing the early years of Reconstruction some in the African American community
held out hope for the circulation of positive images of black men and women. Ac-
cording to Brown, "that a racist pictorial record held sway until the mid-twentieth

century cannot be denied, nor can we ignore the cost to African Americans of the denial of both an informational and expressive popular media. Yet, in the decade following the Civil War, the representation of African Americans in the weekly illustrated press does not appear to have taken the simple, single-minded racist course suggested in most scholarship." Joshua Emmett Brown, *"Frank Leslie's Illustrated Newspaper*: The Pictorial Press and the Representations of America, 1855–1889" (Ph.D. diss., Columbia University, 1993), 199.

8. The historian David Blight has written eloquently on contests over memorializing the war. See Blight, "'For Something Beyond the Battlefield': Frederick Douglass and the Struggle for the Memory of the Civil War," *Journal of American History* 75 (March 1989): 1156–78, the quotation from Douglass appears on 1160–61. Suggestive parallels to the contest over who can claim credit for wartime suffering and sacrifice can be found in the history of postwar Germany. The historian Robert G. Moeller has studied contesting stories of victimization and explored the importance of private experiences in constructing public memory and in fabricating a common history for the Federal Republic of Germany. West Germans collectively mourned the suffering of expellees from eastern Germany and German prisoners of war held in the Soviet Union:

> Their private memories structured public memory, making stories of Communist brutality and the loss of the "German east" crucial parts of the history of the Federal Republic. Focusing on German suffering also made it possible to talk about the end of the Third Reich without assessing responsibility for its origins, to tell an abbreviated story of National Socialism in which all Germans were ultimately victims of a war that Hitler started but everyone lost.

Victims of the concentration camps had no distinctive status. Moeller, "War Stories: The Search for a Usable Past in the Federal Republic of Germany," *American Historical Review* 101 (October 1996): 1013.

9. Thomas Holt, "Marking: Race, Race-Making, and the Writing of History," *American Historical Review* 100 (February 1995): 7. Turning to prisoners' narratives, I follow Barbara Fields in arguing that racism must be understood as part of particular social processes. See Fields, "Race and Ideology in American History," in *Region, Race, and Reconstruction: Essays in Honor of C. Vann Woodward*, ed. J. Morgan Kousser and James M. McPherson (New York: Oxford University Press, 1982), 143–77.

10. Charles J. Stillé, *History of the United States Sanitary Commission Being the General Report of Its Work During the War of the Rebellion* (Philadelphia: J. B. Lippincott and Co., 1866), 307n. The Grand Army of the Republic made prisoners' experiences central to its ritual. Old members covered new recruits in ragged blankets meant to recall the conditions of prisoners and asked them to kneel before a coffin labeled with the name of a soldier who had died in Andersonville and to swear to keep the secrets of the organization. Stuart McConnell, *Glorious Contentment: The Grand Army of the Republic, 1865–1900* (Chapel Hill: University of North Carolina Press, 1992), 94–95.

11. The best study of the publishing industry during the Civil War is Alice E. Fahs, "Publishing the Civil War: The Literary Marketplace and the Meanings of the Civil War in the North, 1861–1865" (Ph.D. diss., New York University, 1993). On subscription publishing, see John Tebbell, *A History of Book Publishing in the United States*, (New York: R. R. Bowker, 1987); and Michael Hackenberg, "The Subscription Publishing Network in Nineteenth-Century America," in *Getting Books Out: Papers of the Chicago Conference on the Book in Nineteenth-Century America*, ed. Michael Hackenberg (Washington, D.C.: Library of Congress, Center for the Book, 1987), 45–75.

12. House Special Committee on the Treatment of Prisoners of War and Union Citizens, *Report on the Treatment of Prisoners of War kept by the Rebel Authorities, during the War of Rebellion: to which are appended the Testimony taken by the Committee, and Official Documents and Statistics, etc.*, 40th Cong., 3d sess., 1869, H. Rept. 45.

13. Five narratives by former prisoners were published in 1887, more than in any single year since 1868. Hesseltine, *Civil War Prisons*, 247–57. Although the numbers are small, a pattern does emerge from the dates listed in bibliographies compiled by Hesseltine, 259–82, and by Frank Byrne in Allan Nevins, James I. Robertson Jr., and Bell I. Wiley, *Civil War Books: A Critical Bibliography* (Baton Rouge: Louisiana State University Press, 1967), 2: 185–206. The number of prisoners' narratives published in each given year are as follows: 1862–5; 1863–2; 1864–4; 1865–19; 1866–7; 1867–3; 1868–5; 1870–3; 1876–2; 1879–3; 1880–2; 1881–1; 1882–1; 1883–1; 1884–1; 1886–1; 1887–5; 1888–3; 1889–1; 1890–4; 1892–1; 1893–5; 1894–1; 1897–1; 1898–1; 1899–2; 1900–3. Hesseltine counted 51 books and articles on prisons published between 1901 and 1910; he found another 27 accounts published between 1912 and 1921. See also Paul H. Buck, *The Road to Reunion, 1865–1900* (Boston: Little, Brown, and Company, 1938),

45–47, 103. On pensions, see McConnell, *Glorious Contentment*, 126–65; Hesseltine, *Civil War Prisons*, 249–50; Megan J. McClintock, "Civil War Pensions and the Reconstruction of Union Families," *Journal of American History* 83 (September 1996): 456–80; and Theda Skocpol, *Protecting Soldiers and Mothers: The Political Origins of Social Policy in the United States* (Cambridge: Harvard University Press, 1992), 102–51.

14. John Ransom, *Andersonville Diary; Escape and List of the Dead, with Name, Co., Regiment, Date of Death and No. Of Grave in Cemetery* (Auburn, N.Y.: John Ransom, 1881). On Ransom, see William Marvel, "Johnny Ransom's Imagination," *Civil War History* 41 (September 1995): 181–89. Without questioning the legitimacy of Ransom's claim about his teeth, Marvel offers evidence to cast doubt on the existence of a prison diary. "Thanks to its widespread distribution as well as its wholesale exaggerations and misrepresentations, John Ransom's diary helped thousands of former prisoners gain their pensions, and Ransom was the first one in line. He also profited from the spectacular sales of his book to both pension lobbies and individuals" (188).

15. Felix LaBaume, "Appeal to Congress," in Ransom, *Andersonville Diary*, 192. Among the narratives inspired by pension legislation were those of Alonzo Cooper, *In and Out of Rebel Prisons* (Oswego: R. J. Oliphant, Job Printer, Bookbinder, and Stationer, 1888); and S. S. Boggs, *Eighteen Months a Prisoner under the Rebel Flag* (Lovington, Ill.: S. S. Boggs, Author and Publisher, 1887).

16. Robert Underwood Johnson, *Remembered Yesterdays* (Boston: Little, Brown and Co., 1923), 194. See also Frank Luther Mott, *A History of American Magazines* (Cambridge: Harvard University Press, 1938), 3: 468–70; and the preface to *Battles and Leaders of the Civil War*, ed. R. U. Johnson and C. C. Clough Buel (New York: Century Co., 1887–1888), 1: ix–xi.

17. T. H. Mann, "A Yankee in Andersonville," *Century* 40 (July 1890): 447–61, and *Century* 40 (August 1890): 606–22. The magazine's attempt at balance is suggested by a reply to Mann from a Confederate veteran. He believed Mann's account, he said, because it so closely resembled what he remembered of his own treatment in a northern prison. *Century* 41 (November 1890): 154. The editors also published material on northern prisons. Articles on prisons include Frank E. Moran, "Colonel Rose's Tunnel at Libby Prison," *Century* 34 (March 1888): 770–90; W. H. Shelton, "A Hard Road to Travel out of Dixie," *Century* 40 (October 1890): 921–49; J. T. King, "On the Andersonville Circuit," *Century* 41 (November 1890): 100–5; Horace Carpenter, "Plain Living at Johnson's Island,"

Century 41 (March 1891): 705–18; John A. Wyeth, "Cold Cheer at Camp Morton," *Century* 41 (April 1891): 844–52; and W. R. Holloway, "Treatment of Prisoners at Camp Morton. A Reply to 'Cold Cheer at Camp Morton,'" *Century* 42 (September 1891): 757–70. The exchange between Wyeth and Holloway suggests how difficult it was to incorporate stories from prisons into the narrative of reconciliation.

18. The narratives I analyze here differ in this respect from the worked memoirs of some of their contemporaries. The historian Anne C. Rose found an impulse to autobiography characteristic of a group of middle-class figures she identified as American Victorians. For them, the war provided a means of ordering private experience. Class privilege seemingly freed them from the narrow confines that brought ordinary soldiers into print. As Rose puts it, "To move from the production of such crafted episodes to a willingness to write full-scale autobiography required not simply longer texts but a conviction that the entirety of one's life was of public interest." Rose, *Victorian America and the Civil War* (Cambridge: Cambridge University Press, 1992), 254. See also McConnell, *Glorious Contentment*, 21.

19. Their stories were designed to appeal above all to their contemporaries—to their families, friends, and neighbors, and to bureaucrats in the pension bureau. As the Russian literary critic Mikhail Bakhtin wrote, "Contemporaneity was reality of the 'lower' order in comparison with the epic past. Least of all could it serve as the starting point for artistic ideation or evaluation. The focus for such an idea could only be found in the absolute past. The present is something transitory, it is flow, it is eternal continuation without beginning or end; it is denied an authentic conclusiveness and consequently lacks an essence as well." Bakhtin, "Epic and Novel," in *The Dialogic Imagination: Four Essays*, ed. Michael Holquist (Austin: University of Texas Press, 1981), 19–20.

20. A. C. Roach, *The Prisoner of War and How Treated* (Indianapolis: Railroad City Publishing House, 1865), 4. An identical passage appears in Willard Glazier, *The Capture, Prison Pen and the Escape; giving a complete History of Prison Life in the South* (New York: United States Publishing Company, 1868), v. Similar promises opened almost every prisoner's narrative. For example, see Amos E. Stearns, *Narrative of Amos E. Stearns, a Prisoner at Andersonville* (Worcester: Franklin P. Rice, 1886); John W. Urban, *Battle Field and Prison Pen, Through the War, and Thrice a Prisoner in Rebel Dungeons* (Philadelphia: Edgewood Publishing Company, 1882); and B. F. Booth, *Dark Days of the Rebellion, or Life in Southern Military Prisons* (Indianola, Iowa: Booth Publishing Co., 1897). Southern

prisoners likewise promised a "plain unembellished account of my experiences as a prisoner of war, wherein I have endeavored to confine myself to a simple detail of facts, avoiding moralizings, eschewing rhetoric, and modestly renouncing my privilege of criticising 'the situation.'" A. M. Keiley, *Prisoner of War, or Five Months among the Yankees* (Richmond, Va.: West and Johnston, 1865).

21. J. Madison Drake, *Fast and Loose in Dixie: An Unprejudiced narrative of personal experience as a prisoner of war at Libby, Macon, Savannah, and Charleston* (New York: The Authors' Publishing Company, 1880), 298.

22. Abbott, *Prison Life in the South*, [7]. Glazier too sat on the ground and wrote on his knee. His story, however, came through the lines concealed in a hat. Glazier, *Capture, Prison Pen and the Escape*, xx. See also William Harris, *Prison-Life in the Tobacco Warehouse at Richmond* (Philadelphia: George W. Childs, 1862), 9. On pencils, see Glazier, *Capture, Prison Pen and the Escape*, 251, and *John Ransom's Andersonville Diary: Life inside the Civil War's Most Infamous Prison* (1881; reprint, ed. Bruce Canton, New York: Berkeley Books, 1986), 97, 217.

23. Ransom, *Andersonville Diary*, 10; Eugene Forbes, *Diary of a Soldier and Prisoner of War in Rebel Prisons* (Trenton: Murphy and Bechtel, Printers, 1865), iv; and John McElroy, *Andersonville: A Story of Rebel Military Prisons, or fifteen months a guest of the so-called southern confederacy* (Washington: The National Tribune, n.d.), viii. Others apparently used the expertise they gained writing about experiences in prison to fabricate careers as professional writers. Willard Glazier, for example, followed his *Capture, Prison Pen and the Escape* with books on battles, exploration, travel, and American cities.

24. Robert H. Kellogg, *Life and Death in Rebel Prisons: Giving a Complete History of the Inhuman and Barbarous Treatment of Our Brave Soldiers by Rebel Authorities, Inflicting Terrible Suffering and Frightful Mortality, Principally at Andersonville, Ga., and Florence, S.C.* (Hartford: L. Stebbins, 1865), 424.

25. W. H. Newlin, *A Narrative of Prison Escape; or an account of the escape of six federal soldiers from prison at Danville, Va.: their travels by night through the enemy's country to the Union pickets at Gauley's Bridge, West Virginia, in the winter of 1863-64* (Cincinnati: Western Methodist Book Concern, 1888).

26. The list of the Union dead at Andersonville had its own curious history. It was compiled by Dorence Atwater, an Andersonville inmate who was paroled to work as a clerk in the surgeon's office and given the task of recording the deaths of all Union prisoners. After the war, the government paid him three hundred dollars for his list but then insisted that he had no right to profit from its publication.

When Atwater refused to return his list to the government, he was court-martialed, dishonorably discharged from the military, and made to serve two months' hard labor at Auburn State Prison in New York. Released from prison, he "immediately set about preparing [the list] for publication, and have arranged to have it printed and placed within your reach at the cost of the labor of printing and material, having no means by which to defray these expenses myself." Dorence Atwater, *A List of the Union Soldiers Buried at Andersonville* (New York: The Tribune Association, 1866), iv. Atwater charged twenty-five cents for his list. A copy of it appeared in Warren Lee Goss, *The Soldier's Story* (Boston: I. N. Richardson and Co., 1875), and Ransom, *Andersonville Diary*.

Lists of captives in other prisons conclude Cooper, *In and Out of Rebel Prisons*; Henry M. Davidson, *Fourteen Months in Southern Prisons* (Milwaukee: Daily Wisconsin Printing House, 1865); Glazier, *Capture, Prison Pen and the Escape*; and Harris, *Prison-Life in the Tobacco Warehouse*.

27. McElroy, *Andersonville*, [preface]; Kellogg, *Life and Death in Rebel Prisons*.

28. On exchange, see Hesseltine, *Civil War Prisons*, 69–113; and James M. McPherson, *Battle Cry of Freedom: The Civil War Era* (New York: Ballentine Books, 1989), 792–801.

29. McPherson, *Battle Cry of Freedom*, 797. Eight pictures of skeletal prisoners appeared in findings published by *Report of the Joint Committee on the Conduct and Expenditures of the War*, 38th Cong., 1st sess., 1864, H. Rept. 65, 35–39. That summer, reproductions of photographs of two of the same maimed prisoners appeared in Republican campaign literature. See John D. Defrees, "Remarks Made by John D. Defrees, before the Indiana Union Club of Washington, D.C., Monday evening, August 1, 1864" (Washington, D.C.: L. Towers, Printer, 1864).

30. Some 29 percent of the men confined in Andersonville died; 34 percent of those held at Salisbury, South Carolina, died. At Elmira, New York, the worst of the Union prison camps, 24 percent of the inmates died. Although northern propagandists made much of southern cruelty, overall death rates differed little. One report made to Secretary of War Stanton held that "26,436 out of a total of 220,000 Confederate prisoners died in northern prisons while 22,576 prisoners out of a total of 126,950 Union prisoners died in the South." Hesseltine, *Civil War Prisons*, 254–55.

31. Hesseltine, *Civil War Prisons*, 133–58; McPherson, *Battle Cry of Freedom*, 800–801.

32. Kellogg, *Life and Death in Rebel Prisons*, 389–90.

33. Anthony Giddens has written on this kind of transfer of trust from individuals to impersonal systems of expertise. See Giddens, *The Consequences of Modernity* (Stanford: Stanford University Press, 1989), 21–27; Steven Shapin, *A Social History of Truth: Civility and Science in Seventeenth-Century England* (Chicago: University of Chicago Press, 1994), 15; and Hayden White, "Fictions of Factual Representations," in *Tropics of Discourse* (Baltimore: Johns Hopkins University Press, 1978), 122–24.

34. United States Sanitary Commission, *Narrative of Privations and Sufferings of United States Officers and Soldiers while Prisoners of War in the Hands of Rebel Authorities* (Boston: Littells Living Age, 1864), 3. The accounts of privation and suffering appeared as the last of the pamphlets published by the Loyal Publication Society. See Frank Friedel, "The Loyal Publication Society: A Pro-Union Propaganda Agency," *Mississippi Valley Historical Review* 26 (December 1939): 359–76. George Templeton Strong remembered the publication as a "weighty and memorable paper." He also recalled that the commission's findings had been denied by "Richmond papers, by rebel representatives on the floor of their so-called Congress at Richmond, and by the Honorable Mason in the London *Times*." *The Diary of George Templeton Strong*, ed. Allan Nevins and Milton Halsey Thomas (Seattle: University of Washington Press, 1988), 315–16.

35. United States Sanitary Commission, *Narrative of Privations and Sufferings*, 12–13.

36. "A Typical Negro," *Harper's Weekly* (July 4, 1863): 429. Private Gordon's picture also appeared on the cover of the abolitionist pamphlet, *The Views of Judge Woodward and Bishop Hopkins on Negro Slavery at the South illustrated from the Journal of a Residence on a Georgian Plantation by Mrs. Frances Anne Kemble* (Philadelphia: Pennsylvania Democratic State Committee, 1863). According to Joseph T. Glathaar, the physicians who examined slave recruits like Private Gordon were shocked by the evidence they uncovered of physical abuse. Glathaar, *Forged in Battle: The Civil War Alliance of Black Soldiers and White Officers* (New York: The Free Press, 1990), 76–78. See also Alan Trachtenberg, "Albums of War," in *Reading American Photographs* (New York: Hill and Wang, 1989), 71–118; and Kathy Newman, "Wounds and Wounding in the American Civil War: A (Visual) History," *The Yale Journal of Criticism* 6 (1993): 63–86. Images of torture and suffering would also have been familiar to those who had read the narratives of fugitives. For example, see Kellogg's illustration of a man hanging

by his thumbs, in *Life and Death in Rebel Prisons*, 334; and Geer's of a prisoner pinned to the ground, in J. J. Geer, *Beyond the Lines; or, a Yankee Prisoner Loose in Dixie* (Philadelphia: J. W. Daughaday, 1864), 211. See also Savage, *Standing Soldiers, Kneeling Slaves*, 23–26.

37. United States Sanitary Commission, *Narrative of Privations and Sufferings*, 4, 32. Northern readers who had worked in abolition would surely understand the power of such sympathetic response. See Elizabeth B. Clark, "'The Sacred Rights of the Weak': Pain, Sympathy, and the Culture of Individual Rights in Antebellum America," *The Journal of American History* 82 (September 1995): 463–93; Philip Fisher, *Hard Facts: Setting and Form in the American Novel* (New York: Oxford University Press, 1985); G. J. Barker-Benfield, *The Culture of Sensibility: Sex and Society in Eighteenth-Century Britain* (Chicago: University of Chicago Press, 1992); and Karen Halttunen, "Humanitarianism and the Pornography of Pain in Anglo-American Culture," *The American Historical Review* 100 (April 1995): 303–34. But a preference for emotional truth did not prevail in postwar America. Several historians have written on the emergence of professional authority in the second half of the nineteenth century. For example, see Thomas Haskell, *The Emergence of Professional Social Science: The American Social Science Association and the Nineteenth-Century Crisis of Authority* (Urbana: University of Illinois Press, 1977); Dorothy Ross, *Origins of American Social Science* (New York: Cambridge University Press, 1991), 53–97; and Kenneth Cmiel, *Democratic Eloquence: The Fight over Popular Speech in Nineteenth-Century America* (Berkeley: University of California Press, 1990).

38. House Special Committee, *Report on the Treatment of Prisoners of War*, 6.

39. Ibid., 6. Warren Lee Goss, *The Soldier's Story of his Captivity at Andersonville, Belle Isle, and Other Rebel Prisons* (Boston: Lee and Shepard, 1865); and Davidson, *Fourteen Months in Southern Prisons*. On the emergence of postwar organizations, see George Fredrickson, *The Inner Civil War: Northern Intellectuals and the Crisis of the Union* (New York: Harper and Row, 1965). On the blend of statistics, eyewitness accounts, and policy recommendation that constituted the protocols of authority in government reports, see Mary Poovey, *Making a Social Body: British Cultural Formation, 1830–1864* (Chicago: University of Chicago Press, 1995), 117. On statistics and social science, see Ross, *Origins of American Social Science*, 59–60.

40. Ross, *Origins of American Social Science*, 62; Samuel Haber, *The Quest for Authority and Honor in the American Professions, 1750–1900* (Chicago: Uni-

versity of Chicago Press, 1991); and Burton Bledstein, *The Culture of Professionalism; The Middle Class and the Development of Higher Education in America* (New York: W. W. Norton, 1978).

41. John Sekora found that "after the Civil War and under the aegis of 'national reconciliation,'" slaves' narratives "were dismissed as, at best, irrelevant and outdated curiosities." Sekora, "Black Message/White Envelope: Genre, Authenticity and Authority in the Antebellum Slave Narrative," *Callaloo* 10 (summer 1987): 482. Perhaps many would-be writers turned their attention to more pressing tasks, building the communities necessary to free life. It is also true that no network of African American publishers had yet emerged to replace the abolitionist intellectual infrastructure that had encouraged publication of black writers. Henry Louis Gates Jr. has explored the connections between artistic expression and political aspiration in the African American community. See Henry Louis Gates Jr., "The Trope of a New Negro and the Reconstruction of the Image of the Black," in *The New American Studies: Essays from Representations*, ed. Philip Fisher (Berkeley: University of California Press, 1991), 321; and Henry Louis Gates Jr., *Figures in Black: Words, Signs, and the "Racial" Self* (New York: Oxford University Press, 1987), 14.

42. House Special Committee, *Report on the Treatment of Prisoners of War*, 6.

43. Urban, *Battle Field and Prison Pen*, 311.

44. Barker-Benfield, *Culture of Sensibility*; and Halttunen, "Humanitarianism and the Pornography of Pain in American Culture," 303–34. See also Fredrickson's discussion of Moncure Conway in *Inner Civil War*, 123–29. My reading of the storytelling and suffering present in prisoners' narratives benefits from the work of James E. Young, particularly his *Writing and Rewriting the Holocaust: Narrative and the Consequences of Interpretation* (Bloomington: Indiana University Press, 1988).

45. Frederick Douglass, *Narrative of the Life of Frederick Douglass, an American Slave* (1845; reprint, New York: Penguin Books, 1986).

46. Abbott described himself "en déshabillé [sic]" on wash days. He had made a skirt of a blanket. Abbott, *Prison Life in the South*, 98–99. Cooper was more specific, describing Abbott as looking like an "old woman." Cooper, *In and Out of Rebel Prisons*, 115.

47. Eric Foner, "Abolitionism and the Labor Movement," in *Politics and Ideology in the Age of the Civil War* (New York: Oxford University Press, 1980), 57–76. On the cultural consequences of racial formations in the antebellum

United States, see Eric Lott, *Love and Theft: Blackface Minstrelsy and the American Working Class* (New York: Oxford University Press, 1993).

48. David Roediger, *The Wages of Whiteness: Race and the Making of the American Working Class* (New York: Verso, 1991), 175; see also Grace Hale, *Making Whiteness: The Culture of Segregation in the South, 1890–1940* (New York: Pantheon, 1998), 9.

49. United States Sanitary Commission, *Narrative of Privations and Sufferings*, 32. Boggs, *Eighteen Months a Prisoner*, [3].

50. John McElroy, *Andersonville, A Story of Rebel Military Prisons, Fifteen Months a Guest of the So-Called Confederacy, A Private Soldier's Experience in Richmond, Andersonville, Savannah, Millen, Blackshear and Florence* (Toledo: D. R. Locke, 1879), ix–x. Lieutenant-Colonel Chas. Farnsworth told a standing committee of the United States Sanitary Commission that the keepers of the Belle Isle prison had acted out, "in their treatment of northern soldiers, the great principle of Slavery and of the South, that the lives of the poor and helpless are in their eyes of no more value than the amount of interest they will produce on capital." Soldiers' lives, in other words, were worth nothing. United States Sanitary Commission, *Narrative of Privations and Sufferings*, 44. Adam S. Johnston also expressed concern that he would not be believed. The sufferings of Union soldiers could not be described "by pen and ink, nor can any artist paint, or tongue give utterance in full, without being challenged." Johnston, *The Soldier Boy's Diary Book* (Pittsburgh: n.p., 1866), 64.

51. On chains, see Geer, *Beyond the Lines*, 4. On instruments of torture, see Boggs, *Eighteen Months a Prisoner*, 18–19. On the "middle passage," see United States Sanitary Commission, *Narrative of Privations and Sufferings*, 6. On patrols, see Roach, *Prisoner of War*, 148.

52. Abbott, *Prison Life in the South*, 99–100; Alvan Q. Bacon, *Thrilling Adventures of a Pioneer Boy . . . While a Prisoner of War* (n.p., 1863), 16; Booth, *Dark Days*, 166–67; Drake, *Fast and Loose in Dixie*, 80–83; and Joseph Ferguson, *Life-Struggles in Rebel Prisons: A record of the sufferings, escapes, adventures and starvation of the Union prisoners* (Philadelphia: James M. Ferguson, 1865), 65–69. A former slave offered Captain Geer extraordinary lessons in avoiding capture by dogs. He advised him to fill his tracks with pepper and explained how to vault through the woods using a pole. Geer, *Beyond the Lines*, 128.

53. Kellogg, *Life and Death in Rebel Prisons*, 218–19; Lessel Long, *Twelve Months in Andersonville, on the March—in the Battle—in the Rebel Prison Pens,*

and at last in God's Country (Huntington, Ind.: Thad and Mark Butler, Publishers, 1886), 177; and McElroy, *Andersonville*, 185.

54. On "dyaesthesia Aethiopsis," see Martin S. Pernick, *A Calculus of Suffering: Pain, Professionalism, and Anesthesia in Nineteenth-Century America* (New York: Columbia University Press, 1985), 155–56.

55. United States Sanitary Commission, *Narrative of Privations and Sufferings*, 80.

56. House Special Committee, *Report on the Treatment of Prisoners of War*, 27.

57. Or as Henry Davidson remarked, "Their Saxon features alone distinguish them from the negro." Davidson, *Fourteen Months in Southern Prisons*, 148–49. Goss, *Soldier's Story*, 73; Forbes, *Diary of a Soldier*, 47; Long, *Twelve Months in Andersonville*, 93. See also Roach, *Prisoner of War*, 208; and House Special Committee, *Report on the Treatment of Prisoners of War*, 995.

58. McElroy, *Andersonville*, 153. See also Roach, *Prisoner of War*, 208. On racial identity and the construction of the "other," see Michael Rogin, *Blackface, White Noise: Jewish Immigrants in the Hollywood Melting Pot* (Berkeley: University of California Press, 1996); Mechal Sobel, "Revolution in Selves: Black and White Inner Aliens," in *Through a Glass Darkly: Reflections on Personal Identity in Early America*, ed. Ronald Hoffman, Mechal Sobel, and Fredrika J. Teute (Chapel Hill: University of North Carolina Press, 1989); Peter Stallybrass and Allon White, *The Politics and Poetics of Transgression* (Ithaca: Cornell University Press, 1986), 5; and Lott, *Love and Theft*, 148–51.

59. Roach, *Prisoner of War*; Davidson, *Fourteen Months in Southern Prisons*, 180–81; Bacon, *Thrilling Adventures*, 27.

60. Lott, *Love and Theft*, 91–100.

61. I borrow from Stallybrass and White, *Politics and Poetics of Transgression*, 49, see also 125–48. Several years ago, the literary critic Steven Marcus argued that Engels's difficulty depicting the filth and poverty of the working class in Manchester exposed a crisis in the consciousness of the European bourgeoisie: "This consciousness was abruptly disturbed by the realization that millions of English men, women and children were virtually living in shit." Marcus, *Engels, Manchester, and the Working Class* (New York: Random House, 1975), 184. See also Mary Douglas, *Purity and Danger: An Analysis of the Concepts of Pollution and Taboo* (1966; reprint, London: Ark Paperbacks, 1984), 2, 35–40.

62. House Special Committee, *Report on the Treatment of Prisoners of War*, 24.

63. Ibid., 25. By the 1880s, such descriptions had lost their hard edge. Compare the congressional committee's phrasing with that of Alonzo Cooper: "These cars had been used for the transportation of beef cattle and had not been cleaned in the least since thus used. It was, therefore, like lying in a cow stable." Cooper, *In and Out of Rebel Prisons*, 39–40.

64. *The Diary of George Templeton Strong*, 306.

65. Stephen Greenblatt, "Filthy Rites," *Daedalus* 111 (1982): 1–16; and Suellen Hoy, *Chasing Dirt: The American Pursuit of Cleanliness* (New York: Oxford, 1995), 35–58. Historians and literary critics who study Victorian Britain have had a great deal to say about the role of cleanliness in class formation. Anne McClintock, *Imperial Leather: Race, Gender, and Sexuality in the Colonial Contest* (New York: Routledge, 1995), 207–218; and Poovey, *Making a Social Body*, 115–31. Both McClintock and Poovey insist on the importance of gender and domesticity (and in McClintock's case, race) for understanding the rhetoric of cleanliness.

66. House Special Committee, *Report on the Treatment of Prisoners of War*, 1102; Cooper, *In and Out of Rebel Prisons*, 46.

67. Thomas Wilson inserted the passage from the former prisoner in the collection of propaganda he published as *Sufferings Endured for a Free Government; or, a History of the Cruelties and Atrocities of the Rebellion* (Washington, D.C.: By the Author, 1864), 73.

68. Booth, *Dark Days*, 247.

69. McElroy, *Andersonville*, 304, 310, 314.

70. For example, see Boggs, *Eighteen Months a Prisoner*, 18–19, 25; Glazier, *Capture, Prison Pen and the Escape*, 211; Cooper, *In and Out of Rebel Prisons*, 148–49; Davidson, *Fourteen Months in Southern Prisons*, 148–49; Geer, *Beyond the Lines*, 4, 122–28; and Newlin, *Narrative of Prison Escape*, 5, 33–37. House Special Committee, *Report on the Treatment of Prisoners of War*, 66, 146–50, 883, 963, 995, 1006–8.

71. Geer, *Beyond the Lines*, 122; and Drake, *Fast and Loose in Dixie*, 95.

72. Abbott, *Prison Life in the South*, 225. See also Bacon, *Thrilling Adventures*, 21–22. On swamps as domains of slavery, see David C. Miller, *Dark Eden: The Swamp in Nineteenth-Century American Culture* (Cambridge: Cambridge University Press, 1989), 90–94. On slaves' knowledge of the landscape, see Rhys Isaac, *The Transformation of Virginia, 1740–1790* (Chapel Hill: University of North Carolina Press, 1982), 52–53.

73. William B. McCreery, *"My Experience as a Prisoner of War, and Escape from Libby Prison." A Paper Read Before the Commandery of the State of Michigan, Military Order of the Loyal Legion of the U.S.* (Detroit: Winn and Hammond, Printers and Binders, 1893), 26. Unlike most memoirists, McCreery avoids dialect, something perhaps explained by the fact that his paper was written to be read aloud. To have spoken in dialect would have made him resemble a blackface performer, turning his account into explicit comedy. Written accounts left comedy implicit, shifting the burden of performance to readers. It was far easier to put dialect in a book than to perform it on stage.

74. John Hadley, *Seven Months a Prisoner; or, Thirty Six Days in the Woods* (1868; reprint, New York: Charles Scribner's Sons, 1898), 116. On former slaves bearing gifts, see also Glazier, *Capture, Prison Pen and the Escape*, 236; Bacon, *Thrilling Adventures*, 24; Drake, *Fast and Loose in Dixie*, 95–96, 98–99; Cooper, *In and Out of Rebel Prisons*, 146; Roach, *Prisoner of War*, 86, 155–57; and Ferguson, *Life-Struggles in Rebel Prisons*, 68.

75. Ransom, *Andersonville Diary*, 217, 224, 220, 236.

76. A fictional narrative published by the writer and abolitionist James R. Gilmore reverses these expectations. Writing as Edmund Kirke, a man who claimed to have found a prison narrative by Henry L. Estabrooks, Gilmore set out to prove that the "negro is not black." To that end, he created a series of characters to whom he granted individual identities—first and last names and specific, if fictional, geographic locations. Henry L. Estabrooks, *Adrift in Dixie; or, A Yankee Officer Among the Rebels* (New York: Carleton Publishers, 1866).

77. Goss, *Soldier's Story*, 127.

78. For Goss, slaves were part of nature, not of culture. See Gates, *Figures in Black*, 96–97.

79. Hadley, *Seven Months a Prisoner*, 155; Cooper, *In and Out of Rebel Prisons*, 149; Glazier, *Capture, Prison Pen, and the Escape*, 296–97.

80. House Special Committee, *Report on the Treatment of Prisoners of War*, 248–49.

81. J. T. Trowbridge, *The South: A Tour of Its Battlefields and Ruined Cities, a Journey through the Desolated States and Talks with the People* (Hartford: L. Stebbins, 1866), 468.

82. Chas. L. Cummings, *The Great War Relic. Valuable as a Curiosity of the Rebellion Together with a Sketch of my Life, Service in the Army and how I lost my*

feet since the War; also many interesting incidents illustrative of the life of a soldier (Harrisburg: George E. Reed, 1887).

83. Some thirty-five thousand men survived war-related amputations, and their demands for compensation for wartime injuries were crucial to the development of the welfare state. As Theda Skocpol has demonstrated, wounded veterans helped nineteenth-century Americans formulate the mutual obligations of the state and its citizens. Skocpol, *Protecting Soldiers and Mothers*, 144–51. Books by injured drunkards include Thomas Doner, *Eleven Years a Drunkard, or the Evils of Intemperance Showing What Whiskey Did for me* (Sycamore, Ill.: Arnold Brothers, 1874); and Festus G. Rand, *The Autobiography of Festus G. Rand. A Tale of Temperance* (Romeo, Mich.: J. Russell, Printer, 1866).

84. Cummings, *Great War Relic*, 9–10. Like Cummings, Charles Williams, a mailman who lost his feet when he nearly froze to death, understood that able-bodied people looked at him with a mixture of pity and curiosity. Their curiosity was his invitation to write. "But the reader can easily imagine, if he has had any of the many little accidents we are all liable to, such as a cut on the hand or a bruise requiring a plaster or bandage, the monotony of repetition in his own case of perhaps a few days, and understand my feelings in telling a story for twenty two years. By the advice of many well-informed people, I have had the present book printed, and offer it not that it contains any particular merit, but that the kindly-inclined may satisfy their curiosity and I derive some recompense for my time." Williams, *Terrors of a Blizzard, by one who has had the experience. The Fate of a Mail Carrier: Or How I Lost my Feet. Written by the Loser* (Oshkosh, Wis.: Castle-Pierce Press, 1902), 2.

85. A story published in *Harper's Weekly*, "The Empty sleeve at Newport: or Why Edna Ackland learned to Drive" (August 26, 1865), offered readers lessons in the proper demeanor toward wounded veterans. The hero of the story "hated the endless questioning and commiseration—the answering of inquiries as to his health, and how and where and when that sleeve became empty. He did not enjoy the role of hero, nor the admiring pity of simpering misses and stout mamas" (534).

86. Nevins and his collaborators describe Cummings' book: "Though void of value, this memoir went through five editions and more than 35,000 copies were purchased by sympathetic readers." Nevins, et al., *Civil War Books*, 1: 77. To Cummings, the book was apparently quite valuable. The market for Cummings's book might well be explained by the increased visibility of the wounded veterans who, in the early 1880s, were campaigning for pension legislation. See Hesseltine, *Civil War Prisons*, 249–50.

87. My thinking about Mr. Cummings and his disability has been influenced by Rosemarie Garland Thomson, *Extraordinary Bodies: Figuring Physical Disability in American Culture and Literature* (New York: Columbia University Press, 1997). I find her discussions of work, race, "otherness," and the ways a culture produces disabled bodies particularly helpful. As she puts it, "That a man might be a virtuous worker one day and an indolent pauper the next doubtless raised uneasy questions about an individual's capacity for unlimited self-determination" (48). On amputation during the Civil War, see Oliver Wendell Holmes, "The human wheel, its spokes and felloes," *Atlantic Monthly* 11 (May 1863): 567–80; Laurann Figg and Jane Farell-Beck, "Amputation in the Civil War: Physical and Social Dimensions," *Journal of the History of Medicine and Allied Sciences* 48 (October 1993): 454–74; Erin O'Connor, "Fractions of Men: Engendering Amputation in Victorian Culture," *Comparative Studies in Society and History* 39 (October 1997): 742–77; and Lisa Herschbach, "Prosthetic Reconstructions: Making the Industry Remaking the Body, Modeling the Nation" (paper delivered at Interuniversity History of Medicine Consortium, New York, January 6, 1999).

88. Cummings, *Great War Relic*, 10, 36–38. January was among the wounded prisoners exchanged in January 1865 and photographed at Annapolis on his return to the North. His picture appeared in *Harper's Weekly* (January 17, 1865): 380. It was reprinted in Abbott's *Prison Life in the South*, 304, and appeared again in McElroy, *Andersonville*, 545. S. S. Boggs repeated January's version of his amputation in his *Eighteen Months a Prisoner*, 53. January's account of his experience appears in House Special Committee, *Report on the Treatment of Prisoners of War*, 1137–38. Crippled soldiers on the lecture circuit included Daniel Kelly, who sold a pamphlet entitled *What I Saw and Suffered* (Buffalo: Thomas, Howard and Jones, 1868). Crippled beggars pretending to have been prisoners of war included George W. Murray, who sold his *A History of George W. Murray and his Long Confinement at Andersonville, Ga. Also the Starvation and Death of his Three Brothers at the Same Place by Himself* (Springfield, Mass.: Sold for the Benefit of the Author, 186?).

EPILOGUE

1. Oswald Garrison Villard, "Sex, Art, Truth, and Magazines," *The Atlantic Monthly* (March 1926): 3.

2. Macfadden seemed to bother genteel editors. How different were their projects, after all, when like him they were busy cultivating advertisers rather than subscribers? Helpful studies on magazines at the end of the nineteenth century include Christopher P. Wilson, "The Rhetoric of Consumption: Mass-Market Magazines and the Demise of the Genteel Reader, 1880–1920," in *The Culture of Consumption*, ed. T. J. Jackson Lears and Richard Wightman Fox (New York: Pantheon, 1983), 39–64; Richard Ohmann, *Selling Culture: Magazines, Markets, and Class at the Turn of the Century* (New York: Verso, 1996); Jennifer Scanlon, *Inarticulate Longings: The Ladies' Home Journal, Gender, and the Promises of Consumer Culture* (New York: Routledge, 1995); and Ellen Guber Garvey, *The Adman in the Parlor: Magazines and the Gendering of Consumer Culture, 1880s to 1910s* (New York: Oxford University Press, 1996).

3. Work on masculinity in the early twentieth century helps explain Macfadden's appeal. Kevin White and Greg Mullins credit Macfadden with helping to invent and to publicize styles of heterosexual masculinity. Kevin White, *The First Sexual Revolution: The Emergence of Male Heterosexuality in Modern America* (New York: New York University Press, 1993), 28–35; and Greg Mullins, "Nudes, Prudes and Pigmies: The Desirability of Disavowal in *Physical Culture*," *Discourse* 15 (1992). See also George Chauncey, *Gay New York: Gender, Urban Culture, and the Making of the Gay Male World* (New York: Basic Books, 1994), 116. Margaret Walsh identifies Macfadden as one of the proponents of "masculine domesticity." Walsh, "Suburban Men and Masculine Domesticity, 1870–1915," in *Meanings for Manhood: Constructions of Masculinity in Victorian America*, ed. Mark C. Carnes and Clyde Griffen (Chicago: University of Chicago Press, 1990), 123–24. For a helpful overview of the problems of masculinity, see Gail Bederman, *Manliness and Civilization: A Cultural History of Gender and Race in the United States, 1880–1917* (Chicago: University of Chicago Press, 1990), 1–44.

4. The historian Robert Ernst has produced the most careful biography of Macfadden, *Weakness Is a Crime: The Life of Bernarr Macfadden* (Syracuse: Syracuse University Press, 1991). See also William Hunt, *Body Love: The Amazing Career of Bernarr Macfadden* (Bowling Green, Ohio: Bowling Green State University Popular Press, 1989); Henry F. Pringle, *Big Frogs* (New York: Vanguard Press, 1928), 117–36; Clifford J. Waugh, "Bernarr Macfadden, the Muscular Prophet," (Ph.D. diss., SUNY Buffalo, 1979); and Jacqueline A. Hatton, "True Stories: Working Class Mythology, American Confessional Culture, and *True Story Magazine*, 1919–1929," (Ph.D. diss., Cornell University, 1997).

5. James C. Whorten discusses Macfadden's role in the fitness craze of the 1890s in *Crusaders for Fitness: The History of American Health Reformers* (Princeton: Princeton University Press, 1993), 296–303.

6. Ernst, *Weakness Is a Crime*; Clement Wood, *Bernarr Macfadden: A Study in Success* (New York: Lewis Copeland Company, 1929), 72; and Alva Johnston, "The Great Macfadden," *Saturday Evening Post* (21 and 28 June 1941). Additional material can be found in three commissioned biographies published as Macfadden toyed with the idea of running for president: Wood, *Bernarr Macfadden*; Fulton Oursler, *The True Story of Bernarr Macfadden* (New York: Lewis Copeland Company, 1929); and Grace Perkins, *Chats with the Macfadden Family* (New York: Lewis Copeland Company, 1929). Late in his life, he was the subject of a three-part *New Yorker* "Profile" by Robert Lewis Taylor. Taylor painted him as a benign aged eccentric with a taste for headstands, bare feet, raw carrots, and parachute jumps. See, Taylor, "Physical Culture," *The New Yorker* (14 October 1950): 39–51; (21 October 1950): 39–52; (28 October 1950): 37–51. Mary Macfadden dissented from Taylor's celebration, and three years later exposed the tyranny of many of her estranged husband's eccentricities. She particularly resented his battles with the medical establishment. See Mary Macfadden and Emile Gauvreau, *Dumbbells and Carrot Strips: The Story of Bernarr Macfadden* (New York: Henry Holt and Co., 1953).

7. For a slightly fictionalized description of Physical Culture City by one as inclined to excess as Macfadden himself, see Harry Kemp, *Tramping on Life: An Autobiographical Narrative* (New York: Boni and Liveright, 1922), 164–74.

8. Pringle, *Big Frogs*, 132.

9. Bernarr Macfadden, *The Athlete's Conquest: The Romance of an Athlete* (New York: Physical Culture Publishing Co., 1901), [1]. Macfadden asks readers to excuse the book's defects because it was "founded on fact." "It was written," he continues, "in the extravagant enthusiasm and idealism of youth, though when the reader realizes that physical culture brought the author from the weakness, emaciation and hopelessness of a consumptive to that condition of superb health necessary in a successful athlete, and has kept him in that condition now for nearly fifteen years, he may excuse the efforts made in this novel to enthuse others to strive for similar rewards" (292).

10. M. Macfadden and Gauvreau, *Dumbbells*, 76. See also Hunt, *Body Love*, 50, 55; and Wood, *Bernarr Macfadden*, 304. E. Radford Lumsden, the public relations counsel for Macfadden publications, reported that his boss never

considered writing difficult. Lumsden, "Bernarr Macfadden—An American Type," *Fifty Years in Business Magazine* 1 (October 1940): 21.

11. On celebrity and publicity in late nineteenth-century America, see Philip Fisher, "Appearing and Disappearing in Public: Social Space in Late-Nineteenth-Century Literature and Culture," in *Reconstructing American Literary History*, ed. Sacvan Berkovitch (Cambridge: Harvard University Press, 1986), 155–88; and Leo Braudy, *The Frenzy of Renown: Fame and Its History* (New York: Oxford University Press, 1986), 450–583.

12. Throughout the odd history of his publishing enterprise, Macfadden maintained control over *Physical Culture*. The publication changed its name to *Beauty and Health* in the early 1940s and continued to appear under various titles into the 1950s. Theodore Peterson, *Magazines in the Twentieth Century* (Urbana: University of Illinois Press, 1956), 243–47, 273–93.

13. A letter published in *The Journal of the American Medical Association* reported the death by starvation of a "fine young Syrian" in Chicago who had followed Macfadden's advice on fasting. "Macfaddism and a Starvation Death," *The Journal of the American Medical Association* 84 (10 January 1925): 136. A year earlier, *The Journal* had warned against Macfadden publications. "Exploiting the Health Interests," *The Journal of the American Medical Association* 83 (25 October 1924): 1340.

14. According to Stuart Hall, "If the forms of commercial popular culture are not purely manipulative, then it is because alongside the false appeals, the foreshortenings, the trivializations, and the shortcuts, there are also elements of recognition and identification, something approaching a recreation of recognisable experiences and attitudes to which people are responding." Hall, "Notes on Deconstructing the Popular," in *People's History and Socialist Theory*, ed. Raphael Samuel (London: Routledge, 1981), 253. Historians have begun to pay more careful attention to patterns of participation in mass culture, although they do not exactly agree on what participation means. See Lawrence W. Levine, "The Folklore of Industrial Society: Popular Culture and Its Audiences," *American Historical Review* 97 (December 1992):1369–99; and T. J. Jackson Lears, "Making Fun of Popular Culture," *American Historical Review* 97 (December 1992): 1417–26.

15. *True Story* (May 1926): 65.

16. *Physical Culture* 23 (May 1910): 509. Several threads likely lead to Macfadden's *True Story*, among them the techniques of advertisers who staged con-

tests in the 1890s to determine how readers responded to their advertisements. Ellen Guber Garvey has written a good account of the development of this strategy in *The Adman in the Parlor*, 51–79.

17. M. Macfadden and Gauvreau, *Dumbbells*, 218–19. Others dismissed Mrs. Macfadden's claim as a tactical maneuver in her divorce suit. Ernst, *Weakness Is a Crime*, 75–76.

18. Werner Sollors has written a helpful introduction to a new edition of Holt's book. Hamilton Holt, ed., *The Life Stories of Undistinguished Americans* (1906; reprint, New York: Routledge, 1990), xi–xxviii.

19. "One Farmer's Wife," *The Independent* (9 February 1905): 294–299.

20. Ibid, 294.

21. "These Men and Women Know the Appeal of the True Story," *True Story* (January 1923): 8. Macfadden promoted a deceptively simple theory of narrative: stories were, to borrow the anthropologist Richard Bauman's phrase, "verbal icons of the events they recount[ed]." Simplicity was crucial to Macfadden's imagined democracy. Richard Bauman, *Story, Performance, and Event* (Cambridge: Cambridge University Press, 1986), 5.

22. "These Men and Women Know the Appeal of the True Story." The phrase *amateur illiterates* is from an article in the *Saturday Evening Post* quoted in George Gerbner, "The Social Role of the Confession Magazine," *Social Problems* 6 (summer 1958): 29.

23. In 1926, Macfadden advertised "8 True Story Pictures," "adapted to the screen from TRUE STORY MAGAZINE. . . . Think, if you will of that vast, pulsating army of enthralled TRUE STORY Readers. . . . More than 2,500,000 copies alone are sold monthly . . . To capable showmen the great box-office results are obvious." *Film Year Book, 1926* (New York: Film Daily, 1926), 326.

"The Girl He Saved from Chinatown's Horrors," (*True Story* [September 1919]: 7) was illustrated by pictures produced by "True Story Films." Read for photographs alone, *True Story* closely resembles the photographic melodramas (*romans-photos* or *fumetti*) so popular throughout the world. Macfadden continued to play with photographic truths on the pages of his short-lived (and personally very costly) tabloid, the *New York Graphic*. When he found it impossible to illustrate a news story, Macfadden instructed his staff to pose for or to construct from existing images a composite photograph. He called such inventions "composographs." Lester Cohen, *The New York Graphic: The World's Zaniest Newspaper* (Philadelphia: Chilton Books, 1964), 95–102.

24. "These Men and Women Know the Appeal of the True Story"; and *True Story* (February 1926): 65. John Stuart, "Bernarr Macfadden: From Pornography to Politics," *New Masses*, 19 (19 May 1936): 8–11. On the mixed messages of mass culture—it is often both liberatory and oppressive—see Hall, "Notes on Deconstructing the Popular," 238–39; and Kathy Peiss, *Cheap Amusements: Leisure in Turn-of-the-Century New York* (Philadelphia: Temple University Press, 1986), 6.

Fascism, incarnated in Mussolini, appealed to Macfadden. In 1930 he visited the dictator (who reportedly told Macfadden, "I, too, am a physical culturalist") and trained a group of Italian cadets in the arts of physical culture. Thomas B. Morgan, *Italian Physical Culture Demonstration* (New York: Macfadden Books, 1932), 25; and Thomas Dixon, *A Dreamer in Portugal: The Story of Bernarr Macfadden's Mission to Continental Europe* (New York: Covici, Friede Publishers, 1934). "Only Dictatorial Powers Can Save Us," Macfadden contended in an editorial published in *Liberty* on March 25, 1933. On fascism and the male body, see John M. Hoberman, *Sport and Political Ideology* (Austin: University of Texas Press, 1984).

According to Kathryne V. Lindberg, George Horace Lorimer, the publisher of *Saturday Evening Post*, also admired Mussolini. Lindberg, "Mass Circulation versus *The Masses*: Covering the Modern Magazine Scene," in *National Identities and Post-American Narratives*, ed. Donald E. Pease (Durham: Duke University Press, 1994), 311.

25. Dorothy Kemble, *Behind the Girl on the Magazine Cover* (New York: Macfadden Publications, 1936), 17–19; M. Macfadden and Gauvreau, *Dumbbells*, 223.

26. For the results of polls conducted by Macfadden and by Fawcett, see Harland Manchester, "True Stories," *Scribner's Magazine* (August 1938): 60. See also William Frank Rasche, *The Reading Interests of Young Workers* (Chicago: University of Chicago Libraries, 1937), 68, 70. On *Popular Mechanics*, see Steven M. Gelber, "Do-It-Yourself: Constructing, Repairing, and Maintaining Domestic Masculinity," *American Quarterly* 49 (March 1997): 83–85.

27. Gerbner, "Social Role of the Confession Magazine," 33. Martin Johnson, "If a Cannibal King Wanted Your Wife for His Harem," *True Story* (July 1919): 10–11, 81. Jacqueline Hatton argues that heterosexual content characterized the magazine for the first five years of its existence. Hatton, "True Stories." Stories told from the man's point of view occasionally appeared in later years. A compilation of *True Stories of 1941* contains at least three tales told by male narrators: "Our Fourth Daughter," "A.W.O.L.," and "Women are Different." Robert O. Ballou, ed. *True Stories of 1941* (New York: Bartholomew House, 1941).

28. *True Story* (February 1926): 41, 32, 34; (May 1926): 32, 63. Janice Radway speculates that the success of commercial fiction, like Macfadden's romances, depended on its "capacity to catch the reader up in a story that seems to propel itself forward with force. The elementary pleasures of plot are the test of achievement here, and, apparently the more accomplished the concealment of the fact that the story has been conceived and ordered by an author, the more intense the necessary experience of transport provided for the reader." Radway, "The Book-of-the-Month Club and the General Reader," in *Reading in America: Literature and Social History*, ed. Cathy N. Davidson (Baltimore: Johns Hopkins University Press, 1989), 276. See also Janice A. Radway, *A Feeling for Books: The Book-of-the-Month Club and Middle-Class Desire* (Chapel Hill: University of North Carolina, 1997).

29. According to the sociologist George Gerbner, in the world depicted in *True Story*, "the flame of rebellion is first kindled, then controlled in scope and divorced from its broader social context, and then doused in jet streams of remorse, sacrifice, and compromise." Gerbner, "Social Role of the Confession Magazine," 40. The historian Regina Kunzel finds that unhappily pregnant girls made good use of *True Confessions*. In 1949, after reading an appeal published in *True Confessions*, some one hundred and fifty young unmarried pregnant women wrote to the United States Children's Bureau asking for assistance. Kunzel speculates that their letters constituted "*true* 'true confessions.'" The popular culture of the confession magazines "might have helped women find the words to make such a confession, as well as the narrative templates with which to plot their own stories." Regina Kunzel, "Pulp Fictions and Problem Girls," *American Historical Review* 100 (December 1995): 1467, 1477, 1486.

30. "Thinking Clergymen Acclaim *True Story*," *True Story* (February 1929): 8.

31. Villard, "Sex, Art, Truth," 5–6; Gerbner, "Social Role of the Confession Magazine," 33; John Tebbel and Mary Ellen Zuckerman, *The Magazine in America, 1741–1990* (New York: Oxford University Press, 1991), 194; and Kunzel, "Pulp Fictions," 1471.

32. On affidavits, see Kemble, *Behind the Girl*, 18–19.

33. "Plagiarism," *True Story* (July 1929): 8.

34. American Economic Evolution (New York: True Story Magazine, 1930), 3, 12, 83. *How to Get People Excited: A Human Interest Textbook* (New York: True Story Magazine, 1937).

35. Michel de Certeau, among others, has called attention to the ways that readers make the texts they read. Michel de Certeau, *The Practice of Everyday*

Life (Berkeley: University of California, 1984), 169. See also Janice A. Radway, *Reading the Romance: Women, Patriarchy, and Popular Literature* (Chapel Hill: University of North Carolina Press, 1984), 6, 48, 68–69, 98, 221. Radway describes readers engaged in the active production of meaning, but several of her romance readers also became romance writers. Elsewhere Radway questions a tendency among scholars of popular culture to privilege song and dance as the cultural forms of the people. "If humans have the inherent capacity to move physically and to sing, do they not also have an inherent capacity to represent and to organize representations, to narrate and to tell stories?" Radway, "Maps and the Construction of Boundaries," *International Labor and Working-Class History* 37 (spring 1990): 22–23.

36. Villard, "Sex, Art, Truth," 6. Some in a first generation of American novel readers took stories literally, constructing a grave in New York for "Charlotte Temple" and decorating it with "wreaths, locks of hair, and mementos of lost loves." Cathy Davidson, *Revolution and the Word: The Rise of the Novel in America* (New York: Oxford University Press, 1986), 73.

37. Jack London, "Confession," in *Novels and Social Writing* (1907; reprint, New York: Library of America, 1982), 193–94.

INDEX

Designer: Nicole Hayward
Compositor: Impressions
Text: 11/15 Bulmer
Display: Bulmer
Printer and Binder: Edwards Brothers